BEYOND THE MIDDLE KINGDOM

A Series Sponsored by the East-West Center

CONTEMPORARY ISSUES IN ASIA AND THE PACIFIC

John T. Sidel and Geoffrey M. White, Series Co-Editors

A collaborative effort by Stanford University Press and the East-West Center, this series focuses on issues of contemporary significance in the Asia Pacific region, most notably political, social, cultural, and economic change. The series seeks books that focus on topics of regional importance, on problems that cross disciplinary boundaries, and that have the capacity to reach academic and other interested audiences.

The East-West Center promotes better relations and understanding among the people and nations of the United States, Asia, and the Pacific through cooperative study, research, and dialogue. Established by the US Congress in 1960, the Center serves as a resource for information and analysis on critical issues of common concern, bringing people together to exchange views, build expertise, and develop policy options. The Center is an independent, public, nonprofit organization with funding from the US government, and additional support provided by private agencies, individuals, foundations, corporations, and governments in the region.

EDITED BY SCOTT KENNEDY

Beyond the Middle Kingdom

*Comparative Perspectives on China's Capitalist
Transformation*

Stanford University Press · *Stanford, California*

Stanford University Press
Stanford, California

Printed in the United States of America on acid-free, archival-quality paper

Library of Congress Cataloging-in-Publication Data

  Beyond the Middle Kingdom : comparative perspectives on China's
capitalist transformation / edited by Scott Kennedy.
      pages cm—(Contemporary Issues in Asia and the Pacific)
  Includes bibliographical references and index.
  ISBN 978-0-8047-6957-0 (cloth : alk. paper)
  ISBN 978-0-8047-6958-7 (pbk. : alk. paper)
  1. Capitalism—China. 2. China—Economic policy. 3. China—
Economic conditions. 4. China—Politics and government. 5. Comparative
economics. 6. Comparative government. I. Kennedy, Scott, 1967-editor of
compilation. II. Series: Contemporary Issues in Asia and the Pacific.
  HC427.95.B477 2011
  330.951—dc22

                                                      2010049968

Typeset by Thompson Type in 9.75/13.5 Janson.

For Gao Hua, a scholar's scholar

献给学者的典范 – 高华

Contents

List of Figures and Tables

Figures

Tables

Acknowledgments

For the uninitiated, edited volumes seem like an ideal form of scholarship. They allow us to address a topic more deeply and broadly than we could by ourselves. Moreover, they are vehicles for building and strengthening communities of experts because of the conferences, letters, emails, and phone calls that typically accompany these efforts. Such communication also ends up improving the work of each individual contributor. On the other hand, what is an ideal form in principle may be less so in practice. The uninitiated soon discovers that the process presents an amazing set of challenges—raising funds, organizing the conference, selecting which papers to include, encouraging revisions, and meeting the demands of reviewers, all of which can make the project extend to more years than anyone could rightly expect to accept. I am lucky to report that in this instance, at least from the perspective of the editor, the reality came very close to matching the ideal. Because of—not in spite of—the challenges, I have become much more appreciative of the good nature and quality of the scholarship of my peers and the collective enterprise required for such a project to succeed.

This book began as a conference, "Capitalism with Chinese Characteristics: China's Political Economy in Comparative and Theoretical Perspective," held at Indiana University in May 2006. IU was supportive in multiple ways. I am grateful to the East Asian Studies Center for helping organize the conference. Its director Jeff Wasserstrom and associate director Margaret Key were instrumental in putting the conference together. Other important contributors to staging the conference include Rachael Brown, Mary Beth Kennedy, Patsy Rahn, Tim Rich, Travis Selmier, and Wang Jianxun. The funding for the conference came from several units on campus: the East Asian Studies Center, the Center for International Business Education and

Research, the College of Arts and Sciences, the Office of the Vice Provost for Research, the Office of the Vice Provost for International Affairs, and the East Asian Languages and Cultures Department. CIBER was also gracious enough to offer their executive meeting facilities gratis, and James Russell from the Political Science Department crafted a beautiful and streamlined website.

Central to the conference's success was the contributions of the paper authors, panel chairs, discussants, and attendees. In addition to those participants whose contributions are in the pages that follow here, I want to also express my appreciation to the other scholars and experts who gave their time and energy to the conference: Marc Blecher, Gardner Bovingdon, Nandini Gupta, Stephan Haggard, Rick Harbaugh, Ho-fung Hung, Hu Shuli, Jason Kindopp, Marjorie Lyles, Barrett McCormick, Andrew Mertha, Ethan Michelson, Barry Naughton, Kevin O'Brien, Scott O'Bryan, Vladimir Popov, Michael Robinson, Heidi Ross, Ben Ross Schneider, Aseema Sinha, Yan Sun, and Yi-Feng Tao. I am indebted to all of you, though special thanks goes to Stephan Haggard for his detailed analysis of all of the papers and help in envisioning a resultant volume.

It has taken several years for the ideas presented at the conference to be refined into the chapters that compose this book. I cannot say enough how proud I am to be associated with the other contributors. They are all excellent social scientists and writers, and each of them has demonstrated an openness to engage different ideas and have been patient and kind with me. We have all benefitted from the suggestions and comments provided by the original conference participants, the anonymous reviewers at Stanford University Press as well as from Harry Harding, Heon Joo Jung, and the students in my Chinese Politics graduate seminar. Wang Qun and Edwin Way provided editing assistance at the tail end of the project. I am extremely grateful to the Editorial Board of the Contemporary Issues in Asia and the Pacific Series for including this volume in their fine series and providing specific suggestions to the manuscript. Particular thanks are due to the series co-editors, John Sidel and Geoffrey White, and to Elisa Johnston, publications manager at the East-West Center. Stacy Wagner has provided amazing support from her position as acquisitions editor at Stanford University Press. She and her colleagues Jessica Walsh and Margaret Pinette guided the book from submission to the production process with the utmost professionalism and care. Without their continuous encouragement and guidance, this book never would have been published.

Finally, this book is dedicated to Gao Hua. A specialist of Chinese modern history at Nanjing University since the 1980s, he taught modern intellectual Chinese history for over a decade at the Hopkins-Nanjing Center for American Studies. From the very first day sitting in his classroom, I knew I had encountered a special person, a man of remarkable knowledge and analytical ability who had developed fortitude from his commitment to the intellectual enterprise wherever it led him. His writings on the history of the Chinese Communist Party and other topics tell it as he sees it, and we should all have eyes as sharp as his. Although Gao Hua's writings and lectures are rich in detail about China, his analysis of modern Chinese history and politics is clearly informed by cross-national comparison. A scholar's scholar, Gao Hua has also been a friend's friend. He and his dear wife, Liu Shaohong, opened their home and hearts to me and my wife, Mary Beth. I enjoyed many evenings sitting in his study asking questions and sharing ideas. As time passed, I learned that I was far from alone in this experience, and that many of us owe Gao Hua more than we can say. Over the course of his life, Gao Hua has endured more than anyone should and has given of himself more than anyone would imagine possible. During the past few years, he has been physically slowed by illness, but he is still as sharp and insightful as ever. One cannot help but be inspired by Gao Hua. For all of this and much more, this book is dedicated to him.

BEYOND THE MIDDLE KINGDOM

INTRODUCTION

Chapter One

Overcoming Our Middle Kingdom Complex
Finding China's Place in Comparative Politics

SCOTT KENNEDY

For those who follow China, the country appears to be a mass of contradictions that defy logic. The People's Republic of China (PRC) is led by a Communist Party, but China ranks only second to the United States in number
of billionaires. The Politburo Standing Committee has extraordinary power,
yet the lowest township and village officials regularly flout national policies.
And, perhaps most surprising of all, despite an economic revolution that
has resulted in China adopting economic policies and institutions found in
capitalist systems and generated social pluralization that includes extensive
transnational linkages, democratization seems less likely than ever. There
is another kind of contradiction, which is not bedeviling China but rather
those of us who study that country. There seems to be a disjuncture between
how quickly China is changing and how slowly we are adapting the way we
study the country's politics.

Don't get me wrong. Over the last sixty years, China specialists have
moved from simply trying to describe Chinese politics to comparing Chinese reality against various theories and offering up new explanations of
politics by drawing on the Chinese case. Yet we rarely use a tool that provides the title of the disciplinary subfield in which many China experts re-
side: comparison (as in "the comparative politics subfield"). The PRC is led
by a Communist Party, but it has rarely been systematically compared with
other Communist countries. China is now awash in capital, but it is only

infrequently compared (or contrasted) with other capitalist countries. And even though nonstate actors, from businesspeople to peasants, are becoming more politically active—around 80,000 protests take place each year—their behavior likewise is rarely directly measured against that of their cousins elsewhere. The goal of this volume is to demonstrate that, in light of China's capitalist transformation, there is greater utility than ever in examining China through different comparative lenses, for what it teaches us both about China as well as about politics more generally.

Studying Chinese Politics and Political Economy: Different Degrees of Theorizing

The comparative politics subfield of the political science discipline—and that is the formal home of comparative political economy specialists—is misnamed. We are all at heart specialists in *domestic* politics and political economy, either of a country or region or of a discrete issue, such as the bureaucracy, democratization, or protest. We are attentive to international and transnational factors but typically only in so much as they shape or are shaped by domestic political processes. Under this umbrella, there is wide variation in scholars' goals, research methods, and scope of the data they collect. Some aim at description of political behavior and systems, while others seek to develop theories that contain causal inferences about politics beyond the specific people or events being studied. In so doing, some aim for grand theories that hold across time and space, while others seek to develop "middle range" theories that hold true under a narrower set of circumstances. Domestic politics and comparative political economy scholars employ a range of methods, from qualitative case studies to large-n quantitative analyses to formal modeling, or a combination of these techniques. And finally, some scholars obtain their data from a single polity and others use data from several countries, either a small number to allow for focused comparison or a wide cross section to facilitate statistical analysis. For those interested in contributing to theories of politics, no one approach is necessarily better than any other, and there is growing sentiment that scholars should employ multiple methods in order to obtain as authoritative findings as possible.[1]

This book's empirical focus is on political economy questions, that is, issues that involve the politics of economics (such as how political institutions shape economic policy and business behavior) or the economics of politics (such as how globalization realigns political alliances), but the insights identified here are highly relevant to students of Chinese politics and society writ large. In fact, the boundary between political economy and comparative politics is increasingly blurred. That is especially true in the China field as a growing proportion of Chinese politics scholars—perhaps a large majority of them—do research that engages political economy questions. Hence, it is difficult to speak about trends among specialists of China's political economy without situating them in the broader China field of which they are a part.

Scholars of Chinese politics and political economy run the gamut in terms of goals and methods. From the earliest studies up through the present, there has been a strong area studies tradition in which description of China in and of itself has been of high importance. Much of this research is straightforward political history, which is perhaps most prominent in work on China's political elites but is also found on other aspects of the political system.[2] There have also been a large number of studies that attempt to faithfully describe certain aspects of the political system that had not been well understood previously, such as China's "democratic" parties and efforts at bureaucratic reform.[3]

Although there are exceptions, the trend toward being more theoretically motivated emerged in the 1980s. Whereas some see description and theory building as entirely competing approaches, it is helpful to consider these research goals along a continuum. Even though few works by Chinese politics specialists have generated new theories of politics that are intended to apply beyond the Chinese case, most scholars are attuned to theoretical issues to one degree or another. At a minimum, they take inspiration from a political theory, concept, or orientation and apply some of its insights to identify regularities or patterns in Chinese politics.[4] Some of these initial efforts then inspired further research that "tested" their original findings. For example, Susan Shirk's argument about the role of the Central Committee as a "selectorate" in shaping the economic policies of the leadership was later examined in detail, with some elements being confirmed and others being questioned.[5]

Since the late 1990s, China scholars have gradually shifted from borrowing theories and concepts to systematically testing them using the Chinese case and even coming up with new theoretical innovations. In some instances, they have done so by offering a new conceptual lens derived from the Chinese experience that can then be applied elsewhere. A prominent example is the concept of "rightful resistance," in which protesters use the formal language of rights created by the state to defend themselves to an extent officials did not originally anticipate.[6] But a more common strategy, particularly with regard to political economy questions, is to divide China into discrete units and compare them to each other, thereby increasing the number of "cases" so that there can be multiple values in either the independent or dependent variables being examined. A few scholars, most notably Elizabeth Perry, divide China historically, comparing and contrasting different eras.[7] More commonly, specialists keep their focus on contemporary China and compare across different regions,[8] organizations,[9] and economic sectors.[10]

In addition to comparative (small-*n*) case studies, China specialists are also increasingly compiling large-scale data sets about individual Chinese people and organizations and subjecting them to econometric analysis to examine a wide range of political phenomena. Many such studies are formal surveys geared to measure popular attitudes toward political and social issues.[11] Others are based on a wide range of primary and secondary written sources, from archives to statistical compendia, to analyze all sorts of political questions.[12] Moreover, there is a growing, though still small, cohort of scholars who employ rational choice concepts and models on issues that involve strategic choices among officials, from the most senior elites to mid-level bureaucrats and the lowest of local cadres.[13]

Often Theoretical but Rarely Comparative

This review so far suggests that the reputation of the field of Chinese politics and political economy as simply narrow area studies is unjustified. China specialists have been integrated into the rest of political science and other social science disciplines. However, there is one way in which the China scholars of today resemble their counterparts of earlier generations. They are still extremely hesitant to engage in cross-national comparative research.

Through the first thirty years of the PRC, the total number of comparative works could be counted on one hand.[14] Their frequency has risen only slightly in subsequent years, with one or two comparative piece of scholarship annually since the mid-1990s. In addition to the infrequency of such work, many of these studies are only weakly comparative. Single-authored studies most commonly explicitly reference the experiences of other countries in the introductory or concluding sections of their books. Doing so helpfully contextualizes their China research, but these authors do not make comparison a central element of the discussion or the basis on which findings are reached, limiting the relevance of the comparisons.[15] There are a number of edited volumes that center around comparing China to another country or region and bring together specialists of China and other countries. But these books share a common weakness, in which the country specialists write only about their own country. Even when authors write on parallel topics, they typically use different concepts or discuss the same issue in just different enough a way so that the reader is left with "apples-oranges" comparisons. The introductory and concluding sections struggle, often unsuccessfully, to bridge these differences.[16]

Since the early 1990s there have been a smattering of comparison-based studies by China specialists, almost all of them comparing the PRC with a small number of countries. These works are spread across a wide range of topics, from democratization to corruption and protest.[17] These initial steps toward comparative scholarship should be welcomed, and they need to be built on. Many of these works are not explicit about the theoretical rationale for why China and the other countries were chosen as cases. Only occasionally is there a discussion of whether the comparison is of "most similar" or "most different" systems, or which variables are being tested through the comparative exercise.

The limited extent of comparison by China politics and political economy specialists has not raised much concern among the field's leading scholars. None of the field's main textbooks contains any significant comparative elements to their narratives.[18] There have been several important reviews of the field over the last quarter century. Most discuss in positive terms the shift from emphasizing description to engaging in theory building,[19] although a recent commentary criticized the faddishness for quantitative skills that has seemed to have caught on among the youngest generation of scholars.[20] Standing almost alone, Harry Harding stressed the need for China politics specialists to engage in cross-national comparisons. Writing over a quarter century ago, he predicted, apparently overoptimistically, that China specialists would have to be comparativists to enter the mainstream of political science.[21]

There are several reasons why Harding's expectations have not been met. First, for Westerners China is an extremely challenging country to study. It requires years of language training to read Chinese media and documents, listen to broadcasts, and speak to informants. When China specialists could not go to China, they closely monitored the media and interviewed emigres in Hong Kong, then still a British colony. Once the gates were opened in the late 1970s, it quickly became a common expectation that extended fieldwork on the ground in the PRC was a requirement of good scholarship. Conversely, the great investment in time and energy honing one's China skills left many experts unprepared to engage in comparisons or at least led them to believe that they could not do justice to the assignment.

A second reason for the limited interest in comparison has been the widespread belief that China is so unique that such an exercise will only lead to contrasts. Not only do the language and culture differ from the West, but a widespread assumption is that the foundations of Chinese society and its political system are a world apart. Observers who want to highlight China's distinctiveness regularly refer to the country as the "Middle Kingdom," a literal translation for the Chinese characters that combine to mean China, *zhongguo*. Historian John King Fairbank, the father of modern Chinese studies, is famous for emphasizing that China was not just a country, but a civilization whose emperor saw his land situated at the center of the universe and who ruled by heavenly authority.[22] For Fairbank and others, the revolution brought less change than meets the eye.[23] Those who share this sentiment believe that, in foreign affairs, China suffers from a "Middle Kingdom complex," in which its leaders feel obliged to recover the country's lost glory and exalted position. Although a new generation of pathbreaking comparative historical research has raised strong doubts about the work of Fairbank and others, those views have not resonated among politics specialists who have witnessed China following its own distinctive path in the last sixty years.[24] China first diverged from the Soviet Union in pursuit of a more "Maoist" revolutionary strategy and then in the late 1980s withstood social forces that brought about the USSR's extinction. Accompanying these trends was the revival in the mid-1980s of interest in the political science discipline on how political institutions shape politics. Neoinstitutionalism has emphasized path dependent trajectories of political life. Many China specialists have embraced the logic and theories of this approach, reinforcing the predilection to see China as distinctive.[25]

This sense of uniqueness is encouraged by China's government. According to the PRC regime, China practices "socialism with Chinese characteristics," which differs substantially from orthodox socialism as envisioned by Marx or Lenin.[26] This allows the regime flexibility and plausible deniability to adopt a wide range of policies and goals that the average person would view as capitalist. In addition, the Chinese government regularly contends that China should not adopt "Western-style" democracy or ensure its citizens basic civil liberties because doing so would be inconsistent with China's "national essence" (*guoqing*). If the Chinese government were to agree that the same rules of social science that shape political and social life elsewhere apply in China, its range of flexibility would be reduced.

An ironic twist to the perception of being unique is that the term *Middle Kingdom* is really a Western invention. In Chinese, the characters for China originally meant "central states," plural, a reference to the several states that existed alongside each other in what is today central eastern China prior to when China was first unified in the third century BCE. The Chinese never use the words *zhongg-guo* to stress the country's distinctiveness or to imply that it is a civilization or empire rather than an ordinary country. Tellingly, the use of the term in the U.S. media has varied unevenly over time. Journalists use it more when tensions between the United States and China rise and when China appears particularly powerful or influential.[27] The PRC may want to become more powerful, but the Middle Kingdom complex is ours, not China's.

The third and perhaps critical source for the disinterest in cross-national comparative research is China's size. As a large country, there is an enormous amount of potentially available data; with such diversity across regions, sectors, and individuals, China politics specialists can be theoretical by leveraging internal variation. China's massive size not only allows specialists to get by without comparison, it also allows them to get away with it. China is an important country in global strategic, political, and economic affairs. There are nontheoretical reasons why it is vital for scholars to understand this country. Political science departments have expanded the number of China positions significantly over the last two decades. Being in high demand, combined with a recognition of the difficulties for doing research on China, means that China specialists face somewhat less pressure to be comparative than their counterparts whose research focuses on smaller, less influential nations. Although often seen as polar opposites, the same logic that applies to China studies may also explain why American politics specialists also rarely engage in comparison.

The Need to Compare China

It may go without saying, but it should be said anyway: cross-national comparison can be an extremely useful research approach that provides insights not available through other strategies. Such studies provide an opportunity to theoretically analyze the causal effect of a number of factors that cannot be observed through subnational analyses, including regime type, national bureaucratic structures, overall state capacity or strength, the structure of central–local relations, patterns of government–business relations, geography and economic endowments, official ideology, political culture, location in the global economy, transnational relationships, international regimes, and the international security environment. These factors can be described without cross-national comparison, but it is difficult to determine their effect, especially relative to each other, without comparing more than one country where the value of these factors vary.

When scholars borrow theories and concepts derived from elsewhere and measure China against them, they are unwittingly engaging in a type of comparison, measuring Chinese reality against foreign ideal types. Such comparisons can yield a warped vision of China. For example, the importance of cultivating personal relations (*guanxi*) to complete a business transaction or obtain a permit is inconsistent with a rational-legal political system where impersonal contracts are taken as given. Yet the Chinese reality may be seen in a different light when compared against the actual use of connections and networks employed by Americans, Germans, Koreans, or Russians. What may be seen as a difference of kind may turn out to be a difference of degree. Without systematic reality-to-reality comparisons, one cannot be certain. And if we cannot be certain, we will never be able to determine if the images of a distinct Middle Kingdom are reality or myth.

Experts of other nations have made excellent use of comparison to put their countries in a different light not available otherwise. Specialists on Latin America, Africa, Southeast Asia, and China's smaller East Asian neighbors engage in comparison as a matter of course. Even Japan specialists, studying a country with an even stronger self-image of uniqueness than

China, are increasingly drawn to comparison to great effect. Stephen Reed's *Making Common Sense of Japan* (1993) busted a host of myths about Japan: the country is not small, it is large by most standards; its crime rate is not abnormally low by global standards; and the LDP's political tactics look surprisingly familiar to students of other parliamentary systems. More recently, Gregory Kasza, who penned this volume's concluding chapter, has demonstrated that Japan's welfare policies, often labeled as distinctly "East Asian," are similar to that of most advanced industrialized countries.[28]

Systematically comparing China with other countries will not necessarily uncover an equal amount of similarities, but it will clarify with greater precision where similarities and differences exist. Not only can we compare outcomes, but we can also compare the relative effect of different factors (independent variables) have on political behavior. For example, corruption levels in China may differ from those in the United States and Nigeria, but a comparison among these countries, or perhaps with others, can help shed light on what factor is most important in determining corruption across different political environments.

China Compared to What?

Having argued for the benefits of comparison, the next step is to identify the range of comparative frameworks we can use. Comparative scholarship on Chinese politics has most often adopted one of four lenses.

The first places China in the context of other (former) Communist countries, with the greatest attention paid to Russia, to understand similarities and differences in their transition away from state socialism. Since the late 1980s, leaving aside a few exceptions, the world's Communist countries have abandoned central planning in favor of fundamental market reforms. The first aspect of this transformation debated by scholars concerns the effect of countries' initial conditions in determining their reform trajectory. Scholars originally assumed Communist countries all started in the same situation, but they have realized that differences in geography, political institutions, elite politics, and other factors could have real consequences for the reform path.[29] The other intensely discussed question is what reform strategy is more effective in creating sustained economic growth. In the early 1990s, the dominant view stressed the need for immediate privatization, liberalization of prices, and lowering of international barriers to trade and investment, what is known as shock therapy because the purpose is to quickly expose economic actors to the full force of market conditions to provide a strong incentive to adapt. Since the latter half of the 1990s, many have come to question the wisdom of shock therapy and have argued for a different sequencing of reforms, in which privatization and financial liberalization are postponed in favor of allowing new economic actors to compete in a controlled environment in which market disciplines are added more gradually to give companies and workers more time to adapt and avoid sudden dislocations.[30]

Research on this question involving China has addressed both issues. A few studies have been comparative, but typically the reality of China's transition is measured against a stylized vision of economic shock therapy.[31] One of the most prominent recent contributions, by Minxin Pei of Claremont McKenna College, argues that China's gradualist transition has become trapped by the national elite who do not want democratization and corrupt officials who have hijacked economic reforms to suit their own interests.[32] By contrast, Vladimir Popov argues that China's economy has outperformed other post-Communist countries during the past two decades because its reform program has strengthened state institutions and capacity far more effectively than others.[33]

As helpful as the transition approach is, it is hampered to some extent by focusing on the gross contrast between plan and market at the expense of overlooking the many possible different destinations of the transition. Recent research has highlighted that capitalist countries come in many "varieties," from liberal systems rooted in competition between firms and an arm's length relationship between state and industry on the one hand, and others in which competitive markets are situated in a wider context of cooperative arrangements among firms and more symbiotic ties with state officials (particularly in the bureaucracy) on the other hand.[34] In addition to these alternative patterns, both of which can generate sustained efficient economic behavior and provide needed public goods, there are also capitalist countries in which rent seeking is common, either by elements of society who depend on clientelist links with well-placed patrons or by officials who themselves are direct participants in the economy.

When asked where China fits, some China scholars are satisfied to pick among these options. Noting a common Confucian cultural heritage, China's interventionist bureaucracy, industrial policies, close government-business ties, and sustained rapid growth, some see similarities with the developmental states of China's East Asian neighbors, especially Japan and South Korea.[35] Others, citing the proliferation of corruption and the widening gap between rich and poor, suggest that China's political economy exhibits many of the pathologies that have stunted sustained development among countries in Southeast Asia and Latin America.[36]

Although some of the scholarship on China utilizing a transition perspective has explicitly compared China to other post-Socialist countries, the vast majority of work situating China in the context of developmental states or crony capitalist countries has done so by measuring China against one of these ideal types.[37] As a result, China is compared against highly stylized versions of these countries that do not sufficiently recognize the gaps between model and reality or how the political economy in East Asian and Latin American countries has changed over time. In the case of China's neighbors, there is a recent rich body of scholarship using previously unavailable sources of data that takes issue with the conventional wisdom most China specialists envision in their comparative work.[38]

The final posture that China specialists take when engaging in comparison is to reject the exercise altogether and instead argue that China is unique. This disdain for comparison, or the finding that all is contrast, comes in several forms. The earliest work stresses how China's distinctive culture and social structure, such as the emphasis on family-based entrepreneurship, have resulted in a particularly "Chinese" style of capitalism.[39] A second brand finds that China's distinctive political institutions, with extensive power given to localities, and the country's weak bargaining position in the post–Cold War global economy, has led to a "capitalism with Chinese characteristics" in which China is growing rapidly while deeper development lags behind.[40] A better-known option, embodied in a book of the same name, argues that China's economic problems are not the product of a weak central government unable to impose its will on localities but rather a Chinese regime bent on state control of the key sectors of the economy. The result is stifled innovation and entrepreneurship, exhibited most clearly in Shanghai.[41] The last version of the "China is unique" school argues that, in fact, China's economic performance of the last three decades is remarkably successful and the result of unprecedented policies and institutions. One observer claims China so clearly violated the tenets of the fabled "Washington consensus" that it has established a new "Beijing consensus."[42] A similar motivation lies behind those now attempting to draw the outlines of a "China model" of development.[43]

Although there are distinctive elements of China's political economy, the contributors to this perspective have not sufficiently defended their assertions, in part because they rarely engage in systematic comparison of China with elsewhere. Advocates of the cultural view have done so, but their starting point for China—small family-owned businesses—is not a full representation of a PRC in which state-owned enterprises and large corporations listed on stock markets account for much of the country's economic activity.[44] Huang goes to the other extreme by stressing the state-owned sector and underplaying the wide variation across regions and industries. And any claim of a Beijing consensus has to cope with the reality that most of China's economic policies are the product of conflict and compromise and that many of China's economic policies are consistent with conventional economic approaches. Unfortunately, regardless of which stripe, application of the adjective "Chinese" has become a short-cut substitute for rigorous comparison.[45] This problem is not unique to China specialists, as students of other post-Communist countries have fallen into a similar habit.[46]

Chinese Economic Policy and Performance

The purpose of this book is to demonstrate the utility of comparison for better understanding Chinese politics by presenting a nuanced picture that is obscured when the country is viewed in isolation. In short, our goal is to move beyond the Middle Kingdom.

Written by some of the field's leading China specialists, the chapters in this book all engage in small-*n* comparisons involving China and a few countries. A wide assortment of cases is used. Russia and China's East Asia neighbors figure prominently, but the chapters depart from earlier works rooted in reality-versus-ideal type comparisons to instead analyze the actual experiences of China relative to the others. Another set of cases discussed in several chapters involves large developing countries. Their similar size and economic level make them good candidates for comparison, allowing us to see the consequences of these common characteristics as well as identify others that may account for distinctive outcomes among this group.

There are many aspects of China's political economy that deserve attention, but the contributions here revolve around two sets of very important issues. The first concerns China's economic policies and the country's resultant performance, and the second set is the sources and consequences of the emergence of interest groups in the context of an authoritarian political system. Both have rightly received a great deal of attention but have not been the subject of sustained comparison until now. In some cases, the authors address problems in which they are already leading authorities, but they break new ground by providing and analyzing a substantial amount of new information about China and then go on to place China in a fresh comparative perspective. In others, the authors venture into entirely new territory, both substantively and comparatively. In either event, every chapter represents a novel contribution to the debate about China and about political economy more generally.

Leading China specialist Margaret Pearson launches the first section by examining China's economic regulatory framework in comparison with that of three other countries with a record of extensive intervention in the economy: France, Brazil, and Japan. Whereas others typically describe one system, she identifies three distinct "tiers" of China's economy in which the state's intervention varies systematically—a top tier of core sectors entirely dominated by state-owned enterprises, a middle tier that combines assertive industrial policy with extensive competition involving domestic and foreign companies, and a bottom tier of sectors in which full competition and entrepreneurship are highly encouraged. Although distinctive in some respects, because of China's Communist legacy, her comparisons with these other dirigiste economies reveals important and unexpected similarities about China's regulatory system.

Arthur Kroeber asks whether China's development approach and performance justify the assertion that China is a developmental state in the mold of its neighbors, Japan, South Korea, and Taiwan. Although he finds common objectives and overlapping tools, China's approach differs in some key respects due to its size, Communist legacy, and a different international climate in which mercantilism is less acceptable than when its neighbors were developing. Moreover, China's record, though impressive, exhibits glaring weaknesses that contrasts with its neighbors, including higher inequality and limited success at innovation.

Andrew Wedeman paints a different picture of Chinese economic policy, though one that complements Pearson and Kroeber, because he focuses on how local–state intervention in the economy is shaped by the nature of interregional competition. His tracing of the evolution of the Chinese and Russian auto sectors highlights a nonlinear process with unexpected positive consequences in China and negative implications for the neighbor to the north. The nature of central–local relations in China pushed local officials and automakers to progressively shift from pursuing rent-seeking opportunities to promoting more efficient producers that compete in national markets. By contrast, Russia's chaotic market environment has left auto firms pursuing short-term opportunities that have made them all inefficient and uncompetitive.

In his chapter, Mark Frazier focuses on social policy, an element of China's political economy that has drawn a lot of attention in the "varieties of capitalism" literature but where China has been barely a footnote in the broader comparative discussion. Frazier compares China's efforts to create a welfare safety net with similar efforts in Asia, Latin America, and Africa. He finds that no single factor, whether regime type, level of industrialization, or the power of labor interests, individually explains the trajectory of the welfare systems of China or other countries. He concludes that China looks less like its East Asian neighbors and more like other "large uneven developers" around the globe.

The Emergence of Interest Groups

The second set of chapters examines the complex emergence of interest groups in an authoritarian context, making them vulnerable to state intrusion and leaving them without the institutional power conferred to social actors by elections. The shift to a market economy has attenuated many segments of society's direct dependence on the state. Most companies' income derives from selling to consumers and businesses, in China and abroad. And with a growing pool of retained profits, companies have greater opportunity to make investment choices that are based on their own preferences and not state industrial policies. But as the chapters demonstrate time and again, China does not have a *free*-market economy and likely will not have one in the future. State actors can affect the life chances of businesses in many ways, through state-owned banks directing loans to some and withholding them from others, adoption of regulations regarding the broader economy or specific sectors and regions, appointments of executives to state-owned enterprises, and discretionary privileges provided by or withheld by well-placed individual officials. As a result, companies have to be aware of state authority and engage officialdom to protect their interests.

Identifying patterns of state-society relations has been a central preoccupation of China scholars since the late 1980s, and they have extensively borrowed conceptual frameworks developed elsewhere. Originally, some scholars believed that economic reforms were leading to the emergence of a civil society that could at a minimum restrain state power and potentially provide impetus for democratization.[47] Others have countered that corporatism, in which the state pushes society to interact with officialdom through state-sponsored organizations, more accurately captured state–society dynamics.[48] Still others have suggested that clientelism, in which the lines between state and society blur, is more on the mark.[49] And, not unexpectedly, some have questioned the application of these concepts or said that a combination of them applies.[50]

Although this research agenda has shed light on important developments and provided a new environment in which these concepts have been considered, almost none of this research has been explicitly comparative. Hence, it has been difficult to determine to what extent elements of Chinese society are organized, active, and influential relative to their counterparts in other countries. Similarly, it has been hard to be sure whether the same economic and political factors shape state–society relations in the PRC and elsewhere.

The chapters in this section attempt to bring the conversation into a comparative light by examining the evolving behavior of business actors vis-a-vis the state. My chapter compares patterns of business lobbying on national economic policy in China, Japan, India, and Russia, finding unexpected similarities and differences across the cases. The analysis demonstrates that both domestic political institutions and economic contexts shape the evolution of business associations, direct lobbying strategies, and the composition of policy coalitions.

Kellee Tsai focuses on the interaction between China's private entrepreneurs and officialdom, particularly at the local level. She shows that their behavior shares much in common with businesspeople in many other authoritarian capitalist countries. As elsewhere, entrepreneurs are not proto-democrats, but they have developed a variety of coping mechanisms, what she terms "adaptive informal institutions," that have still led to enduring, even if less noticed, changes in how business and officialdom interact on a regular basis.

The final chapter in this section considers a specific policy area around which government–business relations revolve. Drawing on comparisons with Mexico and South Korea, Victor Shih applies an interest-group argument to explain why China has been hesitant to permit stakes in domestic banks to foreign interests. He suggests that the greater political clout and higher economic concentration of domestic financial interests in Mexico gave them the resources to persuade the state to permit the sales to foreigners, while the Chinese and Korean financial communities lack similar levels of power, making such sales much less likely to be approved.

Many Chinas but a Consistent Picture

In the book's concluding chapter, Gregory Kasza, a longtime practitioner and champion of the comparative approach, explains why cross-national comparison has not been widely employed by China specialists and how this volume represents a breakthrough for the field.[51] He highlights common themes and patterns that run through the chapters and identifies other types of comparisons that should be pursued in future research on China's political economy. Although he claims the humble role of "outsider," we are all comparativists with a common mission, and his insights and suggestions are highly valuable.

At the same time, it is fitting to identify here some conclusions that emerge out of the book as a whole. Just as the changing angle of the sun affects our view of the landscape, the alternative analytical lenses place China in contrasting lights, confirming Geddes's insight that the comparative cases we choose affect the conclusions we reach.[52] Nevertheless, the various perspectives are surprisingly mutually compatible with each other and offer a picture of China much clearer than any Picasso painting.

Most broadly, China is distinctive but not an outlier. China does not exactly mirror the developmental states of East Asia or its post-Communist cousin Russia, yet there are some parallels with these countries and even more with other large developing countries such as Indonesia and Brazil.

China has a similar aim to promote economic growth as other dirigiste states in East Asia and elsewhere, such as France, and employs some of the same methods, but China's policy process and toolkit are shaped by China's geographic breadth, the Communist Party's ties to the state-owned sector, and the activism of many different stakeholders. Hence, the process in China looks less coherent than in Japan and South Korea. Yet, as Wedeman shows, competition among regional governments in China has escaped the vicious cycle that has hampered Russia, instead evolving into a virtuous cycle of more open, transregional competition that has generated more capable domestic producers. The length of China's high-growth period is particularly long, but, given the mixed record of performance visible when comparing sectors and companies and the high degree of income inequality, China shares much in common with other moderately successful countries around the world.

When attention is turned to the role of interest groups, we see that the move toward capitalism has led business to gain some influence over the state, but it is still less organized and powerful than its counterparts in a wide array of countries. At the same time, the Chinese case magnifies observations from elsewhere that it is common for there to be significant fissures within business and in how companies interact with the state, suggesting that treating industry as a unitary actor is just as problematic as treating the state as a singular entity.

Placing China in comparative perspective not only reveals more about China, it also speaks to the comparative exercise more broadly and allows us additional insight into questions about the relative effect of different factors on countries' political economies. Trying to delineate amongst types of capitalist systems is laudable, but, when attempting to push all countries into two or three categories, it is not a surprise that China either gets lumped in with others with whom it shares many similarities and differences or that China is ghettoized in its own category. But that does not mean that for China either choice is potentially appropriate; rather that the nature of the categorization itself is problematic.

The studies in this volume suggest that a comparison of first-order variables is more valuable. Although some would prefer parsimony, our research lends more support to the conclusion that multiple factors shape countries' economic policies and the behavior of interest groups. A *Communist legacy* is clearly important because of the state's relationship with state-owned enterprises, regardless of whether they have been formally privatized. This creates pressures for path dependence not visible in countries without this history. But state ownership and the resultant ties tell only explain a part of the story, as other factors push and pull in other directions. Similarly, *regime type* (autocracy or democracy) matters, but not absolutely. China and India share similarities in the social policies and in the emergence of industry associations in highly competitive sectors. Conversely, a democratic Russia is attempting to control the political activism of business in ways just like China, for example, with state-controlled chambers of commerce. Several contributors show how the *structure of the bureaucracy*, at the national and local levels, affects the substance and implementation of economic policies.

Economic variables likewise shape policy and outcomes across countries. China's *size*, its most obvious characteristic, provides China developmental opportunities not available to smaller countries, but it also creates enormous complications for central government officials trying to achieve consensus and implement consistent policies. The political economy of sectors and policy issues varies widely in China and elsewhere in part because of the different *distribution of interests* in each area. We see this in the stories related to autos, software, banking, and welfare. The relevant stakeholders and distribution of interests in China's auto sector differs from those in Russia and Japan, and the fact of state ownership of China's banks means they have a different attitude toward foreign acquisitions than their private counterparts elsewhere. Finally, a country's *position in the global economy* shapes its policy options and their efficacy. As a late-late developer, China does not have the luxury of unfettered access to technology and markets that the United States felt more comfortable providing Japan during the Cold War; hence, it has had to be much more open to foreign direct investment. At the same time, the changing cost structure of production has generated opportunities for China to attract investment and its accompanying technology not available to others.

Looking ahead, comparativists incorporating China into their research agendas need to look in even greater depth at the issues analyzed here. There is no shortage of other important topics deserving study, from environmental politics to fiscal policy to Internet regulation. The enterprise would benefit from more first-hand, multicountry field work as well as large-*n* analyses using quantitative datasets. One element of cross-national comparison that could be more fruitfully mined concerns addressing internal variation.

As Kasza points out, China's internal variation, much on display in several chapters here, has been a hindrance to cross-national comparison because of the difficulty of identifying the one Chinese pattern to be used as the basis for comparison and also because such variation itself offers an excellent environment for social science theorizing. Nevertheless, China is not unique in having internal variation. The United States and other large countries have tremendous variation, and so do even smaller countries, a phenomenon no doubt promoted by globalization. The Chinese case and its subnational units can provide inspiration (and data) for scholars to analyze more carefully similarities and differences in patterns of variation within countries more generally.

Certainly this book is not the first word in viewing China's political economy in comparative perspective, but it is hoped that through demonstrating the feasibility and benefits of cross-national comparison, it will generate momentum for further scholarship that confirms the rationale for the path taken here.

PART ONE

Chinese Economic Reform and the Varieties of Capitalism

Chapter Two

Variety Within and Without
The Political Economy of Chinese Regulation

MARGARET M. PEARSON

This chapter examines China's emerging system of economic regulation—
and more generally its system of economic governance—by comparing China
to several other major capitalist economies. In so doing, the chapter attempts
to characterize some of the basic foundations of China's political economy
as it has emerged since the late 1990s, as well as to shed light on a core question of this volume: How can we locate China's political economy in reference
to other capitalist countries? Empirically, the chapter focuses on the most
strategic sectors of the Chinese economy. The chapter's main themes key off
the idea that, contrary to predictions of substantial convergence in forms of
economic governance, there remain significant "varieties of capitalism."[1] But
rather than just arguing that the Chinese case supports the idea of "varieties,"
it goes further to argue that some key elements of China's political economy
in its strategic industries still must be considered to lie outside the rubric of
"capitalism." China is not sui generis, and it has traveled a long distance from
the height of planned socialism, and yet its remaining differences must be
kept center stage to properly understand the system.

More specifically, the chapter examines variance in China's emerging
regulatory state in two contexts. First, it discusses the commonsensical but
underemphasized point that China does not have a singular political economy. Rather, China actually has several economic systems, or "tiers." Each
of these tiers is characterized by its own version of the "regulatory state."

The point should not surprise us, as any continental economy can be expected to have great internal diversity of economic form. Yet it is a point that analysts of the Chinese political economy have too often ignored. In response to this deficiency, the chapter's first section lays out a generalized heuristic understanding of China's three-tiered economy and their associated systems of regulation.

Second, focusing on the top two of the tiers, the chapter compares some of the core regulatory institutions and norms in China with their counterparts in several capitalist systems. The analysis engages two comparative reference points not often made by Chinese political economy experts: Europe (especially France) and the major economies of Latin America (especially Brazil). Reference is also made to the "developmental states" of East Asia, specifically Japan, which although a more common point of comparison nevertheless continues to help bring into relief key features of Chinese economic governance. These points of comparison are chosen because they appear *ex ante* to share some basic features with China, most notably a history of state intervention in the economy. This prior impression of similarity is upheld in the comparison. Yet important differences in the Chinese political economy remain—differences stemming from the remaining commitment to state ownership at the apex of the economy.

Before proceeding with discussion of China's considerable internal variation ("tiers"), it is useful to give a brief overview of the international state of regulatory thinking and the global context of Chinese regulation, both institutionally and normatively. When the Chinese reform leaders embarked on the path to a market-driven system and declared the twilight of the era of ministry-led economic governance typical of the distributive state, it was clear that some form of "regulation" would have to come into being. Thus, regulation in China (as elsewhere) is a key aspect of the state's control of the economy, helping to delimit where to assert and intervene over markets and where to draw back. In other words, a regulatory state serves the function of economic governance that ministries, wholesale public/collective ownership, and state provision of services had carried out previously. In replacing the structures of a command economy with a regulatory state, the Chinese leadership—taking account of the existing institutional and political landscape—has had to make myriad decisions about what direction to move, in terms of regulation.

The Chinese leadership's redrawing of the system of economic governance must be understood as part of a "global wave" of regulatory reform. Outside of China, privatization movements that swept Europe, Latin America, and East Asia accompanied the end of regulation as a process of "steering the economy" toward a more minimalist view of the state's role as creator of a context for fair market competition. Many aspects of the emergent regulatory states were modeled on an idealized version of the American system. Institutionally, the hallmark is the independent regulator—regulators who are substantially autonomous from political organs as well as being separate from and impartial to the firms they regulate. The job of the independent regulator is, in this view, to referee a level playing field between market players without regard to the makeup of the players. If rules are transparent and applied evenly, and in concert with certain procompetitive policies, competition should be enhanced by government regulation. The tool deemed best to promote this goal, and applied to some degree in the European context, is "competition policy" in specific sectors and/or overarching procompetition state institutions.[2]

Whether independent regulators actually make expert decisions independent from government and business is, unsurprisingly and with merit, debated.[3] Nevertheless, the vision of the procompetitive independent regulator, underlain by the normative idea that the regulatory state is *the* modern system of economic governance, is the hegemonic ideal; no legitimate alternative model currently exists. This hegemony is perpetuated by all major international organizations whose work touches on issues of economic regulation, including the World Bank, the International Monetary Fund, the World Trade Organization (WTO), the Organization for Economic Co-operation and Development (OECD), and the Asian Development Bank. It is a core part of the advice offered countries as diverse as South Korea, Mauritania, Serbia, and Vietnam by private and public consultancies in international economic development.[4] The push for international diffusion has been underway for the past decade.[5] Numerous European countries have established independent regulators in multiple sectors. As Majone has commented, "Statutory regulation by independent agencies—sometimes called, for historical reasons, 'American-style regulation'—is rapidly becoming the most important mode of regulation, indeed the leading edge of public policymaking in Europe."[6] International agencies, notably the OECD, have been mainly responsible for this diffusion across Europe.[7] A similar story of international diffusion of the international regulator model by international agencies can be told for Latin America.[8] The Chinese government, too, has been made much aware of this model, in large part through its contacts with the international organizations named previously.[9]

Yet, in actual practice, among those countries that have adopted the independent regulator model there has yet to be convergence of practice across countries. Rather, we have institutional isomorphism—the same institutional form adopted but with very different ancestries in each country and, ultimately, different outcomes.[10] As we shall see, despite discursive convergence between the ideal of the independent regulator and the stated goals of many governments, convergence to the ideal in practice is limited. Indeed, certain patterns of deviation from the model are shared across many systems.[11]

It is not only internationally that we see variance in regulatory forms. Internally, China exhibits a variety of regulatory practices, depending on the nature of industries involved and their status in the eyes of the Chinese party-state. These "tiers" are examined in the next section.

China's Tiered Economy

Many analyses of China's political economy overlook a very basic fact: as a continental economy engaged in a wide range of productive and consumptive activities, there is no *single* Chinese political economy. Nor does China's economy contain a single model of regulation. It is more useful instead to think of China's political economy and, by extension, its system of regulation, as having three tiers.[12] The top tier consists of China's "lifeline" (*mingmai*), or "commanding heights" industries. The third, or bottom, tier is constituted by the vast majority of China's private and collective firms. It also contains many of the country's approximately 90,000 smaller state firms, some of which have been sold to private or foreign investors. The middle tier is made up of firms that are both considered important by the state and are sometimes governed by explicit industrial policies. And yet in the middle tier the state asserts less control in terms of foreign direct investment and local ownership than in the top-tier lifeline industries.

REGULATORY CHARACTERISTICS OF THE TOP TIER

The top tier of China's economic and regulatory structures is made up of the largest companies, all state-owned, and those that the government considers most strategic. Pursuant to the 1993 Company Law, many state-owned enterprises have been reorganized into joint-stock corporations or limited liability companies.[13] Stock shares of a portion of these companies' assets were issued to nonstate and state actors, primarily to raise revenues and (perhaps) gain international legitimacy. Yet the state intends to maintain dominant ownership and, especially, control of these strategic firms. Moreover, they have been subject to pressure by the government to consolidate into large enterprise groups. This goal was ensconced in the Tenth Five-Year Plan, approved by the National People's Congress—China's legislature—in 2001. The plan calls for the development of a number of large companies and enterprise groups in each sector that focus on the core business of the sector. The top three companies in each major sector are to be state-owned, moreover. The target by 2010 was to have between thirty and fifty state-owned firms as "national champions."[14] For the top-tier industries, the effort to foster national champions is related to the desire to limit competition for China's largest state firms. The related slogan *"zhua da fang xiao"* ("grasp the big, release the small"), endorsed at the 15th Party Congress in 1997, captures the effort to concentrate state assets in large state firms, ideally getting rid of poorly performing assets in these companies, and at the same time spinning off (selling or consolidating through mergers) medium and small enterprises. It is important to emphasize that these policies do not, as often characterized, reflect bureaucratic inertia and a vested interest in propping up state-owned dinosaurs. Rather, they reflect a conscious effort by the Chinese government to concentrate and consolidate China's main state enterprises, and to make them profitable, as a key element of its ongoing development strategy. Key goals are to prepare Chinese enterprises to compete on global markets and to preserve the value of state assets.[15]

With regard to regulation, many industries in the top tier have witnessed the establishment of new independent regulators.[16] The government has set up regulatory commissions governing key infrastructure sectors (electric power, telecommunications, and aviation) and financial services (securities, insurance, and banking). Most of these regulators were carved out of or morphed from previous ministerial level agencies. The establishment of new regulators has been supported by corporate governance laws, which have also aimed to separate regulators from the businesses they regulate. (For example, the insurance regulator's former ministerial persona, the Bank of China, also previously had direct control over the largest insurance company, and the company with former monopoly power—People's Insurance Company of China [PICC].) These efforts to separate regulator from firm—to avoid business "capture" of the regulators—have been supported by government-sponsored rhetoric to the effect that regulatory independence is desirable.

Yet a number of bureaucratic and institutional features of the Chinese system have prevented the independent regulator model from being fully articulated. In particular, regulatory authority remains weak, and separation of regulators from "politics" has not been successful. In terms of institutional design, two main gaps with the independent regulator model are most evident. First, supraregulatory bodies remain exceptionally powerful. These companies' assets have been placed under the control of the State-Owned Assets Supervision and Administration Commission (SASAC). SASAC has substantial authority over assets, including the privatization, sales, and purchases of businesses and business units and the appointment of top managers. Most of these firms, in addition to being on SASAC's list of strategic companies, are also overseen by the even more powerful National Development and Reform Commission (NDRC). The NDRC remains the source of most industrial policy and in addition must approve major investments and industry decisions.

Finally, the Chinese Communist Party (CCP) retains substantial authority over strategic state enterprises. This authority is realized in two areas: appointment of top executives to major state-owned firms and placement of Party members on the board of firms. Efforts to improve corporate governance through corporatization of state enterprises has proceeded with some success in the past decade. Moreover, it is not necessarily true that the Party will influence decisions that contravene the efforts of corporate governance reform; as pointed out by John Thornton (who, among many hats, is board member of one of China's largest telecom firms, China Netcom), "The chairman of Netcom likes to say that he does not see a contradiction between Party influence and the protection of [non-Party] minority shareholders because the goals of the two are the same—namely, Netcom's success as a business."[17] Nevertheless, it is clear that the Party still has influence in appointing top executives, as the Organization Department of the Party remains involved.[18] At a minimum, its members retain veto power over appointments and major policy decisions.

These supraregulatory institutions can easily justify their involvement in regulatory activities because they retain ultimate responsibility for overall economic performance of the economy and its most strategic sectors. Moreover, they are the source of policy goals that must be implemented by regulators—a function that in Western economies is often served by national legislatures. The main dysfunction arising from the presence of supraregulatory authorities is that their authority vis-à-vis the formal regulators is poorly defined, and their power often trumps that of the industry-specific regulator. Ironically, SASAC's authority is also not clearly demarcated, as many of the firms it oversees are themselves huge conglomerates, often the offspring of former ministries that control massive amounts of resources and have high-flying ties to political leaders.[19]

The weakness of regulators is further exacerbated by a second institutional feature just noted with regard to SASAC: new regulators' need to continue to compete with other agencies that never lost authority to regulate a particular sector. The telecom sector provides the most egregious example, with at least ten other government bodies (including the Ministry of State Security) retaining a say over telecom decisions.[20] In short, regulatory decision making in China's top tier remains fragmented and contested, and the coordination that must occur, in fact, between these multiple contestants leads to a very fragmented and poorly enforced regulatory regime.

Thus, the attempt to add in new institutions, processes, and ideas and even to eliminate some of the old hindrances has not created a seamless transformation to a brand-new system of economic governance. Rather, the new system has been grafted onto the rest of the system—but not granted sufficient, or sufficiently delineated, authority. The extremely fragmented politics characterized by protracted bargaining between interested bureaucracies remains a fact of regulatory life, as does the hyperconscious attention to formal government hierarchy and a unit's location in it.

In addition to these institutional features emanating from China's former planning system, the current regulatory environment contains normative preferences to limit competition (by managing industry structure) and to name winners. Indeed, the upper echelons of the party-state retain a keen interest in the performance of the state-owned firms on which it has banked much of its vision for the future of China's economy, as well as much of its own legitimacy. This keen interest means it must care which firms survive—leading to continual efforts to optimally structure the market and avoid what it perceives to be wasteful competition. One clear result of the desire to avoid "excessive" competition is that the state has actively structured the strategic industries, breaking up the former monopolies into four or five pieces, rotating assets in and out of them like a shell game to optimize the structure.[21] Rumors are rife that in the telecommunications industry (which in the past few years has been consolidated into four major players), one of the major firms will be further broken up and folded into another of the existing companies, leaving three dominant players.[22] NDRC and SASAC, in addition to the formal regulator (MIIT), are the dominant actors in these matters, which involve decisions about not only industry structure and disposition of state assets but also the allocation of technical modalities between state firms, as well as the choice of both Chinese and foreign partners in any upcoming joint ventures.

REGULATORY CHARACTERISTICS OF THE MIDDLE TIER

Regulation of the middle-tier firms shares with that of the top-tier firms a primacy for state ownership and desire for creation of national champions. Nevertheless, there are differences that give firms in this tier a different character. There is substantially more diversity in regulatory structure and governance of firms in the middle tier. Some firms in this tier are centrally owned and thereby supervised by the central offices of the NDRC and SASAC, and the central Party, as in the top tier. Others are owned by municipal governments or provinces and so more controlled by local offices of the NDRC, SASAC, and the Party. Examples of industries in the middle tier include automobile and pharmaceuticals production, as well as chemicals. The auto industry, the empirical focus of this discussion, usefully illustrates not only the key characteristics of the middle-tier industries but also the internal diversity of the tier itself.[23]

Unlike most of the industries in the first tier, a sector-specific regulator does not oversee China's auto industry. Nevertheless, the industry is governed by industrial policy promulgated by the NDRC's predecessor (the State Planning Commission) in 1994. The government is cognizant of the multiplier effects, and related employment effects, of such industries and so wishes for them to be successful.[24] Hence, the auto industrial policy mandated that China have three or four major auto manufacturers, and, although it would not force the elimination of competitors, it would encourage mergers. The NDRC was the dominant voice in deciding which companies should become "national champions" and which should merge.

There is an implicit recognition with regard to the auto industry that, while it makes sense to have the government structure the industry and supervise assets, these industries should be given more leeway. Why? Three factors are important. First, in contrast to the industries in the first tier, the government has recognized that the auto sector could not succeed without being integrated into the global supply chain and without joint ventures. This recognition was tempered by the desire for substantial local content requirements for JVs. Shanghai municipality in particular worked hard and with some success to develop a local supply chain.[25] Yet over the years Chinese government efforts to enforce Chinese production of inputs for auto JVs has waned, or relaxed, considerably. (There have been substantial efforts to close foreign firms out of distributorships, however.) Second, perhaps because the government could not, and should not, limit consumer demand, it acquiesced in the idea that more of the auto industry would be market driven.

Third, the industry contains state-owned firms that are both centrally owned and owned at the municipal level (Shanghai and Beijing municipal governments). There is also one substantial private firm (Geely). Because municipalities have a significant role in development of the industry, the center has yielded somewhat the notion of comprehensive authority. With regard to regulation, central SASAC oversees the assets of the large centrally owned auto producers, whereas the municipal SASAC branches oversee those firms owned by Beijing and Shanghai municipal governments and do not report directly to the center. In short, the hyperintensity of central regulation in this sector is less than for the strategic industries. As a result, although industrial policy has been aimed at creating national champions, the designation of national champion is won more through competition and consolidation of existing firms than designation from the top.[26]

REGULATORY CHARACTERISTICS OF THE BOTTOM TIER

Regulation of the vast majority of Chinese businesses in terms of numbers—notably, medium and small manufacturing, personal services, and retail firms—is quite distinct from the style of regulation evident in the top two tiers. During the reform era, small and medium firms have either sprung up outside the state—what Naughton calls "growing out of the plan"—or, if previously existing, have moved out of the crosshairs of the comprehensive regulatory agencies through the process of *fangxiao* ("letting go of the small").[27] Many firms in this tier are small scale and involved in personal services or the sale and manufacture of consumer goods and other light industries. The majority of China's export-oriented firms fit into this group. Others are small scale locally owned firms that are not "strategic," such as coal-mining. These firms are not subject to efforts at economic regulation or of industrial policy. They are not subject to oversight by a sector-specific independent regulator. [28]

However, firms in the third tier are subject to other types of regulation. The first types of rules aim to give the state approval rights for certain standard issues involving business scope and operations. Often, these restrictions originate at the local level.[29] The major "regulatory agency" to oversee matters of market regulation for most Chinese enterprises is the State Administration for Industry and Commerce (SAIC), a bureaucracy charged with stabilizing the market and also combating local protectionism in order to enhance the market. SAIC's operations were centralized from the local level to the provincial level in the late 1990s,[30] yet it is far from being premised on the independent regulator model.

These small and medium enterprises of the third tier also are increasingly subject to "social regulation" designed to protect consumers from fraud, overpricing, and discrimination, as well as to protect workers. Led by high-profile cases of pharmaceutical fraud, pyramid schemes, and workplace accidents, and driven by popular demand and media focus, social regulation has gained much attention in China in the past decade. As a result, institutions for social regulation have gained currency. Two areas for such regulation are notable. The first is the regulation of food, food labeling, and drug safety, which has resulted in the establishment of the State Food and Drug Administration (SFDA, modeled on the U.S. Food and Drug Administration). The fake baby formula scandal of the 1990s, which led to numerous deaths among infants, was a major spur for this institutional development.[31] A second is the efforts to regulate coal mine safety through the State Administration of Coal Mine Safety (established in 1999). Deaths from coal mine accidents have received tremendous publicity within China in the past decade, spurring regulation. Both regulators are designed to be separate from the administrative segments of the state that long were involved in production ("independence from business").[32] In their early years, fragmentation and poor definition of regulatory authority, as well as spotty implementation, have marred these regulation efforts.

The previous discussion has given evidence of considerable variation in the systems of governance of the Chinese economy. It has highlighted the effort of the Chinese government to disaggregate its regulatory system based on considerations as varied as sectoral characteristics (such as monopoly versus competition), degree of integration with the global economy, and perceived strategic importance. Within each tier, there has been some attention to creating complementary institutions.[33] For example, the top-tier institutions providing oversight on behalf of the regime complement the limited competition in industry structure, whereas in the bottom tier the relative lack of regulatory oversight is complemented by the relative fluidity of the labor market. A fascinating question is the degree to which the different tiers complement each other or whether there are substantial costs to the lack of coordination. The Chinese reformers implicitly, in launching market reforms in differential phases and even more in attempting to carry out a policy of "grasping the big and releasing the small," have for the time being pronounced the effort at producing overall complementarities in a planned system less effective than segmenting the economy and aiming for complementarities within tiers.

The following section focuses on China's top tier firms. The task is to locate the ideational and institutional parameters of these firms in comparative perspective.

Locating Chinese Patterns of Economic Governance in the Top Tiers— Comparisons with France, Japan, and Latin America

Comparative political economy has long attempted to categorize economic systems according to type, such as capitalist (state capitalism, coordinated capitalism, market capitalism) and socialist (planned socialism, market socialism). These heuristic and comparative efforts received an injection of new life in the late 1990s with the emergence of the "varieties of capitalism"

literature. A core emphasis of this literature is the persistence of differences between nominally similar politicoeconomic systems—differences
that reflect institutional history—despite pressures from globalization; convergence is unlikely.[34] The underlying theme of the varieties of capitalism
literature—of nonconvergence and remaining differences—is helpful for beginning to understand China's political economy, which is very ambiguous
in its capitalism vis-à-vis much less unambiguously capitalist ones. The second half of this chapter has two goals. First, it attempts empirically, if only
briefly, to show how China's system of economic governance in the top tiers
shares similarities with other systems—Japan, France, and (with less speci-
ficity) countries of Latin America—that have undergone regulatory reform
in the recent past.[35] These countries share both ideological and institutional
features that limit the independent authority of new regulatory agencies. As
a result, in some strikingly similar ways all deviate substantially from the
Anglo-American ideal of the market-enhancing independent regulator. Second, the discussion highlights the differences that remain in China's economic system that, stated bluntly, cause its top tiers to remain much closer
to state socialism than the other countries considered—despite substantial
reform over the past twenty-five years.

It must be noted, of course, that comparisons across systems are difficult
in small-n studies, as the differences quickly come into high relief. What is
striking about this set of cases is that, in the era of globalization, privatization, and decentralization, the role of the state, in terms of ideology and
institutions, remains prominent in these systems.[36] The state role is most
prominent in China, perhaps, but understanding the state's prominence in
other more "mainstream" countries allows us to see China as much less of an
outlier—less sui generis—than those who study China's political economy
are often tempted to do, even if in the end crucial differences remain.

CROSS-NATIONAL SIMILARITIES

Many elements of China's economic and regulatory reforms in its top tiers
appear similar to reforms found in other countries. As discussed previously,
the spread of the independent regulator model has been extensive in Europe
and Latin America. These reforms have gone hand-in-hand with partial
privatization and a scaling back of the state's economic role. As in China,
both European and Latin American governments adopted versions of the

independent regulator model in the 1980s and 1990s. The idea that the state should encourage competition among newly privatized firms, so that private monopolies did not simply replace public ones, was one key rationale for adoption of this model. The adoption of this model was weaker in Japan. Regulatory reforms in Japan in the 1980s brought a modicum of improvement in market competition in strategically designated sectors and some privatization. Another surge of regulatory reform occurred in Japan in the wake of the 1997 Asian Financial Crisis. China's adoption of the ideal model was perhaps more earnest than in Japan—in part because China was less insulated from outside pressures such as WTO accession—but less earnest than in Europe and Latin America, as the task of grafting the model onto a situation where there had been less privatization posed substantial problems.

Deviation from the ideal-typical model is not surprising. It is more instructive to examine the common modalities of deviation from the ideal model. Here, I compare ideational and institutional similarities between China and, alternately, France, Japan, and Brazil.

Policy Ideas

Simply stated, China shares with France and Japan, and to a lesser degree with Brazil, a continuing affinity for state guidance of the top tiers of the economy, even if there has been substantial privatization. As is consistent with its formal ideology of market socialism, China remains the strongest advocate of state intervention. But China is not alone in its affinity for dirigisme. The comparison with Japan and the developmental state model is obvious because it captures some of the ways the Chinese state is attempting to regulate the economy. The model not only places the state at the center of the action, it tolerates substantial government intervention to structure markets, often in favor of particular firms whose failure would impose unacceptable social costs. With regard to Japan in particular, while the country has made significant reforms, it has been widely concluded that these reforms have not significantly reduced the government's control over business. The government encourages market stability, and discourages "excess competition" that might reduce profits of favored firms.[37]

Comparison with France is also apt. In contrast to the deep American ambivalence and even hostility toward state intervention, there has been a normative acceptance, even to a large extent by the French right, of mixed economies and state intervention, particularly to control competition.[38]

Commenting on Western Europe as a whole, Majone concludes that "the commitment to competition policy has never been as strong in Europe as it has in the United States."[39] Despite substantial privatization carried out in the 1980s, and often running against the currents of EU integration, the French government maintains a position that state intervention, if not ownership, then relatively close control, is acceptable.[40] This is the case, for example, in the French telecommunications sector, which retains significant state ownership or control. As Schmidt states, "The policy programme of French governments on the left and right from the mid-1980s to the late 1990s encountered problems related to the fact that, while they consistently emphasized the necessity of neo-liberal reform in their discourse, they barely spoke of its appropriateness other than to reiterate time and again without much conviction that they were defending traditional values of social solidarity."[41] In Brazil, too, despite the presence of market-oriented reformers (notably President Cardoso in the early 1990s), ambivalence about privatization remained. There were neither opinion leaders nor a strong conservative party committed to privatization. The converse has largely been true: even relatively weak states have been prone to be quite interventionist in the economy.[42] The current resurgence of statism, seen in the form of a renewed popularity of state control of strategic industries, brings Latin America even closer to the Chinese path.

Institutions

The greater faith placed in statist control of strategic industries finds its counterpart in institutional preferences for the restriction of competition, particularly (though not exclusively) competition by multinationals, and the concomitant structuring of markets and development of national champions. As previously discussed, the late 1990s in China saw a resuscitation of the ideal of national champions, including efforts to sustain WTO-compatible industrial policy. Whereas some predicted after the Asian Financial Crisis that the era of state-protected business groups of the "East Asian Miracle" would become defunct, this has not proven to be the case in China, just as they have by no means disappeared in Japan (or Korea, in the form of *chaebol*).[43] Hence, the Japanese state has preferences as to the specific market actors and favors in particular those firms that stand to enhance the international competitiveness of national firms. Similar to China's effort to promote large enterprise groups, both France and Brazil show continuing affinity for large enterprise groups. European cartels and restrictive agreements have been "traditionally accepted either as an expression of the freedom of contract, as in Britain, or as instruments of rationalization and industrial policy, as in Germany."[44] French privatization involved the sale of controlling shares to *noyaux durs* ("hard cores") of strategic investors with close ties to the government.[45] While industrial policy per se has been eschewed by the French state, it has fostered a

> mixed economy in which cross-shareholdings and interlocking directorships ensure that French business now looks much like the German in terms of banking–industry partnerships and like the Japanese in terms of affinity groups of industries, banks, insurers, and other service providers, and suppliers.[46]

In Brazil, the structuring of markets and concentration of industry was part and parcel of nationalization and monopoly status of strategic industries (notably oil, electric power, telecommunications, mining, and steel) that existed from the 1950s until the late 1980s.[47] Yet the pattern continued under privatization, as public enterprises were sold to existing large industry groups, prior to the advent of any procompetition regulation. Thus, a concentrated market structure was reified under private ownership.[48] (Notably, though, Latin American conglomerates often bring together quite unrelated business lines under the rubric of a "group."[49] The pattern of Chinese conglomerates is largely unstudied.) Brazil's pattern of privatization-before-regulation suggests the uncertainty surrounding the establishment of independent regulators and further fostered a number of the problems for regulators—lack of autonomy and authority, albeit from societal groups (the age-old problem of regulatory "capture").

As discussed previously, regulatory agencies in China's strategic industries have made significant adaptations to the Chinese political environment. They remain subject to many competing stakeholders, including the former and present state-sector owners of the industries, such that regulators must account not only to politicians who set policy directions (as is natural) but also are accountable to the many other interested bureaucratic players who continue to have a place at the regulatory table.[50] Moreover, they are often subordinate to comprehensive agencies designed to supervise state assets and keep industries aligned with the CCP's vision of development. All this translates into problems gaining authority and independence. Such problems find counterparts in Europe, Latin America, and Asia, even if the context of each system adds unique elements. The need for extensive regulatory coordination with other parts of the state bureaucracy and with industry is visible in France. French business–government relations are marked by very close links and need for cooperation between the formerly dirigiste state and industry.[51] Throughout Latin America, including in Brazil, extensive coordination between states and business associations is a major hallmark of the political economy.[52] Indeed, Brazilian regulators are poorly insulated from the executive, as well as from business.[53]

In both France and Brazil, moreover, there is a "revolving door" between business and regulators (as is true even in the ideal-typical U.S. regulatory system). The French system of training both bureaucratic elites and business elites in the same few schools means many business elites have ties to top state actors and may readily enter the business world.[54] Similar ties between business and government bureaucrats exist in Latin America.[55] A revolving door has the advantage of bringing expertise and, often, capacity to the regulatory realm. Yet it remains a structural impingement on the independence of new regulators. China's version of the revolving door is inherent in a system in which the government maintains power of appointment over the business executives of strategic firms. Although in China the revolving door involves state actors more than business groups located outside the state, business influence on policy is growing in China through the advent of lobbying by firms and business associations.[56] China's situation is not yet close to that of Latin America and Europe, where regulation is by and large the story of tripartite influence of government, business, and labor.[57] In China, organized labor (at least as yet) does not have a voice beyond the Party, and the voice of business is still more tied to the state than not. Yet the common thread through all three cases is that the regulatory systems are quite porous, greatly limiting the autonomy of regulators.

The lack of independence feeds into problems of insufficient regulatory authority and legitimacy. The powerful influence of China's supraregulatory agencies—NDRC, SASAC, and the Party—have counterparts in Japan's political economy. In contrast to Europe and Latin America, Japan's industrial policies typically are carried out, with significant autonomy from political or civil forces, through comprehensive or sector-specific bureaucracies, Japan's MITI (now METI) being the archetype.[58] Indeed, this foundation of the Japanese developmental state has cast a long shadow over Japan's more recently sanctioned regulators and has resulted in more than a modicum of bureaucratic rigidity.[59] In Europe, in France as well as in Germany, the tradition of ministerial direction of major industries means that both countries have faced problems extricating bureaucratic interests from the regulatory area. In France in particular, ministries retain substantial levers over regulators, even if not able to enforce industrial policy.[60] The rise of the European Union as a supranational regulator has ameliorated this pressure somewhat but by no means completely.[61] The competition between Latin America's weak regulatory institutions and the large state enterprises or private enterprise groups has limited the independence of the former. This situation has resulted in relatively weak legitimacy for Latin American regulators.[62]

IN WHAT WAYS DOES CHINA'S REGULATORY SYSTEM REMAIN UNIQUE?

If the previous discussion has allowed us to understand the ways in which problems in China's "modern" regulatory system have counterparts in other industrial economies, we must also consider ways in which China's system of economic governance remains quite unique. The main source of China's uniqueness, leading to its superbly ambivalent adoption of "capitalism," is its Communist past and the fact that policy movements toward capitalism have been carefully constructed (albeit gradually) by Party leaders and in the absence of chaotic discussions within or between state and society. More accurately, while the Chinese leadership has not been able to control many elements of reform, it has monopolized the terms of debate (in contrast to debates led by competing parties in the comparison countries in this chapter), and it has monopolized much of the reforms of institutional structures. Hence, China's system of continuing state ownership and structure of Party control—at least over strategic industries—means that in crucial ways China remains an outlier and not even yet ready to be included as a "variety of capitalism." Both explicit and implicit in the previous discussion are four major "differences": the continued important role of state ownership; the remaining hypersalience of superagencies with authority over the economy; the absence of a politics of transparent electoral politics and coalition building; and *concertation* between the state, business and labor.

China's top tiers of government have been shielded from extensive privatization; if other countries considered here have been ambivalent, China's government, for its strategic industries, has largely avoided it. In short, ownership matters. As Barry Naughton notes, "The Chinese government has never unambiguously embraced privatization and continues to avoid the term in favor of vague circumlocutions such as 'restructuring'."[63] As a result, despite the restructuring of the state-ownership system such that ministry-controlled firms are now "corporations," firms in the top tiers remain primarily owned by the state, and managers of these firms ultimately are responsible to state interests.[64] (Complete privatization, particularly through sales to insiders—workers and especially management—has become widespread in China since the late 1990s but in the small and medium size firms, especially those in the lowest tier, that were to be "let go.")

Although the interests of the state are in theory no longer to be exercised through a broad range of interested government offices, the weak and fragmented authority of regulators leaves open much space for political interference. At the same time as the old state agents have not been cleared from the picture, new life has been breathed into supranational state agencies such as SASAC and the NDRC. Even the Party's role, if mostly limited to personnel appointments and broad supervision, has been clarified. As a result, though new regulators are to create a level playing field, it is far from clear that they can do so when the firms they are regulating are themselves owned by the state and overseen by the same agencies responsible for preserving state assets. Despite extensive reform in the system of enterprise management, then, China's remaining state ownership and the interests of the state in the performance of the firms appear more intense than in Japan, France, or Brazil, where much more extensive privatization has occurred. Ownership differences do not necessarily mean Chinese regulators operate more or less effectively than their counterparts where privatization is more thorough; both stray from the ideal. Yet in Latin America, for example, where privatization preceded the establishment of independent regulators, the regulators are often playing catch-up in uncharted territory; their weakness is vis-à-vis society.[65] In China, in contrast, the regulators are still deeply mired in the politics of the state and are weak relative to other state players.[66]

When reviewing the vast literature on regulation and economic reform in Europe, Latin America, and Asia, two core (and related) elements quickly reveal themselves to be absent in China, electoral politics and coalition building. In those democratic countries, it is clear that politicians' efforts to please major constituencies and build coalitions for (or against) reform dramatically influence the outcomes of reform. The establishment of the institutions of a regulatory state, for example, is often part of a political platform designed by political parties striving to win elections. In France, much of the dynamic of deregulation and privatization must be understood at least in part through the prism of left–right party competition in the 1980s and 1990s. In Brazil, it was a reformist electoral coalition surrounding various presidents, most notably Cardoso, that drove reform.[67]

Closely related to the need for reform programs to deal with nonstate actors via electoral politics has been the interaction, outside of China, between reform programs and the major nonstate forces of business and labor. Forms of coordination between the state, business associations, and labor groups—variously termed *concertation*, pacts, and societal corporatism—that are core to the political economy of reform in Latin America and Europe are often at the heart of analyses of reforms in those countries.[68] In China, we are only beginning to see direct evidence of the sort of coordination with actors outside the state, and the interlocutors are state and business, with labor excluded. Kennedy in particular has written of lobbying by industry groups and firms themselves, which he puts in comparative perspective in his chapter in this volume.[69] Interestingly, we know that extensive coordination must happen over regulation and reform in China. This was illustrated in the previous discussion of the lack of autonomy. But much of what we know concerns the need for coordination within the state. Deep exploration of patterned coordination between major business groups and the Chinese state still awaits students of Chinese political economy. Nevertheless, the continued strength of the state in China's strategic industries allows for skepticism that influence of nonstate actors will reach the point found in privatized industrial economies.

How does this comparison, and the findings of both similarities and differences, help us to locate China's economy in relation to other developed, capitalist economies? In some respects, China's nascent regulatory state has many of the same aspirations and shortcomings of those of other countries. Comparisons with France, Brazil, and Japan make evident how the transition away from a heavily state-dominated model of political economy is not as smooth as would be deemed advisable by those who promulgate the international model of the "independent regulator."

Chapter Three

Developmental Dreams
Policy and Reality in China's Economic Reforms

ARTHUR R. KROEBER

This chapter considers two major questions. First, what is the best way to describe China's economic development path? Second, how successful has this path been, not only in generating high GDP growth, but in respect to three other criteria: (1) acquisition of technology and development of innovative capacity; (2) development of competitive domestic firms; and (3) acquisition of political power in the international trading system.

I argue that Chinese economic development since 1978 is partly explicable by the model of the "East Asian developmental state" devised to describe common features of the development experience of Japan, South Korea, and Taiwan after World War II. But the Chinese case differs from that of its East Asian neighbors in at least three important respects. First, the task of building a modern industrial economy was accompanied throughout by the task of dismantling an inherited communist economic system while maintaining the Communist Party's monopoly on political power. Second, China's enormous physical size and legacy of relatively autonomous local governments and local production units made it far more difficult for the central government to enforce the cartels and national industry restructuring plans that were important elements of Japanese and South Korean industrial development. Finally, China's reform-driven economic takeoff from 1978 onwards took place during a time when international trade and investment rules were rapidly liberalized. Unlike Japan, South Korea, and Taiwan before it—all of which enjoyed broad access to the United States market while keeping their own markets relatively closed to imports and foreign investment—China has permitted a relatively high degree of participation in its domestic market by foreign firms. Economic reformers in China have also used foreign participation in the economy as a catalyst for reforms that might otherwise have been stalled by domestic political deadlocks.

The East Asian Developmental State

The best starting point for an understanding of China's political economy since 1978 is a comparison with the "East Asian developmental state" as represented by Japan (1950–1990), South Korea, and Taiwan (1965–1995).[1] The purpose of this comparison is not to assert that China conforms to some ideal type or that Chinese leaders self-consciously modeled their economic policies on East Asian precedents.[2] The point is simply to establish a "family resemblance" of shared characteristics and to argue that it is more useful to appraise Chinese development with reference to the other members of this "family" than by using comparisons with developing countries with very different characteristics (for example, in Latin America or Africa) or by attempting to apply a teleological framework such as a "transition from Communism to capitalism."

The East Asian developmental states are characterized by features which I group into four major categories: economic, social, and political *conditions* at the outset of the economic takeoff period; development *goals* espoused either explicitly or implicitly by national policy makers; policy *mechanisms* for achieving those goals; and development *outcomes*. These are listed as follows:

- *Conditions*: A high national saving rate, relatively high levels of literacy and education, equitable land distribution, a historical legacy of effective bureaucratic states and secular political culture, and ethnic homogeneity.
- *Goals*: Rapid economic growth through comprehensive industrial development (rather than the maximization of profit through comparative advantage), and technological autonomy.
- *Mechanisms*: State control (direct or indirect) of a financial system that commandeers national saving and allocates it to sectors defined

by industrial policy; reliance on market prices for most goods other than key inputs such as energy (thereby mitigating the inefficiencies of directed capital allocation); encouragement of exports (ensuring that recipients of directed credit are internationally competitive rather than subsidized wastrels); closure of the domestic market to foreign investment and to imports of final-consumption goods (though imports of industrial and technological goods—often for the purpose of reverse engineering—are encouraged); and private ownership of most industrial companies (to ensure distinctive spheres of action for state and enterprise).

- *Outcomes*: High economic growth; relatively equal income distribution; broad-based industrialization; structural goods trade surpluses; internationally competitive firms with leading positions in global markets; a relative lack of competitiveness in service industries; and inefficient financial systems that tend to fall into crisis once the structural rate of economic growth falls.

China's Developmental Path

In starting point (mid-1970s) conditions and in national policy goals, China fits fairly well with the description given in the preceding paragraphs. A decline in the fertility rate beginning in the early 1970s led to a decline in the dependency ratio and hence an increase in the national saving rate. Literacy and public health were at relatively high levels thanks to Mao-era health and education campaigns, and after the breakup of the commune system, beginning in 1978, land-use rights were more or less equally distributed among the entire rural population. On the policy front, the Four Modernizations program (dating from the mid-1970s) clearly articulated the goals of rapid economic growth, broad-based industrialization (as opposed to the pursuit of economic efficiency per se), and technological autonomy.[3] These goals have been persistently reiterated in the past three decades. The most famous statement of the primacy of broad-based economic development over other goals was the statement by Deng Xiaoping during his tour of south China in 1992 that "development is the only hard truth."[4] Evidence for the importance of these policy objectives can also be found in the periodic long-term plans for various industrial sectors such as automobiles, steel, and semiconductors published by the State Planning Commission, its successor the National Development and Reform Commission, and other industrial ministries. Most recently, the ideal of technological autonomy was articulated in the long-term science and technology plan issued in 2006 by the Ministry of Science and Technology, which called for programs supporting "indigenous innovation" (*zizhu chuangxin*).

When we turn to policy mechanisms, however, China displays some similarities with its neighbors and many differences. The most obvious similarities are a financial system that allocates credit in large measure to serve industrial policy goals defined by central and local governments, encouragement of export production, and reliance on competition and market pricing for most final consumption goods in order to keep the recipients of low-cost credit competitive. Some of these mechanisms, however, took many years to perfect. In the 1990s a major function of the state banking system was to finance social welfare by keeping afloat hopelessly inefficient and overstaffed state enterprises, something that Japanese and Korean banks were never required to do. Similarly, it took nearly two decades—from 1978 to the mid-1990s—to eliminate the old socialist system of planned prices for most goods.

China's economic mechanisms diverge sharply from the developmental-state model in several other broad ways. First, economic decision making in China is extremely decentralized, and the ability of the central government to limit the number of participants in a market or orchestrate cartels is far more constrained than was the case in South Korea or Japan, as an examination of the automobile industry will presently show. Second, foreign direct investment, far from being constrained, is strongly encouraged and played an enormous role in building China's export industries. Finally, a very large proportion of firms, accounting for nearly 40 percent of business sector output, is controlled directly by the state and will continue to be so.

The first of these differences arises in part from China's sheer geographic size, which tends to enable a relatively strong role for local governments. Another cause was the decentralized nature of Chinese economic organization during the Mao era (1949–1976). In contrast to the highly centralized economy of the Soviet Union, in which centrally controlled enterprises accounted for the vast majority of production, the Maoist economic model stressed local industrial self-sufficiency, with the result that most production came from units controlled by local governments. As Andrew Wedeman points out in his contribution to this volume, this legacy of local control generated a progression from local protectionism and rent seeking in the 1980s to fierce competition and price wars in the 1990s. As a result, China developed an imperfect but vibrant market for most consumer and industrial goods, in contrast to the oligarch-controlled black markets characterizing post-Soviet Russia or the cartels that prevailed in Japan and South Korea.

The second area of divergence—China's relatively high openness to foreign direct investment—is very striking. Japan, South Korea, and to a lesser extent Taiwan all discouraged foreign investment in the domestic economy; whereas in China openness to foreign investment on a large scale has been an integral part of its development strategy from the beginning of the reform era. The earliest economic reforms included a law on Sino–foreign joint ventures (1980) and the establishment of export-oriented, foreign-friendly special economic zones (1981). Deng Xiaoping explicitly linked openness to foreign trade and investment to reforms in the domestic economy through his slogan *"duiwai kaifang, duinei gaohuo"* (open up to the outside, invigorate the domestic economy), later condensed into the formulation *gaige kaifang* (reform and opening), which remains the standard official catchphrase for the economic reform process.[5]

This formulation strongly implies that domestic reform is impossible without openness; and because the phrase derives from Deng Xiaoping himself, it is politically impossible to jettison it; hence, openness is likely to remain an intrinsic, rather than transitory, feature of the Chinese economy. The centrality of the openness concept has enabled economic reformers within the government to use opening mechanisms to force through domestic reforms that otherwise would have been far more difficult or even impossible, most notably via China's accession to the World Trade Organization in December 2001.

China's relative degree of openness is illustrated first by Figure 3.1, which shows exports, imports, and total trade as a percentage of GDP. These figures are quite high for a large economy: China's total trade ratio peaked in 2006 at 65 percent of GDP, more than triple that of Japan or the United States (although similar to Germany's).[6] The trade ratio fell sharply, to 45 percent in 2009, largely as a result of the global financial crisis and a reorientation of Chinese economic policy toward stimulating domestic demand. Even so, China's trade ratio remains high for a continental economy. Table 3.1 compares China's openness to foreign direct investment (FDI) and

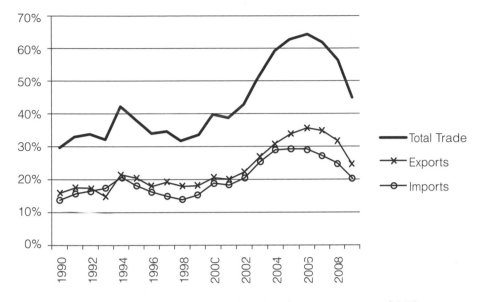

Figure 3.1. China exports, imports, and total trade as a percentage of GDP
Source: National Bureau of Statistics, author calculations.

TABLE 3.1
FDI and import openness

	China 1985–2005	South Korea 1970–1990	Taiwan 1975–1995	Japan 1955–1975
FDI, avg % of GDP	2.9%	0.6%	0.4%	<0.1%
	China 2006	South Korea 1981	Taiwan 1995	Japan 1975
Imports, peak %* of GDP	29.2%	32.9%	35.0%	5.0%

*During economic takeoff period, defined as 1978– for China, 1965–1995 for Korea and Taiwan, and 1950–1980 for Japan. Import/GDP ratios have risen sharply for all Asian countries in recent years, partly because they are more mature consumer economies and partly because of changes in intra-Asian trade patterns. The import ratios for South Korea, Taiwan and Japan in 2005 were respectively 33%, 53%, and 11%.
Source: CEIC database.

imports relative to its East Asian neighbors. As a percentage of GDP, FDI was five times higher in China from 1985 to 2005 than it was in South Korea at a comparable stage of development, seven times higher than in Taiwan, and around fifty times higher than in Japan. At its peak in 1994 through

TABLE 3.2

Foreign enterprise share of China's export and trade balance
(percentage of total)

Year	Exports	Trade balance
2000	47.9%	9.0%
2001	50.1	32.7
2002	52.2	31.8
2003	54.8	33.0
2004	57.1	43.9
2005	58.3	55.6
2006	58.2	51.4
2007	57.1	51.9
2008	55.3	57.8
2009	55.9	64.8

Source: PRC Ministry of Commerce.

1997, FDI accounted for an average of 15 percent of annual investment in China. China's peak import ratio was also six times higher than that of developing Japan. While developing South Korea and Taiwan achieved slightly higher peak ratios than China, the comparison is not a fair one because they are small countries that must import virtually all of their crude oil and many other natural resources, whereas China as a continental economy enjoys a far higher degree of natural resource self-sufficiency.

Unique to China among large trading nations is the enormous share of exports and the trade balance accounted for by foreign invested enterprises (FIEs), as shown in Table 3.2. FIEs have accounted for more than half of China's exports every year since 2001; their share peaked in 2005 but is still around 56 percent, with no clear downward trend discernible. The FIE share of China's trade surplus rose steadily over the past decade and neared 65 percent in 2009. These figures are without doubt by far the highest for any major economy.

The third area of divergence—the high degree of state ownership—is mainly a consequence of the fact that China, unlike its East Asian neighbors, is a postcommunist transition economy. Beginning in 1978, China gradually disassembled the Soviet-style planned economy it had set up in the 1950s and 1960s. A key difference between this reform effort and those of Eastern Europe and the former Soviet Union in the years after 1989 was that in China the Communist Party succeeded in maintaining its grip on political power, and this grip remains undiminished. China is an almost unique example of a postcommunist economy with continuing Communist Party government (Vietnam is the other instance).

The most significant economic difference between China and other postcommunist economies came in privatization of state-owned enterprises (SOEs). Instead of the varieties of mass privatization executed in Eastern Europe and many of the states of the former Soviet Union, China deliberately avoided privatization and focused on deregulating prices and creating competitive markets. There was no large scale privatization effort until after the 1997–1998 Asian financial crisis, and even then this privatization focused on smaller enterprises while leaving untouched the main, centrally controlled state enterprises as well as major province-level SOEs. A decade later, the state sector still controls around 40 percent of business-sector output, and state firms dominate many key industries, including aviation, shipping, steel, oil, chemicals, telecoms, coal, metals, and power generation.[7]

Private entrepreneurship played a crucial role in China's development, especially in the 1998–2003 period of SOE restructuring when tens of millions of SOE employees were laid off and small-scale private enterprises provided new job opportunities. But although China has a huge number of private companies, they are mostly tiny; there are virtually no large private business groups able to exercise political influence at the national level in any way comparable to the South Korean *chaebol* or the large Japanese industrial and trading conglomerates. Meanwhile the party-state has done an impressive job of restructuring and rationalizing the largest state enterprises, evidently with the view of keeping these business groups firmly in state hands but at greatly increased levels of profitability and global competitiveness.[8]

One of the biggest unknowns of China's future development path is how the relationship among the party-state, the top-tier state enterprises, and the rapidly growing private sector will play out. Although there is significant debate on this subject, it seems clear that at present the party-state has no intention of divesting itself of the 140 or so largest state enterprise groups.[9] Thus, the central government intends to continue exercising control over substantial elements of the national economy through direct ownership of operating companies. Meanwhile, private-sector companies will increasingly be encouraged, as they are the principal engine of job creation as well as the main mechanism for meeting demand in consumer markets.

Consequently, as Margaret Pearson's chapter in this volume shows, China now has a three-tiered political economy consisting of strategic or "lifeline" industries dominated by a oligopolies of large centrally controlled firms, competitive manufacturing and service industries dominated by small-scale private firms, and an intermediate tier of industries such as autos, chemicals, and pharmaceuticals where state, private, and foreign-owned firms all operate within a framework of industrial policy that is less stringently enforced than in the strategic industries.

Although this mixed economy now achieves impressive results, one is entitled to ask what occurs when the interests of the entrenched state sector and the up-and-coming private sector conflict. Up to now, such conflicts have been minimal, partly because the economy is divided into sectors where state dominance is presumed and barriers to private-sector players are high and other sectors where competition is virtually unrestricted. State enterprises can survive in these latter sectors but only by competing on more or less equal terms with private firms.[10] As a result, private firms and "strategic" state enterprises have separate spheres of operations, and conflicts are avoided.

In addition, the party-state attempts to limit conflicts between the state and private sectors through a conscious strategy of co-opting private entrepreneurs, either through financial mechanisms or by membership in the Communist Party. An example of the former is telecommunications firm Huawei, which in 2004 received a concessional ¥ 10 billion (US$1.2 billion) line of credit from the China Development Bank, a state policy-lending institution. As detailed in Tsai's contribution to this volume, co-optation via Communist Party membership, long an informal practice, was formally reinstituted in 2002 when a thirteen-year-old ban on inducting entrepreneurs was eliminated from the Party constitution.[11]

Consequences: Policy Reality

The constraints imposed by China's large geographical size, its postcommunist reform imperatives, and its unusual openness to FDI mean that, while a broad consensus exists in the central government in favor of developmental state objectives (diversified industrial development and the creation of large-scale, internationally competitive Chinese companies), progress toward these aims has arguably been far messier than in other East Asian countries.

There is, first of all, the question of how economic policy is formed and implemented. Japan and South Korea centralized power in a small number of influential bureaucratic institutions—in Japan principally the Ministry of International Trade and Industry and in South Korea the Ministry of Commerce and Industry and the Economic Planning Board.[12] These agencies had considerable leeway in formulating economic policy and a relatively high degree of effectiveness in enforcing their mandates.

In China a far larger number of actors are involved in making and implementing policy, with the result that policies are often more haphazard and the divergences between central-level policy and local-level developmental reality are far greater than was ever the case in the other East Asian economies. Because of China's postcommunist reform imperative, much economic policy that emerged in the 1980s and early 1990s was the result of political battles between economic reformers and old-style central planners, and most measures represented complex compromises rather than elements in a grand developmental strategy. Local governments, meanwhile, often interpreted central government laws and regulations very loosely and promoted local economic interests in ways that sometimes converged with but frequently diverged from the aims of Beijing. And as both state-owned and private business groups grew in size and in autonomy in the 1990s, they became more influential actors, again pursuing their own commercial advantage in defiance of central policies.[13] This relatively chaotic policy mechanism, combined with relative openness to foreign investment, meant that China has had far less ability to limit competition in key industrial sectors than Japan, South Korea, and, to some extent, Taiwan did earlier.

It is important to note that these differences between China and its neighbors are often more of degree than of kind. Economic planners in Japan and South Korea did not have a magical ability to pick winners: Honda Motors is one famous example of a firm that achieved a powerful position in both domestic and international markets despite its defiance of MITI's plans.[14] And in all East Asian countries, central policy was frequently constrained or modulated by local political imperatives. Nonetheless, it is clear that China's more decentralized structure of economic decision making meant that local governments and companies had more room to pursue their own agendas, and the central government a less effective ability to promote and protect national champion firms, than was the case in Japan or South Korea.[15]

A second crucial difference lies in the relationship between the central government and corporations. In other East Asian countries, a rather cozy and fairly straightforward relationship evolved between government agencies and large corporations: privately owned corporations received low-cost credit and other benefits from the government, which also ensured that domestic competition was limited and profit margins were kept high. In return, companies did not simply pursue profit maximization through efficiency and comparative advantage but instead complied with state goals such as the exploitation of export markets and the development of indigenous technologies to substitute for established international technologies.

In China the relationship between the government and the corporate sector is far more tortured, because of: (a) the central government's enduring commitment to a high degree of direct state ownership of productive enterprises in a wide range of economic sectors; (b) the state's ambiguous relationship to the private sector, which is valued as a source of employment creation but feared as a potential source of independent political power; and (c) the state's inability to prevent cutthroat competition in most sectors. As a result, China's corporate landscape differs dramatically from that in the rest of East Asia. Unlike Japan and South Korea, it has not so far fostered internationally competitive and technologically advanced multinational firms. Just as striking, it has also failed to produce internationally prominent family-run conglomerates, which are the distinctive form of corporate organization among the Chinese diaspora in Southeast Asia.[16] Instead, China has two dominant forms of corporate organizations, large-scale state firms and focused, small-scale private entrepreneurial firms.

To illustrate the concrete effect of the unique Chinese environment on industrial development, let us briefly consider the automobile industry, a favorite of industrial planners throughout the developing world. The success of the Japanese car industry spurred efforts in South Korea, Taiwan, and mainland China to create similar car industries that could dominate domestic markets and gain an increasing share of export markets. These efforts succeeded in South Korea, failed in Taiwan, and have produced as yet highly ambiguous results in China.[17]

When South Korea decided to shift to full-scale domestic auto manufacture in 1972, the government followed an interventionist procedure. It formulated a Long-Term Plan for Motor Industry Promotion, shut down small assemblers, and limited the number of car manufacturers to three (Hyundai,

Kia, and Daewoo). In the early 1980s it further reorganized the industry, forcibly merging some smaller producers into the major groups and compelling Kia to abandon passenger-car manufacture while giving it a monopoly over light trucks. Artificially high prices in the domestic market, which was closed to imports, enabled manufacturers to subsidize export sales.[18] The result was the achievement of 90 percent local content in cars sold in South Korea and, in the late 1980s and 1990s, a fairly successful export performance by Hyundai. In Taiwan, by contrast, comparable plans drafted in the late 1970s to create a major auto firm using 90 percent local content and targeting export markets collapsed—in stark contrast to the success of Taiwanese industrial development policies in the steel, petrochemicals, and electronics industries. Key factors in the failure were the government's inability either to forcibly merge or close the seven preexisting car assemblers or to impose a total ban on car imports, as was done in South Korea.

The aims of China's auto industry policy (released in 1994 and subsequently amended in 2002) were clearly modeled on Japanese and South Korean precedents: the goal was to create a small group of "national champion" firms, similar to Toyota and Hyundai, that would dominate the domestic market and gain significant shares of major export markets. In accordance with the idea that major industries should be directly controlled by the state, the three firms selected as future national champions were Changchun-based First Auto Works (FAW), Wuhan-based Dongfeng Motor Corp., and Shanghai Automotive Industry Corp. (SAIC)—all state-owned firms.[19] The idea was that these companies, whose own technology was very backward, would first form joint ventures with global automakers and thereby gain technology and expertise. Through improved technology and economies of scale, they would gradually drive China's hundreds of smaller vehicle manufacturers out of business, consolidating their hold on the domestic market. Eventually they would start producing vehicles under their own brand names, outside the original joint-venture arrangements, which would be sold both domestically and abroad.

It has not worked out that way. The Big Three formed multiple joint ventures with multinational auto firms, which assembled local versions of Volkswagen, General Motors, Toyota, and Nissan cars.[20] None of the Big Three has succeeded in developing a new independent line of cars sold under its own brand (something that Hyundai achieved within five years after the establishment of the Korean automobile industry plan). Meanwhile, large chunks of the domestic auto market have been seized by joint ventures in cities that, according to the national auto policy, were not even supposed to have auto industries at all: Beijing and Guangzhou. Here municipal governments, following local development imperatives, acted as passive investors in joint ventures with Hyundai and Honda, respectively, in which the foreign partners called all the shots and there was no meaningful transfer of technology to an autonomous domestic partner. These are classic instances of local governments obeying the letter of national policy—namely that foreign investment in the auto sector had to be in the form of 50-50 joint ventures—while flouting the policy's larger aims in favor of narrower local development objectives.

In addition, as the passenger-car market expanded in the early 2000s, new independent automakers began to pop up in unexpected locations. These included Geely, a privately owned firm in Zhejiang; Chery, a company based in the Anhui city of Wuhu and supported by the local government; and BYD, a Shenzhen-based battery maker that expanded into auto production and has ambitions to pioneer the development of electric vehicles. All three firms quickly gained a significant share of the low end of the domestic market (with models that relied heavily on the theft of designs and parts from the multinationals' joint ventures). None has yet convincingly demonstrated potential for successful export, at least to developed-country markets.

The result of this complex development path is that China has created a large domestic auto industry characterized by fierce competition and falling prices. Instead of the expected consolidation among a small handful of carmakers, market share has become more fragmented: in 1996 the SAIC–VW joint venture controlled 56 percent of the domestic auto market, while by 2006 its share had fallen to around 20 percent and at least six other manufacturers had market share of 5 percent market or more. A large majority of the passenger cars sold in China are made by Sino–foreign joint ventures and bear brands and designs created and controlled by the foreign partners. The Big Three have failed to develop vehicles under their own brand names, and no Chinese automaker is a serious producer of passenger vehicles for export.[21]

The auto industry exemplifies the way in which an industrial policy modeled on East Asian precedent wound up producing unprecedented results in China. The factors at play included China's geographic size and decentralized economic decision making, which enabled local firms and governments to continue operating outside the national policy; the constraints imposed by the government's insistence that national champions be state-owned firms, which resulted in a decision to throw central government support behind dinosaur SOEs rather than more nimble privately owned firms; and the policy of openness to FDI, which enabled multinational auto makers to gain commanding positions in the market.

Although Wedeman in his chapter is correct that China's auto sector is more mature than Russia's, the ultimate outcome in China is still unclear. Both Japan (in the 1920s) and South Korea (in the 1960s) went through phases during which most domestic auto assembly was controlled by foreign firms or joint ventures, and both succeeded in displacing the foreign firms with domestic national champions. This outcome is conceivable for China but unlikely (at least in the short term) because of the immense political cost that arbitrary limitations on or expropriations of foreign automakers would exact. A high level of foreign participation in the auto market is the price that China pays for using Sino–foreign joint ventures as a catalyst for technological development in the sector. It is also a cost of undergoing development during a period in which international trade and investment rules are rapidly liberalizing and the bargaining power of established multinational corporations increases.

Viewed from an economic welfare perspective, there is nothing wrong with this. If the auto industry thrives and creates employment and wealth, then it should not matter whether the owners of the firms are domestic or foreign. China's auto industry has clearly thrived, and, despite the failure of a Chinese Toyota to emerge, China has created several successful domestic firms. These include the privately owned auto-parts maker Wanxiang (which supplies auto assemblers both in China and abroad) and the assemblers Chery, Geely, and BYD, which despite their limitations are more successful than any independent carmaker in Taiwan or Southeast Asia. Yet the government's repeated insistence on creating national champion auto assembly firms demonstrates that it is concerned not simply with the economic welfare of its citizens but also with the industrial breadth and the technological autonomy of the economy as a whole—that is, concerns that we have previously identified as central to the "East Asian developmental state" model. These concerns are also legitimate: in Mexico, for instance, a thriving base of locally owned auto component firms was wiped out after the North American Free Trade Agreement enabled multinational auto assemblers to bring in

their home-country suppliers. Thailand's very large auto-components industry also consists almost exclusively of foreign firms. A similar phenomenon
exists to some degree in Guangzhou, which is now an assembly base for the
three largest Japanese auto companies, all of whom have encouraged their
major Japanese suppliers to locate plants there.[22] To the extent that industrial
clusters simply become enclaves of foreign-owned firms, it is possible that
backward linkages into the domestic economy may fail to develop, and the
technological development of domestic firms is permanently retarded. Arguably, this is occurring in the electronics industry: China is now the world's
largest producer, by volume, of a wide range of electronic goods, including
notebook computers. Yet the production chain is controlled almost exclusively by foreign firms (in this case, Taiwanese component makers and assemblers working under contract for American and European brand hold-
ers), and it is far from clear that Chinese firms are making much headway in
carving out niches in the industry.[23]

Measuring Success

The Chinese economic development path, therefore, shares many of the
starting conditions and industrial policy goals that are identified by the "East
Asian developmental state" literature. But, because of differences in geography, institutions and economic and political history, outcomes in China have
diverged significantly from those in Japan, South Korea, and Taiwan: while
China is well on its way to creating a broad-based industrial structure, individual industrial sectors tend to be much more fragmented than in other
East Asian countries; state rather than private ownership tends to predomi-
nate; and China has yet to produce a significant number of firms that are
competitive in developed-country markets.

It remains for us to assess in more detail how successful China's economic
development has been on the four criteria we identified at the outset: GDP
growth, acquisition of technological and innovative capacity, creation of internationally competitive firms, and acquisition of power in the international
trading system. In terms of economic growth the question is easy to answer.
Between 1980 and 2008 China's GDP grew by an annual average rate of 10
percent. No other country (including Japan, South Korea, and Taiwan) has

ever sustained that rate of GDP growth for such a long period of time. It is not within the scope of this paper to disentangle the various contributions of policy, demographics, and other factors; it is sufficient to suggest that in the context of such spectacular growth, it is unlikely that policy played a negative role and probable that it played a positive one.

Success in acquiring a domestic technological and innovative capacity and in creating internationally competitive Chinese firms is not so clear. For one thing, measuring technological and innovative capacity is extremely difficult. Popular proxy measures such as the number of patents filed or scientific papers published have never been demonstrated to correlate to actual technological attainment; and, in any case, the proliferation of junk patents and plagiarized research papers in China makes such measures worthless. A better yardstick is disaggregated merchandise trade data. As the technological sophistication of an economy increases, so should the technological sophistication of its exports. And if the domestically produced content of these more sophisticated exports increases, it is fair to assume that the innovative capacity of domestic firms is increasing and enabling them to capture more lucrative parts of the value chain.

Between 1980 and 2010 China leapt from being a negligible trader to the world's biggest exporter. This was accomplished in large measure by policies designed to attract export-oriented foreign direct investment. These policies were enormously successful; as previously noted, foreign enterprises accounted for well over half of China's exports in 2005, and the foreign share has been rising. Moreover, as shown by Table 3.2, the foreign contribution to China's trade surplus, quite modest in the 1990s, has became dominant in recent years. The most likely explanation is that foreign enterprises were heavy importers of capital equipment in the 1990s, as they were installing their factories. While these imports continue, they are now outweighed by the production value of exports from the installed base.

Two additional points need to be made. The first concerns the role of processing trade. More than half of China's trade is processing—that is, final assembly of imported materials and components. Processing's share of total trade has declined somewhat in recent years but still accounts for nearly half of all exports and essentially all of China's trade surplus. Chinese trade growth, and by extension overall economic performance, are quite reliant on this relatively low value-added processing trade. An important shift

TABLE 3.3
China's processing trade

Year	Total exports US$bn	Processing/ total exports (percent)	Implied local value added in processing exports (percent)
2001	266.2	55.4%	36.3%
2002	325.6	55.3	32.1
2003	438.4	55.2	32.7
2004	593.4	55.3	32.4
2005	762.0	54.7	34.2
2006	969.1	52.7	37.0
2007	1,218.0	50.7	40.2
2008	1,430.1	47.3	44.0
2009	1,201.7	48.9	45.1

Source: PRC Ministry of Commerce.

since 2006 is that the apparent local value-added component of processing increased significantly, from an average of around 35 percent in 2001–2006 to 45 percent in 2009 (see Table 3.3). This clearly suggested that the technological capacity of China-based firms is increasing. However, it is likely that much of this increase reflects the increasing integration of local supply chains in the consumer electronics industry; these supply chains remain overwhelmingly dominated by Taiwanese firms, and there is little evidence that domestic Chinese firms have substantially increased their participation in these supply chains.

This hypothesis is validated by data on trade in goods classified as high-tech. In 2008, 85 percent of China's high-tech exports were generated by foreign firms—and 68 percent by *wholly owned* foreign firms, in which there is no formal mechanism for technology transfer to a local partner. FIEs are now significant net exporters of technology goods, while domestic firms continue to be net importers (see Table 3.4). On a more qualitative basis, there is little evidence that Chinese firms are producing significant innovation in core technologies, manufacturing process, or design—either in high tech goods or in any other sector. The primary Chinese comparative advantage continues to be production at low cost and on a large scale. Chinese companies that have demonstrated international competitiveness, for instance steel producer Baosteel, telecoms equipment maker Huawei, and auto components maker Wanxiang, have done so not on the basis of new technology or inno-

TABLE 3.4
China's high-tech merchandise trade, 2002–2008

Year	Total high-tech exports US$bn	FIEs US$bn	Percentage	Domestic US$bn	Percentage
2002	67.7	55.6	82.1%	12.0	17.9%
2005	218.3	192.0	88.0	26.2	12.0
2008	415.6	354.1	85.2	61.5	14.8

Year	Total high-tech balance US$bn	FIEs US$bn	Percentage	Domestic US$bn	Percentage
2002	(15.0)	0.6	−4.0%	(15.6)	104.0%
2005	20.5	34.0	165.6	(13.5)	−65.6
2008	73.8	80.5	109.1	(6.7)	−9.1

Source: PRC Ministry of Science and Technology, author calculations.

vative manufacturing process, but mainly by their ability to manufacture to an acceptable standard at very low cost.[24]

How big a problem is this? Even from a developmental-state point of view (where the acquisition of a domestically controlled technological capacity is a goal), it could be argued that in the long run China will achieve its goals even if it appears to be falling short in the near term. Because of its unique cost and scale advantages, China can generate enormous increases in employment and incomes simply by commoditizing an ever-wider range of technologies invented elsewhere. As Figure 3.2 demonstrates, this widening of China's industrial base—represented by China's trade balance in five major goods categories—is proceeding rapidly. By 2008 China became a net exporter of heavy industrial goods, after many years of being a net importer. Most of this improvement represented exports of metal products (such as steel) and vanished in 2009 when the global financial crisis reduced world demand for basic materials. The clear long-term trend, however, is toward a greater volume and sophistication of capital goods exports. Ultimately, these large concentrations of manufacturing capacity, and the development of a richer and more demanding domestic consumer market, are likely to prompt domestic technological innovation. These factors are strongly supported by an array of government policies to increase funding for both basic and applied research, to sharply raise both the quantity and quality of university

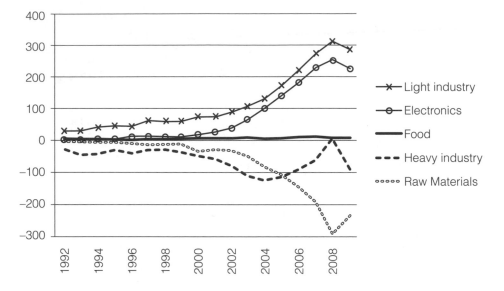

Figure 3.2.   Composition of China's trade balance (in billions of U.S. dollars)
Source: National Bureau of Statistics, author calculations.

graduates, and to systematically improve the linkages between universities and research institutes doing basic research and companies developing commercial applications.[25]

Yet from the point of view of Chinese officials and economists who define success in terms of maximizing "comprehensive national power" and would like to create local versions of Toyota and Sony, the picture is distressing.[26] When Chinese planners talk of "internationally competitive" firms, they do not simply mean companies that can compete effectively in international markets, which, as we have noted, some Chinese firms can already do. Rather, they mean companies that possess: (a) globally recognized brand names; (b) intellectual property rights from which they can reap price premiums, royalties, and license fees; and (c) control of distribution channels in foreign markets. In other words, Chinese officials apparently reject the Taiwanese development path, whose greatest success was the creation of thousands of small, nimble manufacturing firms that operate mainly on a contract basis with the owners of brands and distribution channels in developed-country markets. Instead they favor the creation of Japanese- or Korean-style multinational firms.

Common themes of government pronouncements now are the undesirability of China remaining "locked into low-value assembly production" and the desirability of developing indigenous intellectual property so that Chinese firms can collect rather than pay royalties and license fees. This concern has spawned a number of strategies, including incentive packages for technology industries, the promotion of domestic technology standards, and government procurement rules mandating purchase of domestic hardware and software. The most prominent example of the first was State Council Document 18, published in 2000, which provided a wide range of tax and other benefits for domestic producers of semiconductors and software. These were attacked by U.S. semiconductor makers as an illegal subsidy and were rescinded in April 2005.

The problem with these sorts of policy measures is that by constantly trying to create explicit or implicit discrimination between foreign-owned and domestic enterprises, the government converts what ought to be industrial policy into a trade issue. The two things most required for domestic innovation to flourish and for Chinese multinationals to grow are: (a) an improvement in the rewards system for innovation (including improved intellectual property protection and more flexible capital markets); and (b) and consolidation of industry so that the most efficient players can focus on research and development and well thought-out international expansion, rather than fighting vicious price wars at home to maintain market share.

A final consideration is to what extent China's growth has enabled it to gain power in the international trading system. In that it is now the world's third-largest trading nation, China obviously wields influence over the trade policies of many of its partners. Yet, as a new entrant into the WTO, it has not as yet gained a significant role in setting the rules of international trade; and, insofar as it is perceived as a heel dragger in meeting its WTO obligations, its impact on further adjustments in the WTO regime is likely to be limited, except in a negative sense (blocking WTO rules on matters that Beijing sees as helpful protectionist tools, such as government procurement policies). This relatively low level of influence does not yet seem to be an issue of great concern in Beijing, where policy makers are far more engrossed in domestic reform issues than they are in securing a favorable operating environment for Chinese firms abroad. China's interest in taking a more active role in WTO rule setting will presumably grow in tandem with the presence of Chinese multinationals in international markets. It is likely, however, that such international concerns will continue to take a back seat to domestic considerations for some years to come.

Conclusions

This brief survey suggests two main conclusions. First, while China shares important "family resemblances" with the developmental experiences of postwar Japan, South Korea, and (to a lesser extent) Taiwan, its development course is unique: it will not proceed in accordance with established models, nor does it provide a useful model for any other economy. The influence of factors such as China's geographic and population size, and its postcommunist economy governed by a nominally Communist Party, is so enormous as to preclude grouping China with earlier development stories. For the same reason, countries that try to emulate the "China model" will quickly discover that vast differences in basic conditions preclude anything more than piecemeal borrowing of Chinese policies. In short, it is difficult to identify a meaningful "Beijing consensus" developmental model that stands ready to replace the neoclassical (and perhaps equally phantasmagoric) "Washington consensus" economic model of the 1990s.

Second, while China has achieved high-speed economic growth and broad-based industrialization, it has proven—so far—less successful than its East Asian predecessors in generating a domestic technological base and globally competitive firms along the lines of Toyota, Sony, and Samsung (although it has been notably *more* successful in developing an indigenous technological base than the newly industrializing economies of Southeast Asia— Thailand, Malaysia, and Indonesia). This relative underperformance creates acute anxiety among policy makers, who now focus much of their energy on rectifying them. To the extent that these policies aim to enhance China's technological and commercial autonomy (rather than to increase national wealth by allowing comparative advantage to run its course), they suggest that policy makers remain committed to a developmental-state approach. Yet it is developmentalism with a twist because in China there remains a political imperative that most "national champion" firms should be state owned. The successful East Asian multinationals are universally private firms; although they benefited enormously from state support of various kinds, at the end of the day they had enormous incentives to focus on commercial success.

State firms in China, by contrast, constantly face pressure from their state stakeholders (both their direct shareholder entities and other government agencies that assert some kind of regulatory interest) to pursue noncommercial objectives. Furthermore, the implicit rejection of a leading role for private enterprises means that an enormous amount of entrepreneurial energy is simply wasted because private firms can never reach the scale necessary to maximize their success.

Chapter Four

Crossing the River by Feeling for Stones or Carried Across by the Current?

The Transformation of the Chinese Automotive Sector

ANDREW WEDEMAN

Scholars of China's post-1978 economic reform confront two seemingly diametrically opposed realities. On the one hand, the Chinese economy has outperformed all expectations, with per capita gross domestic product (GDP) growing a total of over 630 percent between 1980 and 2005, compared to a global average of 53 percent.[1] Stunning economic growth has, however, also been accompanied by a surge in corruption, rent seeking, and local protectionism, leading some to believe that reform will spawn a degenerate and mutated form of "crony capitalism with Chinese characteristics" based on "the marriage between unchecked power and illicit wealth," "market communism," and "massive corruption."[2] Others, however, see reform as creating a new class of "cadre entrepreneurs" and "market-oriented" local governments and a form "neomercantilist," "local state corporatism" that will create a quasi-capitalist "developmental state."[3]

These divergent views are based, ultimately, on whether their authors focus on the reality of rising dysfunctionality and fear that reform will fail or whether they focus on the reality of rapid growth and believe that China will somehow overcome the imperfections of its ad hoc reform program and will produce some sort of pseudo, ersatz capitalism. Regardless of which view may be more accurate, characterizations such as these are problematic because they rely on static "snapshot" characterizations of what is actually a dynamic and evolving process. Moreover, they have not proven particularly accurate. Despite repeated predictions that the negative consequences of partial reform will lead to collapse, spawn degenerate hybrids, or cause the transformation process to stall out short of full marketization, reform has never really bogged down. Instead, it has pushed inexorably forward, albeit at variable rates. The reform process has thus exhibited an internal dynamic only partially hinted at by Chen Yun's famous description of the reform process as involving the "crossing a river by feeling for the stones."[4]

According to mainstream thinking, despite uncertainty about how to reform the economy and some degree of ambivalence about the desirability of the capitalist model, the reformers have moved steadily forward, sometimes taking a step backwards for every two steps forward and sometimes dragged forward by "bottom-up" forces they could not fully control.[5] Conventional wisdom thus sees a process wherein "reform begets further reform," thereby moving the economy progressively closer to full marketization in an incremental and ad hoc process in which the partial dismantling of prereform institutions unleashed forces that responded not only to intentional structural changes but also produced secondary and tertiary changes triggered by structural contradictions. In this construct, reform is not a step-by-step progression from one "bank" to another but rather, according to Jin and Haynes, an "evolving, co-evolving, chaotic, self-organizing, path dependent and mutually catalytic" "phase transition" that produces change "at the edge of order and chaos."[6] If we accept that reform is a potentially open-ended dynamic and at least partially chaotic process, it follows that, rather than treating seemingly dysfunctional behaviors as consequences and potential threats to the continuation of reform, we ought to view them as endogenous to the reform process itself.

In an effort to illustrate what I see as the complex dynamic nature of the reform process in China, I draw on evolutionary economics and a comparison with Russia to analyze the transformation of the automotive sector. Like many other sectors, the automotive sector witnessed a process wherein the relaxation of tight central controls not only gave managers greater control but also unintentionally enabled local governments to imposed restrictions on internal trade. Thus, in the early stages of reform, "local protectionism" spread rapidly as "economic warlords" carved up the old command economy into a series of local fiefdoms. Nevertheless, by the late 1990s a functioning market economy had emerged. In this chapter, I argue that local protectionism actually helped generate a more open economy by forcing automotive producers to engage in extensive regional diversification. Diversification enabled them to "jump over" local trade barriers. It also weakened the ties that bound local governments to local producers that had given rise to local protectionism in the first place. In Russia, by contrast, the elimination of most formal institutional controls led its automotive sector to shift from a command economy to an oligopoly characterized by extensive black marketeering and nonmarket manipulation. In key respects, therefore, the ad hoc Chinese approach to reform was actually more successful than the "big bang" program adopted in the former Soviet Union.

Evolutionary Chaos

Evolutionary economists reject what they deemed to be the "mechanistic" assumptions of mainstream economics. Conventionally, economists assume that market activity will develop into stable, coherent patterns (equilibrium) and that these patterns will be sustained until some exogenous shock creates instability and change. Following such a shock, instability and change will continue until the behavior of the constituent actors harmonizes and a new equilibrium is reached.[7] Change occurs, therefore, in a punctuated manner.

Evolutionary economists argue that economic systems never achieve steady state equilibrium, and what might appear to be stable and repeated patterns are at best partial or imperfect equilibrium. Not only are structures assumed to be imperfect, it is also assumed that the system's actors are constantly probing the system's limits in search of new ways to game the system to their advantage. As a result, change occurs continuously rather than episodically. Marginal change occurs as actors exploit new opportunities or avoid negative outcomes. More dramatic change occurs when systemic parameters either fail or are revised. The magnitude of systemic imperfections affects the magnitude of incremental change. Drawing on chaos theory—or, more accurately, "deterministic chaos"—this approach suggests that small imperfections beget behaviors that can swell into forces that produce major or even cataclysmic change. Even small "accidents" ("butterfly effects") may prove to have profound ramifications over the long run because they have the potential to amplify the contradictions in existing structures and even small parametric changes in existing structures, thereby producing a cascade of rapidly accelerating change.[8]

Systems characterized by highly incongruent structures will, of course, generate high levels of "dysfunctional" behavior. Even relatively coherent structures are, however, subject to decay and revision. Catastrophic systemic change can result not only from exogenous, bolt-from-the blue shocks but also from the cumulative effects of endogenous "dysfunctional" behavior. Evolutionary economists, therefore, stress the centrality of holistic dynamic analysis, focusing not only on the factors that produce change but on how change reverberates over time, producing not only temporary instability; they also focus on how changes cascade over time to cause further change, arguing that change is both cause and effect because it occurs in a circuitous chain of causality.[9]

Evolutionary economics bears at least superficial similarity to the Marxist dialectic. But whereas Marxism assumes teleological progress toward a more perfect system, evolutionary economists reject the assumption that change selects "optimal" behaviors. Instead, they assume that "error making" and reactive behaviors may produce suboptimal "Pangloss" outcomes.[10] Moreover, they reject the notion that suboptimal responses will be selected out or that efficient responses will crowd out inefficient responses.[11] Because outcomes are assumed to be inherently unstable and at best imperfectly sticky, both suboptimal and Pareto optimal outcomes are assumed to be transitory and subject to continued revisions.[12]

In addition, evolutionary economics explicitly recognizes that systemic dynamics are driven both by structural parameters and the reaction of individual actors to both those parameters and by the ongoing struggle among the system's constituent actors to either maintain or revise those structural parameters. The direction and flow of change is thus largely driven by behaviors that either stabilize or destabilize the system.[13] Thus small perturbations may produce significant short-term fluctuation, but over time the trajectory of change will return to a "chreodic" or "homeothesis" path whose general trajectory exhibits a relatively orderly evolution over the long run.[14] Chaotic change is thus imperfectly path dependent and tends to occur in a "nonlinear" manner.

Although offering an attractive alternative to a stylized "mechanistic" equilibrium analysis, evolutionary economics and the idea of deterministic chaos do not necessarily provide a particularly clear analytic construct for analyzing systemic change. It instead serves up a series of metaphors and concepts that may be difficult to reduce to an easily articulated "model."[15]

Yet, even as a set of metaphors, the central concepts of evolutionary economics offer a powerful means for describing the dynamics of reform in post-Mao China. In particular, evolutionary economics demands explicit recognition of the reform process as one involving recursive feedback loops and the emergence of partial and transitory "equilibrium" wherein the process unfolds as series of "phases," each of which is ultimately destabilized by its own internal contradictions in a continuous evolutionary process. In abstract, this suggests that we assume that the Chinese economy is evolving toward a more marketized structure but in complex and semi-indeterminate manner.

From Local Protectionism to Price Wars

Analysis of the evolution of local protectionism provides an illustration of the extent to which "dysfunctional" responses to structural reform have been "symptoms" of deeper forces.[16] A direct and logical consequence of a combination of partial price reforms that created a series of rents, fiscal decentralization that gave local governments incentives to seek these rents, and partial market reforms that allowed local governments to monetize and capture these rents, local protectionism flourished during the late 1980s, particularly during the recession of 1989–1990. In the mid-1990s many of its most overt manifestations seemed to disappear as the economy boomed. When the economy slowed in the later 1990s, many of the sectors in which local protectionism had been widespread in during 1989–1990 experienced vicious prices wars as producers sought desperately to unload unsold inventory. Although the use of administrative power to protect local interests and aggressive, cutthroat discounting may seem logically opposite responses to deteriorating market conditions, the shift from local protectionism to price wars flowed directly from shifts not only in the ability of local governments to interfere in the market but also from shifts in the relationship between local governments and local enterprises.

   To illustrate my claim, I focus on the automotive sector. I select this sector for five reasons. First, automotive production is a capital intensive sector with relatively high barriers to entry. It is also a "prestige" sector. Second, the sector is dominated by state-owned enterprises and hence firms that we assume a priori have intimate connections to local governments. Third, automotive production underwent tremendous expansion during the reform

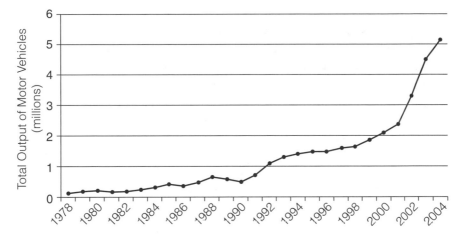

Figure 4.1. Expansion of the automotive sector
Source: *China Statistical Yearbook* (Beijing: Tongji Chubanshe, various years).

period (see Figure 4.1). By the mid-1990s, over 100 enterprises were assembling automobiles. Fourth, automotive production is characterized by a combination of widely dispersed production but also significant levels of spatial concentration. Fifth, during the early reform period, the automotive sector was characterized by high rates of profit and hence was widely seen as a "cash cow." This combination of factors is such that we should expect extensive governmental intervention and efforts to control and manipulate market access.

By the mid-1990s, China had 120-odd automobile manufacturers and vehicles were produced in twenty-six provinces, twenty-four of whom had designated auto making a "pillar" industry.[17] Substantial investment in upgrading and expanding production facilities led to rapid increases in productive capacity, with the result that by 1999 installed capacity had reached 3 million units per year. Four years later capacity rose to 3.5 million and was predicted to reach 4.7 million in 2005. Demand, however, lagged behind capacity so that utilization rates hovered around 50 percent in 1997.

Despite the substantial overhang created by excess capacity, competition was slow to develop. Prior to the mid-1990s, relatively few vehicles were sold to individuals (most vehicles were bought by state or collective units), and it was not until the later 1990s that a substantial consumer market for vehicles emerged. So long as private sales were limited, it was relatively easy for local governments to ensure that locally produced vehicles were favored. As consumer sales increased, local governments predictably slapped "imported" vehicles with a variety of ad hoc fees that ensured that they were more expensive to buy and operate than locally made vehicles.[18]

The auto market was not, however, carved up into a series of local fiefdoms dominated by a single local manufacturer. To begin with, the automotive sector was less fragmented than suggested by the raw figure of 120 vehicle manufacturers, and as it developed the sector became more concentrated.[19] Whereas in 1991 the top fifteen manufacturers accounted for 78% of total vehicle output, in 2001 they accounted for 91 percent.[20] Among passenger carmakers, the Shanghai Automotive Industries Corp. (SAIC) and First Automotive Works (FAW) accounted for 74 percent of sales in 2000, 70 percent in 2001, and 65 percent in 2001 (see Table 4.1), while the top five producers accounted for 96.5 percent of sales in 2000, 91 percent in 2001, and 86 percent in 2002.[21] By 2003–2004, eight enterprise groups dominated the automotive sector. Combined, they controlled forty-eight out of 120 automakers and accounted for nearly 80 percent of all vehicles sold and 90 percent of passenger car sales. Only seven independents produced passenger cars.[22] Thereafter, the sector became less and less concentrated as the big three lost significant market share to other producers (SAIC, for example, had lost more

TABLE 4.1

Passenger car manufacturers' market share (percentage of total sales)

Manufacturing group	2000	2001	2002	2006	2007
SAIC	41.28%	41.00%	38.11%	19.05%	18.11%
FAW	32.84	28.82	26.69	22.93	22.00
Chang'an	8.61	7.18	10.20	7.19	8.28
Dongfeng	8.48	7.37	6.26	13.29	14.29
Guangzhou Honda/Toyota	5.26	7.12	5.10	5.37	8.32
Geely			3.48	6.73	5.38
Zhengzhou Nissan			3.36		
Nanya			2.08		
BYD			1.43	1.78	2.41
CAIC			1.26		
BAW/Beijing Hyundai	0.75	0.67	0.78	7.01	5.21
Chery				7.87	7.20
Huachen	2.50		0.77		

Source: Auto in China, retrieved on April 6, 2006, from www.cacauto.com/english.asp; and FOURIN, "China's Vehicle Production/Sales Monthly Data," retrieved on May 1, 2009 from www.fourin.com/chinaautoweekly/.

than half its market share as of 2007), including to Chery, which got its start as an unauthorized venture backed by the Wuhu city government.

As supply and demand grew, the conglomerates that dominated the automotive sector began to expand, not only by adding capacity to existing plants but more critically by diversifying regionally.[23] Initially, China's largest car manufacturer, SAIC, had most of its operations concentrated in Shanghai (Shanghai VW, Shanghai GM, and Shanghai Huizhong) and had built up local parts production in a conscious effort to localize its supply base.[24] In 1998, however, SAIC expanded outside the city by forming a joint venture with General Motors in Guangxi (SAIC GM Wuling). The following year it set up a new venture (Shanghai Yizheng) in Jiangsu. In 2000, it bought a stake in Anhui-based Chery.[25] In 2004, SAIC and GM bought plants in Shandong (Yantai Dongyue) and Liaoning (Jinbei Automotive, which became SAIC GM Beisheng).

FAW started out with a core of subsidiaries mostly located in and around Changchun, Jilin.[26] In the mid-1990s, however, it took over Harbin Light Duty Trucks and Hainan Auto Works, which produced Mazda sedans in Haikou, formed a joint venture with Mazda to produce sedans in Jilin, and absorbed Jilin Light Duty Vehicles. During 2001–2002, FAW took over Tianjin Huali and Tianjin Xiali (one of China's major passenger car producers); formed a new joint venture with Toyota (Tianjin FAW Toyota); and set up a new subsidiary in Chengdu, which it then used to buy Sichuan Station Wagon and thereby gain control of Sichuan Toyota. In 2003, FAW formed a second venture with Mazda in Jilin.

Dongfeng, meanwhile, expanded its facilities in Wuhan in 1990 with a joint venture with Peugeot (Dongfeng Peugeot Citroen), while also buying Liuzhou Automotive (aka Chenglong) in Guangxi. In 1998, Dongfeng acquired Jiangsu-based Yueda-Kia. Two years later, it teamed up with a Taiwanese auto company, Yulon, to form the Aeolus Corp. (aka Fengshan) in Guangzhou. In 2001, it established a new subsidiary, Dongfeng Rongcheng, in Shandong. Two years later, Dongfeng entered into a joint venture with Honda to produce SUVs in Wuhan.

China's fourth major automaker, Chang'an, owned two major plants, Chang'an Suzuki and Chang'an Ford, in Chongqing and subsidiaries in Anhui (Anhui Tongbao), Jiangsu (Nanjing Chang'an), and Hebei (Hebei Chang'an Shengli). Though a relatively small producer, China Aircraft

TABLE 4.2
Retail sales, passenger cars; average market share, 2003–2005

	National	Chengdu	Yantai	Xi'an	Shenyang	Yunnan	Shanghai	Beijing
BAW	9.07%	0.51%	0.50%	5.99%	7.22%	1.84%		2.12%
BYD	0.41	6.39	0.19	0.67		1.98		1.87
Chang'an	9.66	21.91	1.39	9.49	0.64	10.39	3.96	6.17
Chery	1.71	4.75	0.47			8.70	5.32	5.92
CAIC	6.80	9.17		13.03	5.92	4.57		5.98
Dongfeng	10.34	6.66	3.19	1.21	2.47	5.27	8.51	20.03
FAW	20.23	6.70	10.57	3.66	18.45	15.86	4.14	38.23
Geely	1.82	2.84	0.24	0.21				4.14
GAC	3.46		1.94			3.20	0.82	0.43
SAIC	17.27	3.13	11.63	4.67		15.32	38.65	8.62

Source: Beiya Automarkete, available at www.beiyacheshi.com; FOURIN China Auto Weekly, "China Automotive Monthly Statistics," February 7, 2005; and Autoindex, "World Car Catalogue," available at www.autoindex.org.

Industries Corp. (CAIC) had its operations spread across five provinces— Liaoning (Shenyang Aircraft Co.), Shaanxi (Shaanxi Hanjiang and Xi'an Volvo), Jiangxi (Changhe Suzuki), Heilongjiang (Harbin Hafai), and Guizhou (Guizhou Aviation). Beijing Auto Works and Guangzhou Honda, on the other hand, remained concentrated in their respective home towns.

By 2004, regional diversification, combined with a spate of new entries, had created a complex sectoral geography with an admixture of the major conglomerates and independents in most provinces. Regional diversity is also apparent in the limited available data on retail sales, which show that while particular manufacturers enjoyed a disproportionate market share in some cities, no manufacturer had exclusive or even dominant control over any of the markets for which sales data were available (see Table 4.2). Moreover, the data show strong sales by upstart makers such as Chery, which was largely owned by the Wuhu city government, and Geely, which was a private company.

Regional diversification blurred the political geography of the automotive sector. During the 1980s, connections between automakers and particular governments were reasonably clear. FAW, Dongfeng, and China National Heavy-Duty Truck Corp (CNHDTC) came under the direct control of the State Planning Commission, making them "central" units. SAIC, Tianjin Automotive Works (TAW), Beijing Automotive Works (BAW), and Guangzhou Auto Works (GAW) were owned by their respective municipal governments. NORINCO and CAIC were part of the defense industry and hence belonged to the Ministry of Defense.[27] By 2004, however, most of the major firms had been transformed into joint stock companies (Dongfeng, FAW, SAIC, Huachen, CNHDTC, and Chang'an were publicly listed), and the state's ownership rights had been transferred to state asset management commissions or state holding companies.[28] Most were also involved in joint ventures with foreign partners. The connection between state agencies and enterprises that putatively lies at the heart of local protectionism, the link that ties the financial interests of the local governments to the profits of local firms, was thus attenuated. Moreover, because most automakers were now operating in multiple provinces, they had incentives to form alliances with multiple governments. The presence of multiple automakers in the same locality, conversely, meant that local governments faced cross pressures from rival "local" producers. As a result, the correspondence between "local" enterprises and their local government counterparts became blurred and convoluted.

During the early 1990s, high tariffs (upwards of 100 percent) and the lack of a retail market (most vehicles were purchased by units rather than private individuals) allowed domestic manufacturers to keep prices high.[29] High profit margins, naturally, induced excessive production, and by the mid-1990s carmakers found themselves facing increasing inventories. But rather than look to local protectionism to wall off segments of the domestic market, producers began to cut prices. After some preliminary cuts in 1994, the auto price war began in earnest in 1996 when Shanghai VW reduced the price of its Santana by almost 20 percent. Others followed suit. At the same time, the introduction of relatively cheap compacts such as the Tianjin Xiali, Chang'an Alto, and the Guizhou Yunque created a new threat to higher priced sedans.[30] The war intensified in 1998 when the government relaxed price controls and replaced state-regulated prices with price guidelines but failed to enact effective enforcement mechanisms. Facing only superficial penalties, manufacturers were quick to cut prices, which the central government then rubber-stamped.[31]

Absent systematic price data, it is difficult to fully document the extent of price cutting. Nevertheless, it is clear that competition drove prices down sharply. During 2000, for instance, Shanghai GM cut prices 6 percent, Dongfeng 5 to 9 percent, Shanghai VW 10 to 13 percent, Tianjin Xiali 12 percent, and Nanjing Yuejin 16 percent.[32] The trend in 2001 was the same, with prices for many popular models falling 10 to 20 percent (see Table 4.3).

TABLE 4.3
Price cuts, 2001

Manufacturer	Model	Original price	New price	Amount cut	Percent
Geely	Haoqing	44,900	39,900	5,000	11.1%
TAW	Xiali TJ7101	48,900	39,800	9,100	18.6
Geely	Merrie	59,900	55,500	4,400	7.3
Chang'an	Lingyang	112,700	98,800	13,900	12.3
FAW-VW	Jetta	117,000	99,800	17,200	14.7
TAW	Xiali 2000	119,980	97,000	23,000	19.2
Shanghai GM	Sail	125,000	115,000	10,000	8.0
FAW-Hainan	Mazda	126,000	116,000	10,000	7.9
Dongfeng-Citroën	Fukang	141,000	133,000	8,000	5.7
FAW	Red Flag	240,000	218,000	22,000	9.1
Shanghai VW	Passat	245,000	225,000	20,000	8.1
Guangzhou Honda	Civic	300,000	270,000	30,000	10.0
Dongfeng Aeolus	Sentra	310,000	260,000	50,000	16.1
Tianjin FAW Toyota	Camry	390,000	350,000	40,000	10.2
Average					**11.3**

Source: *China Online*, January 22, 2002.

Thereafter, price cutting continued as Shanghai VW cut the Santana's price 7 percent. Shanghai GM lowered the Sail's price 7 percent. Tianjin Xiali cut the Charade's price 13 percent and that of the Vela 18 percent during 2002.[33] Prices for the twenty-five top-selling vehicles in Beijing dropped an average of 7.6 percent in 2003 and 8.7 percent in 2004. Of the forty-five models sold in both 2002 and 2003, prices for thirty-one (69 percent) averaged 9 percent less in 2003. The following year, prices for forty-eight out of fifty-eight models (83 percent) sold in both years fell an average of 14 percent.[34] Among the twenty-two models for sale in all three years, prices for twenty-one fell an average of 22 percent, and the average price for ten best-selling cars fell 30 percent from Y120,000 to Y84,000. China's entry into the World Trade Organization (WTO) in 2002 put additional pressure on car prices by progressively reducing customs duties on imported cars from 70 to 80 percent in 2001 and from 25 to 28 percent in July 2006.[35] In addition to lowering prices, manufacturers upgraded existing models and introduced new models, thus offering buyers more value for their money.

In sum, we confront evidence of both local protectionism and stiff market-driven competition in the automotive sector. Faced with excess production in the mid-1990s, automakers responded by cutting prices and seeking new customers, including private buyers for the first time. Price cutting and product upgrading increased as new domestic producers entered the sector and existing producers set up new production facilities. Corporations undoubtedly sought the assistance of local governments in controlling access to markets. In some cases, government intervention was quite substantial, as is evident in the case of SAIC, where the Shanghai municipal government clearly manipulated local regulations to give SAIC a significant edge.[36] In Wuhan, the municipal government ordered taxi companies to buy locally built Dongfeng sedans, thus providing it with a captive market for close to half its total output during the early years of its joint venture with Peugeot.[37]

The use of local protectionism, however, appears secondary to a more generalized resort to the classic market tactic of lower prices in hope of undercutting the competition and gaining market share. This is not necessarily surprising because, whereas local protectionism might cordon off a firm's home market and hence provide protection for small and midsize producers, it could not help larger firms expand into new markets unless, of course, these firms were able to forge alliances with other local governments. Regional diversification, on the other hand, allowed producers to "jump" over potential barriers. Regional diversification also created complex networks of interests connecting the major producers to a wide range of local governments, while at the same time confronting local governments with rival claims for "assistance." The evidence thus suggests that, although local protectionism continues to exist within the automotive sector, it exists in an increasingly marketized context wherein automakers must rely more heavily on market tactics as they fight to expand market share.

Analysis

The shift from local protectionism to price wars in the automotive sector was replicated across many sectors. In the late 1990s, in fact, price wars were reported in at least sixty sectors, suggesting that by the late 1990s the Chinese economy had moved a considerable way from the plan and toward the market.[38] The evidence of continued local protectionism in the automotive sector, however, also shows that it remained a "market with Chinese characteristics"—that is, an economy that combined contradictory features. The economy was characterized by informal trade barriers that split the national market into a series of localized markets. These barriers did not, however, eliminate competition because regional diversification meant that most market segments contained multiple producers, each of whom was apt to cultivate local governments. Thus, whereas local protectionism, which had been a standard response to glut conditions in the past, was rapidly replaced by cutthroat price competition as the major national conglomerates and their "local" subsidies battled for market share. In short, even though local protectionism may not have been eliminated and the national market remained fragmented, for all intents and purposes the automotive sector was largely marketized.

What drove this transition from the plan toward the market? The trite answer is that it was a complicated process driven in part by top-down policy reforms and spontaneous bottom-up responses to these policy changes. I say "trite" because ultimately it seems obvious that any major change will involve interplay between that which policymakers intend and what ultimately emerges out of an attempt at significant reform. Recognizing that centrality of the interaction between top-down policy change and bottom-up response, however, brings to the fore the chaotic and evolutionary character of reform in China. It also highlights the extent to which outcomes have rarely approximated what reformers envisioned when they implemented reforms.

Originally, the central government envisioned a highly centralized automotive sector. As noted previously, at the beginning of the reform period, FAW and Dongfeng dominated passenger car production with a number of smaller producers located in Shanghai, Nanjing, Jinan, and Beijing.[39] In the 1970s, new production lines were opened in Tianjin, Shenyang, and Wuhan. Local government, meanwhile, set up small production lines, with the result that in 1978 China had fifty-six carmakers. Most, however, were small scale and produced obsolete and technologically inferior vehicles that sold locally. In 1984, faced with a surge in automobile imports and smuggling, the central government announced plans to move away from autarkic local production and build up large-scale production of technologically modern cars. It designated the auto industry a "pillar" sector in 1986 and ordered a consolidation of the sector. Under the new plan, FAW and SAIC were designated as the primary makers of midsize passenger cars, and Dongfeng would be the primary maker of compacts.[40] Provincial governments were forbidden to establish new local plants, and public security bureaus were ordered not to license cars produced by unauthorized plants.[41] The central government, however, immediately ran into resistance from the Beijing, Tianjin, and Guangzhou governments and gave in by recognizing Beijing Jeep, Guangzhou-Peugeot, and Tianjin Xiali as the "small three." It then caved into the Ministry of Defense's demand that its joint ventures with Japanese carmakers be recognized as the "tiny two."[42]

In 1988, the central government drew up a new plan that again called for the auto industry to be dominated by three major producers (FAW, Dongfeng, and SAIC) and three smaller producers (Beijing-Jeep, Tianjin-Charade, and Guangzhou-Peugeot) with the big three acting as "national champions."[43] In 1994, the central government issued yet another set of guidelines that reiterated its vision of a sector dominated by a few major producers.[44] Six years later in 2000, the State Council announced that no new passenger car factories would be authorized, and the following year "The Tenth Five-Year Plan of the Automotive Industry" once again called for consolidation with an industrial structure in which two or three companies would account for 70 percent of total passenger car production and for an end to the pattern of "scattered investment, small production scale and low technical" quality.[45] Most of the remaining 118 car makers were to be either shut down or shifted over to other production.[46]

Throughout the 1980s and 1990s, therefore, the central government sought to prevent decentralization of the automotive sector and to maintain the dominance of the big three and to thus create a quasi-oligarchic market for passenger cars. As Thun demonstrates, the central government's two-decades-long attempt to eliminate smaller producers and to force a consolidation of the sector failed largely because the center was never able to force local governments to shut down local producers.[47] Nor was the center able to prevent local governments from sponsoring new ventures with the ultimate result that market concentration dropped by half, with the big three's market share falling from 80 percent in 1993 to 40 percent in 2004.[48]

The central government's failure to consolidate the Chinese auto industry can be explained as a function of the chaotic consequences of a partial relaxation of control and rent seeking.[49] Early on in the reform period, the central government increased local governments' control over economic decision making. At about the same time, fiscal reforms made local governments more independent from the central government. Both reforms sought to increase local governments' incentives to promote local economic development and increase their tax revenues. The central government, however, shied away from a comprehensive price reform and retained high import tariffs, with the result that a series of rents were carried over from the pre-reform period. In the case of the auto sector, these included high passenger car prices. High state-mandated prices were then backstopped by chronic shortages caused by a lack of investment in automotive production in the prereform period. As a result, when local governments were given greater autonomy over investment decisions, they naturally sought to move into sectors where prices and profits were high. High technical barriers and capital costs associated with automotive production, however, meant that only those local governments with access to capital could consider investing in the auto industry. Moreover, new start-up producers faced the threat of competition from established producers who were themselves subject to rent-seeking incentives and hence were seeking to expand their productive capacity. Rents also lured in the military, which had been granted permission to convert parts of the defense industry to profit-making production.[50] Thus, even though the central government's plan called for a consolidated auto industry, the lure of rents resulted in proliferation.

So long as demand exceeded supply, competition between existing and newly established automakers was limited. Localities with upstart producers were able to manipulate regulations governing the sale and licensing of cars in ways that discriminated against "imports" and in favor of "local" cars. The major producers, on the other hand, could avoid markets walled off by "local protectionism" and expand into markets where there were no local competitors. Local protectionism had limits, however. Although a local government might be able to cordon off the local market, once a local car market's production reached levels sufficient to saturate local demand, it could not force other markets to open up.

Market saturation thus triggered a secondary unintended cascade of change. In this stage, producers resorted to a combination of spatial diversification, setting up new plants in markets they wanted to expand into and using them to "jump over" local trade barriers. At the same time, they turned to discounting—a classic free-market strategy—to grab market share from rival producers. China's accession to the World Trade Organization and the resulting lowering of import tariffs put additional downward pressure on prices.[51] Cutthroat price competition, in turn, eviscerated what remained of the central government's price fixing system, thus forcing price decontrol. Because there were limits to how far carmakers could cut prices, these conditions also created pressures on the major producers to upgrade the quality of their vehicles in hopes of edging out low-price, low-quality rivals. The unintended consequences of the first round of reforms (the proliferation of automakers and a rapid expansion in productive capacity) thus triggered a secondary set of unintended consequences (regional diversification, marketization, and product upgrading) that moved the Chinese auto sector closer to the market.

Even before price wars erupted, changes in the tax system weakened local governments' incentives to protect local manufacturers. During the early 1990s, the central government reformed the "extrabudgetary" system by designating net enterprise income as "profit." Prior to these reforms, most net income had belonged to the governmental unit that "owned" the enterprises.[52] Once net income became enterprise profits and was subject to regular taxation (including the VAT, which was collected by the central government and then shared with local governments), the proprietary links between local enterprises and local governments became attenuated, and, even though local governments lost their right to the profits of local enterprises they "owned," they gained the right to taxes collected from enterprises operating within their jurisdiction, including enterprises that were nominally owned by other local governments. Ownership rights were further attenuated by the conversion of most state-owned enterprises into joint stock companies and the transfer of ownership from individual state units to a network of state asset management commission and holding companies. With less incentive to protect local producers and new incentives to cultivate profitable producers, local governments' incentives to resort to local protectionism were thus lowered, allowing for greater openness. Between the late 1980s and the present, therefore, the auto sector did not evolve in the direction intended by the central government but instead moved along a chaotic and unintended path that led from the old command economy and toward a more efficient marketized economy.

It is important to recognize, however, that the current "equilibrium" is itself unstable. Despite its failure to force consolidation, the central government is likely correct that, in the long run, China cannot support a large number of medium-sized carmakers and that ultimately the auto sector must move toward a greater degree of oligopoly. If and when this occurs, it seems likely that, rather than result from central government attempt to "pick winners," it will result from a prolonged period of intense competition that will force less efficient producers to either move out of the sector or merge into one of the major auto conglomerates.

In sum, China's auto sector was carried from the plan toward the market by a combination of top-down formal reforms (fiscal decentralization, administrative devolution, reform of the extrabudgetary and tax systems, and the corporatization of the state sector) and bottom-up responses (rent seeking, proliferation of productive capacity, local protectionism, aggressive regional diversification, and vicious price cutting). The process was chaotic in the sense that it was uncontrolled. But it was hardly a random walk. On the contrary, initial top-down reforms created disequilibrium and triggered a dynamic, evolutionary process that created a new partial equilibrium, which was in turn destabilized by secondary top-down initiatives. Although the individual steps and shifts might appear to be "random," the general direction of movement was, however, surprisingly predictable based on some relatively simple economic logic. The interaction between top-down initiatives and bottom-up responses created a process of continuous dynamic change whose precise outcome was never entirely clear but whose general direction clearly moved the Chinese auto industry toward a stylized "market economy."

The Russian Auto Sector

China's muddled but seemingly inexorable movement toward a competitive, if imperfectly marketized, economy stands in rather stark contrast to Russia's transition from a centrally planned socialist economy to an anarchic economy dominated by private oligarchs. The divergence of the two economies seems particularly ironic because, after all, China's cautious reformers sought only to partially marketize their economy and retain considerable state control while the reformers in Russia embraced a "big bang" strategy that called for the wholesale and immediate abandonment of economic controls and rapid privatization. Ultimately what we see in the case of the Chinese auto sector is the emergence of an imperfectly competitive market economy, while in the Russian auto sector we see movement from a planned economy into a black market economy controlled to a very considerable extent by organized crime.

Structural differences explain much of the divergent trajectories of the Chinese and Russian economies. Whereas the Chinese economy had been fragmented into a series of semiautarkic "cells," the Soviet economy had been highly centralized. As a result, when the Chinese initiated economic reform in the early 1980s, their economy was populated by a multiplicity of what many considered redundant "midgets." Russia, by contrast, entered into reform with an economy populated by "giants." At the time reform was begun, for example, a single firm, AvtoVAZ, accounted for close to 90 percent of total passenger car production, while two smaller producers, GAZ and AKLZ, accounted for virtually all remaining production. All three produced poor-quality vehicles based on obsolete designs. Even so, demand greatly exceeded output, and consumers faced long waits for cars.[53] Unlike their Chinese counterparts, the three Russian producers were all tied directly to Moscow through the central economic bureaucracy (GOSPLAN) and operated on a national, not a regional scale.

Given chronic shortages and the abrupt dismantling of the command economy, conditions ought to have favored an influx of new producers in the early 1990s and a surge in production by the three existing producers. The reality was quite different. Rather than increase production to meet demand, the big three Russian automakers continued to restrict output and to operate well below capacity. In the mid-1990s, AvtoVAZ was reportedly running its factories at about 70 percent of capacity, while GAZ was operating at roughly 75 percent of installed capacity.[54] Moreover, AvtoVAZ exacerbated domestic shortage by continuing to export substantial numbers of vehicles, preferring to earn hard cash rather than sell them for rapidly depreciating rubles.[55]

Although a number of foreign and domestic firms sought to exploit the deficiencies in the Russian auto sector, most new ventures enjoyed only marginal success. In fact, fifteen years after the Soviet planned economy was dismantled, AvtoVAZ retained over a 70 percent market share, while number two GAZ had only a 5 percent share. AKLZ had gone bankrupt and been replaced by IZH, whose versions of the Lada, Moskvitch, and the Kia Spectra accounted for 4 percent of sales. KamAZ (maker of the Oka minicar) and UAZ (a SUV maker) each held a 3 percent share. Combined foreign joint ventures TagAZ (Hyundai), VAO (Ford), Avotar (Kia), and Avtoframos (Renault) controlled only 9 percent of the market.[56] Production, meanwhile, increased slowly, rising only about 40 percent between 1992 and 2005, a fraction of the ninefold increase in production in China. For the most part, quality remained extremely poor.

Not only did the sector not experience a major restructuring, the dismantling of state controls led to the emergence of a highly controlled black market dominated by organized crime syndicates. Even before the collapse of the Soviet Union, chronic shortages of automobiles had created a black market in which managers took delivery of "consignments" of cars straight off the assembly line, paying the heavily subsidized factory gate price and then immediately reselling them to dealers at much higher prices. Mobsters, often working in concert with managers, soon muscled their way into the back-door distribution system. In late 1980s and early 1990s a network of "wholesale dealers," most of whom were fronts for organized crime and in which both factory managers and local police were given a financial interest, controlled the movement of cars from the assembly line to ramshackle roadside dealerships. Members of the syndicates moved into the assembly plants and designated specific cars as theirs or simply hijacking them as they rolled off the assembly line.[57] At both the wholesale and retail levels, violence was regularly used to wrest control over market shares and eliminate competition.[58]

In 1993, an upstart businessman with ties to the Chechen mob, Boris Berezovsky, began "marketing" AvtoVAZ cars. Together with AvtoVAZ director Vladimir Kadannikov,[59] he formed a company named LogoVAZ and then negotiated a deal whereby LogoVAZ would take large blocks of cars on consignment, paying only 10 percent of the cars' US$3,321 price. LogoVAZ dealerships would then sell the cars for US$4,590, thus earning the company an immediate profit of $1,269. Under the terms of the deal, however, LogoVAZ did not have to pay AvtoVAZ the US$2,989 it owned for the cars for two years, by which time the valuing value of the ruble would cut the outstanding debt to just US$360. LogoVAZ thus made a total profit of US$3,898 on the sale of a US$4,590 car, or 85 percent of the total sales prices, while AvtoVAZ earned only 15 percent, too little to cover the cost of production.[60] Mobsters linked to Berezovsky, meanwhile, "restricted" retail competition, thus helping to maintain AvtoVAZ's hegemonic position even as the company went bankrupt. When that happened, Berezovsky ultimately bought a 34 percent stake in AvtoVAZ, using monies originally raised from mom and pop investors to fund a new company.[61]

Other means were also used to reap windfall profits at the expense of AvtoVAZ and other assembly firms. AvtoVAZ cars listed for export, for example, were "exported" from the factory to wholesale dealer storage yards in Togliatti, then "re-imported" and sold to retail dealers. By falsely exporting and then importing these vehicles, the wholesaler paid an "export" price that was fixed considerably below the "domestic" wholesale price. By falsifying production records, managers reportedly allowed wholesale dealers to evade taxes on an estimated 20,000 "undocumented" Ladas.[62] Other sources claimed that AvtoVAZ underreported its output by as much as 200,000 cars a year by using duplicate serial numbers to disguise the number of cars built.[63]

Not only were profits hijacked by mobsters and middleman traders, cash-strapped assemblers often found it necessary to resort to barter deals in which they gave away vehicles at below wholesale prices. KamAZ, for example, "sold" its Oka minicar to parts suppliers at a value of 21,000 rubles. The suppliers would then resell them to "dealers," some of whom were actually their own subsidiaries, at a small markup, and these dealers would then resell the cars on the "gray" market for 28,000 rubles, 3,000 rubles less than the price charged by official dealers.[64] AvtoVAZ also found it had to trade cars for parts, with the cars going for 30 percent below market value.[65]

In Russia, even though there is no apparent analogy to local protectionism and we have little evidence of organized, institutional collusion between producers and local governments to create and scrape off rent, we see ample evidence of rent seeking. In the Russian auto sector, however, rents were extracted from producing firms by a variety of private interests, including managers, gangsters, and corrupt local officials. As argued earlier, the divergence paths can be ascribed to critically important differences in the structure of reform in China and Russia. In China, reform incrementally relaxed controls without entirely dismantling controlling institutions. In Russia, reform eliminated the institutions that had controlled the economy during the Soviet era. As a result, while China moved from an ordered, planned economy toward a market economy characterized by a combination of order (regulation) and chaos (free market competition), Russia leapt straight from order into anarchy (see Figure 4.2). Unconstrained by effective regulatory institutions, "businessmen" cum gangsters used force and intimidation to game Russia's emerging laissez-faire economy. In key respects, therefore, the Russian equivalent of local protectionism was the "protection racket."

Eventually, the government restored a semblance of order by cracking down on overt criminal activity and launching a political offensive against oligarchs. The break from oligarchy and anarchy was not, however, complete or immediate. Berezovsky's crony Kadannikov, for example, retained the leadership of AvtoVAZ until 2005. By the mid-2000s, however, the auto sector was beginning to experience a transition, and AvtoVAZ was beginning to face a series of challenges both from rival Russian producers and, perhaps more critically, from imports. Its share of total sales dropped

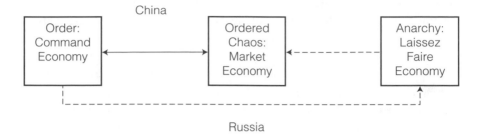

Figure 4.2.   Divergent paths from the plan toward the market

from 70 percent to 40 percent after the government drastically reduced the tariffs behind which it has sheltered since the beginning of reform. Rising incomes also allowed Russian car buyers to switch from cheap Russian models to more expensive imports and foreign designs produced within Russia.[66] The number of foreign-built cars sold in Russia increased, thus, from 225,000 in 2004 to 575,000 in 2005.[67] The Siberian Aluminum (Sibal) corporation, meanwhile, had begun to knit together a network of automakers, including number two GAZ, into a potential challenge to AvtoVAZ's domination of domestic production.[68] Hyundai's joint venture with TagAZ, Kia's joint venture with IZH, and Ssangsang's joint venture with Severstal (which had acquired UAZ) also seemed poised to challenge AvtaoVAZ. SOK, a parts maker, meanwhile had begun taking over some of AvtoVAZ's share of Lada production at its Roslada plant. By early 2006, moreover, both AvtoVAZ and KamAZ were becoming de facto state-owned companies.[69] By the mid-2000s, therefore, it appeared that the anarchy that had characterized the Russian automotive sector since the 1992 reforms had begun to settle into the more ordered chaos that typifies a functioning market economy.

Conclusion

As argued earlier, reform in China was hardly a linear process guided by top-down policy changes but rather a complex and often chaotic process. But the process was not a "random walk." On the contrary, as anticipated by evolutionary economics there was an inner logic to the process, one that has its roots in the law of supply and demand but that was very much governed by institutional rigidities. Lower levels of institutional rigidity, by contrast, caused the Russian automotive industry to take a radically different path, one that arguably moved it away from a market economy rather than toward it.

From a theoretical perspective, by destabilizing the old command system, partial reform created a set of incongruent incentive structures and hence spawned reactions that were dysfunctional relative to the maintenance of the system envisioned. In particular, by granting local governments greater autonomy and forcing them to become more fiscally self-reliant while at the same time creating a price system that contained a series of rents, the first round of reforms not only led to substantial increases in investment and production, which the reformers desired, but also high levels of rent seeking, a response that was itself critically important to spurring increased production. Increased production and rent seeking, in turn, eliminated many of the chronic shortages created by the misallocation of investment in the Maoist period but then led to glut. Glut then begat local protectionism. Local protectionism was, however, only a short-term solution to the problem of excess production and ultimately producers, many of whom had been transformed into profit-driven corporations in the interim and had to turn to alternative means to defend and expand market share. Acting much like corporations in advanced market economies, firms were led to begin aggressively discounting their products, forcing others to follow suit. The resulting prices wars, finally, dissipated those rents that had not been eliminated by formal price reforms.

The process was not, however, a neat linear progression governed by the laws of neoclassical economics. On the contrary, the informal ties that bound local producers to local governments were never eliminated, either by repeated central diktats ordering an end to local protectionism or by corporations' attempts to use discounting to break into new markets. As a result, corporations were forced to "localize" themselves by acquiring subsidiaries within particular market segments and then forging new alliances with local governments. The net result was a segmented market economy, in the sense that local protectionism continued to hamper interregional trade, but in which most market segments fierce competition had become the norm.

In this process, both top-down policy change and bottom-up "spontaneous reform" were necessary, but neither was sufficient. It was instead the dynamic interaction between top-down reform and bottom-up response that drove the process, but in a distinctly nondialectic manner. The effects of a number of critical policy changes, in fact, did not manifest themselves immediately, and in some cases reforms appeared to produce little substantial change when they were enacted. The conversion of SOEs into corporations, which seemed to have little initial consequence, is a case in point. The decision to retain state ownership of a substantial—but shrinking (due to the more rapid growth of the nonstate sector)—part of the economy is often considered to be one of the major shortcomings of China's reforms. And yet it was the fact that *some* SOEs did transform themselves into market-oriented companies and began to look to mergers, acquisitions, and discounting as fundamental business strategies that was likely the single most important factor in pushing the economy closer to a market-driven system when boom gave way to glut in the latter 1990s. Once these corporations penetrated existing market segments and began cutting prices, other firms either had to capitulate or follow suit—that is, they had to transform themselves into market oriented corporations—or die. But not all firms had to transform to survive because of the fact that, to become competitive, many SOEs had to restructure their operations, shed redundant workers, and shut down inefficient operations and because the politics of industrial transformation were such that some local governments—and the central government to a not inconsiderable extent as well—were willing to protect "their" client enterprises by providing subsidies. Market forces alone thus could not weed out all of the stunted "dinosaurs."

In conclusion, the process of reform has been anything but a linear, neat, or even necessarily logical process. On the contrary, the attempt to reform China's Marxist economy by incremental adjustment has given rise to a myriad of dysfunctional responses, including rent seeking, corruption, and abuse of power. But these "pathologies" are not necessarily "dead ends." On the contrary, in key respects these dysfunctional behaviors drove the reform process well beyond the cautious steps envisioned by China's conservative reformers and in a different direction than occurred in Russia. By thus pushing the reform process "off the stones" and into a more swiftly flowing current of reform, they not only made it almost impossible to turn the process around or halt it half way across the "river," they actually helped carry the reform process much closer to the "other bank."

Chapter Five

Welfare Policy Pathways Among Large Uneven Developers

MARK W. FRAZIER

Assessments of welfare policy effectiveness in a high-growth economy can be highly subjective. On the one hand, China's rapid growth has lifted per capita gross domestic product from $674 in 1978 to $4,726 in 2003. Moreover, 220 million rural Chinese, possibly more, have moved out of poverty.[1] On the other hand, it is clear that China suffers from vast and growing inequalities of wealth, deplorable environmental protection, collapsing rural education and health care, informal or underground employment for an increasing number of urban residents, and a rapidly aging population without solid prospects for adequate pensions and elderly care. Coping with these "externalities" of rapid growth has become the core political objective of the Hu Jintao administration. Policy makers and think tanks talk of creating a "welfare state" with universal health care and old-age pensions by 2049.[2] Yet the political pressures at play in China suggest that universal coverage will arrive well before the centennial of China's socialist revolution. This chapter looks at the politics of welfare-state building in China by placing China's recent experiences and debates over welfare policy in the perspective of large, high-growth economies with enduring social and economic divisions.

Discussions of welfare policy in China that have attempted to place China in a comparative context have most often turned to the experience of the East Asian "developmental states," in which governments pursued an export-oriented strategy of rapid growth and consciously avoided all but the most basic welfare provision and social spending.[3] After the expansion of political rights through democratization, eligibility for health care, pensions, social assistance, and other programs was no longer based on employment but on citizenship. This sequence of high growth, democratization, and eventually universal welfare rights stands in contrast with the Russian and East European socialist cases, in which universal welfare rights *preceded* democratization. Fiscal pressures generally led these new democracies toward welfare retrenchment. For these reasons alone—putting aside population, size, and interregional diversity—we cannot get very far in comparing China's welfare policy and its shortcomings with either East Asian or postsocialist economies.

The most rewarding insights into welfare policy outcomes in contemporary China can be gained by placing China in the context of a group that I term "large uneven developers." Large, diverse countries that experience sustained economic growth often do so with serious regional imbalances and other forms of inequality. Indeed, their very size and diversity create inherent inequalities in terms of resources and production factors. Countries such as Brazil, Indonesia, India, and South Africa were highly stratified socially, economically, and politically before undergoing economic growth, and their generally positive economic performances brought increases in inequality. As Kuznets and other development economists have shown, development is often closely associated with growth in income inequality.[4] Regardless of the precision (or lack thereof) with which we can measure inequality, what matters as much is the perception among politicians and the public that income gaps have widened. The political responses to uneven development vary considerably.

As the discussion in this chapter will show, China stands out among the cases for the crucial, albeit unintended, sequence of labor and social policy reforms. The gradual liberalization of labor market policies in the early 1990s was followed by the rapid dismantling of all but the largest firms in the public sector. This created inexorable pressures for welfare policies in the form of social insurance to provide pensions, unemployment, and minimum income benefits to those left jobless or relegated to informal sector work in cities. Financing of these programs came largely through the rapid expansion of social insurance coverage to urban enterprises. This sequencing led to an important political outcome in the form of "leveling" labor hierarchies by, on paper at least, providing the same welfare coverage to all urban workers (including migrants), regardless of their occupation or sector. While implementation was uneven and certain employees (such as civil servants) enjoyed vastly better pensions and health care, the introduction of social insurance has created an important platform on which China's welfare state will evolve and very likely expand.

By significant contrast, authoritarian rulers in South Africa in the 1930s and Brazil in the 1970s adopted universal and in some cases noncontributory pensions and other welfare programs for all citizens (an admittedly restrictive concept in South Africa prior to the 1990s). At the same time, Brazil and South Africa retained extensive labor regulations and large public sectors. India and Indonesia represent cases at the other end of a continuum of coverage for welfare programs. Both have maintained highly conservative welfare regimes based on provident funds designed in colonial eras. Their governments until very recently have been reluctant to expand social policy coverage beyond the core of large firms in the formal sector, and restrictive labor policies remain firmly in place. In terms of welfare coverage, China falls short of the universal rights to health care and pensions found in cases such as Brazil and South Africa, but it has moved considerably away from the narrow, exclusionary welfare regimes found in India and Indonesia.

If the sequencing of urbanization, labor market liberalization, and state sector downsizing is crucial to China's distinctive welfare policy outcomes, what allowed China and not other large uneven developers to take this path? Part of the reason lies in the gradual nature of China's socialist transition. As the Chinese government, beginning in the early 1980s, permitted alternative forms of industrial enterprises (such as rural collectives, foreign-invested enterprises, and private firms) to grow alongside the state sector, declining profits put pressures on SOEs to scale back production costs. Money-losing SOEs could be propped up with subsidies and bank loans, but not indefinitely. Some shrinkage of the state sector was inevitable in China's transition from state socialism, but the choice of welfare policy dominated by social insurance was not. China retained some of the same sharp distinctions in welfare eligibility and coverage that are found in many developing countries that privilege core sector workers and civil servants, but the expansion of social insurance beyond the core labor force has created momentum to expand such coverage to the entire working population.

The argument presented in the following pages stresses the importance of structural inequalities as facilitating conditions for the development of new welfare policies. It differs somewhat from the explanation of welfare policy evolution found in Stephan Haggard and Robert Kaufman's study of middle-income countries of Latin America, East Asia, and Eastern Europe. Haggard and Kaufman argue for the importance of legacy effects arising from earlier political realignments in the twenty-one countries in their comprehensive study.[5] (Their study includes Brazil but not China or the other three large uneven developers discussed in this chapter.) One of the critical inflection points in Haggard and Kaufman's account of welfare policy evolution is when new political elites attempt to incorporate or exclude left-wing, labor, and peasant groups. This initial incorporation or exclusion created welfare policies that would become the source of political pressure to expand or to retrench in subsequent decades, depending on fiscal capacity and to some extent regime type. Haggard and Kaufman make the important point that regime type is a kind of second-order effect or contingent on legacies and fiscal conditions at the time of democratization for many of their cases.

The discussion of large uneven developers presented here also shows that regime type is of secondary importance relative to initial conditions and policy legacies, but my account stresses to a greater extent the ability of ruling coalitions in these cases to maintain relatively narrow, exclusive welfare coverage to favored constituencies at the expense of the rural sector and labor market outsiders. The analysis also stresses the political design of welfare policy, such as the emphasis on pensions in Brazil and South Africa as well as in China, an outcome that reflects a political calculus to introduce popular programs that do little to challenge entrenched economic interests and have few discernible effects on income inequality.

Like the cases in the Haggard and Kaufman study, welfare policies adopted in the 1930s and in the post–World War II, postcolonial era among large uneven developers provided narrow coverage to loyal political constituencies such as civil servants, military personnel, and public or formal sector workers.[6] In their welfare policy pathways, the large uneven developers discussed here most resembled the pattern that Haggard and Kaufman identified for Latin America. Social welfare and labor legislation adopted in the first half of the twentieth century by governments in Brazil and South Africa secured the support of labor in the formal, organized sectors but had the effect of deepening the labor market dualism and marginalizing informal sector and rural workers.[7] China, India, and Indonesia in their postrevolutionary and postcolonial settings saw governments adopt labor and social legislation that also privileged the urban, formal or state-owned, industrial sectors at the expense of the rural.

The established linkage between employment in the "commanding heights" sectors of such economies and access to various social policy programs was crucial. The expansion of welfare coverage and benefits could occur either through the weakening or the dismantling of core industrial sectors or through a decline in their political influence. As the following section shows, in China the introduction of policies to liberalize or dismantle the public sector and to create more flexible labor markets strongly influenced the scope and content of future welfare provision. The absorption of rural labor into labor-intensive, export-based firms extended coverage because these workers were joining the formal sector. At the same time, the dismantling of state enterprises created a spike in informal employment. This conjunction of state sector retrenchment and the growth of the nonstate sector created conditions for the rapid expansion of social insurance in China. After showing in some detail in the next section how reforms to labor markets drove reforms in social welfare policy in China, the discussion then turns to the contrasts and similarities between China's welfare policy pathway and those of other large uneven developers.

The Transformation of Welfare Policy in China

China's welfare state during the command economy period (1949–1979) reflected both state-building goals and the ideological pursuits of state socialism. State sector workers enjoyed broad benefits including housing, education, health care, and pensions. Civil servants and Communist Party officials received even higher levels of benefits. The rural population, by contrast, relied on collectives for minimal medical care and educational resources. While the welfare state of the command economy possessed features that made it unique within state socialist cases, at a broader level of generality, China's prereform welfare state conformed to the practices of others in the developing world. Particular segments of an already small urban sector (full-time state enterprise workers, civil servants, Party and military officers) received welfare provisions, to the exclusion of the rest of the population. Gordon White, in making comparisons between China's command economy and the East Asian capitalist cases, characterized prereform China as a "communist developmental state aiming at high levels of accumulation and unwilling to spend large amounts of funds on welfare benefits which were not directly productive."[8]

There is little question that China's reform-era development strategy prioritized high growth at the expense of other public goods such as health care, education, and environmental protection. Several scholars have noted the importance of giving local governments in China the fiscal and political incentives to promote growth. Jean Oi makes explicit comparisons between the East Asian developmental states and the "local developmental state" in China.[9] Local officials possess rights to revenues and to assets of firms within their jurisdiction. Local officials are also assessed and promoted by Chinese Communist Party personnel evaluators based on the level of economic growth they can generate in their area. Social welfare measures, other than social stability, are usually disregarded in cadre evaluations.

China's welfare policy was driven by two crucial events in the 1990s, state sector restructuring and the introduction of labor market flexibility. With de facto privatization and restructuring, the state sector workforce declined from about 109 million in the mid-1990s to 66.2 million by 2003.[10] The *danwei*, or work-unit, essentially dissolved as state enterprises turned over functions of health care, pensions, housing, and other once-free welfare provisions to urban governments.[11] Contract labor, introduced in the mid-1980s, ended the institution of lifelong employment, and the 1994 Labor Law created a new set of labor market institutions with provisions for labor contracts, dispute resolutions, and social security measures.[12] Following the law's passage and formal implementation in 1995, the Chinese government instituted a system of social insurance in which local governments collected fees from local firms and pooled funds to pay for retirement benefits, health care, unemployment, workplace injury, and maternity leave. Local governments also began to administer minimum income payments for the urban poor.

Amid the many changes in economic and labor policy have come rapid transformations in demographics and social structure. In 1980, the distribution of China's urban and rural residents in the total population was at roughly 19 percent and 81 percent. By 2003, the urban share rose to 40.5 percent. The rural population actually shrank in absolute terms, from 796 million in 1980 to 768 million in 2003.[13] Yet these official figures mask the fact that a considerable portion of the rural population live in or near urban areas, through migration or through the absorption of rural townships and villages by adjacent cities. For example, the rural labor force in 2003 was 488 million, but the number of workers in "primary industry" (agriculture, fisheries, and forestry) totaled 365 million—a difference of 123 million that gives a crude measurement of the size of the rural labor force now working in industry or services, most of which are located in urban areas.[14]

The rural–urban divide shows most clearly how the evolution of Chinese welfare policy has created "the tendency to privilege the stronger and the bias toward marginalizing the disadvantaged."[15] Urban workers and residents are generally covered under contributory social insurance and other welfare programs, while rural residents are not. During the planned economy, this asymmetry in welfare eligibility was at least partially offset by the provision of commune-based services in rural areas. However, with the dismantling of collectives, rural health care collapsed.[16] The rapid urbanization of rural areas surrounding major cities has made this contrast in welfare provision more visible and more acute.

The Chinese government at various levels has responded to the pressures and demands stemming from SOE restructuring and from demographic changes by rapidly increasing social spending. Social expenditures for China's provincial governments averaged 3.1 percent of GDP in the 1990s and rose to an average of 3.9 percent of GDP from 2000 to 2004. Since 2002, social expenditures have exceeded 4 percent of GDP. (By Chinese statistical reporting standards, these calculations include education, public health, social assistance and relief, civil service pensions, and social security subsidies.) Distributions from China's locally managed social insurance funds, which generally pay for pensions and medical insurance reimbursements, represented an additional 2.8 percent of GDP for 2004.[17]

This expansion in social expenditures is directly related to the behavior of urban governments. At the same time that urban officials reduced the state sector through mass layoffs and bankruptcies, they took over the functions of administering welfare programs that had once been delivered by state enterprises. Within a broad policy framework of national regulations, urban governments enjoyed considerable flexibility in determining the payroll levies and benefits for programs such as pensions, health care, and so forth. Pensions are the most significant and sizeable element of these new social programs because they allow urban officials to collect a considerable amount of extrabudgetary revenue, which many urban governments need to cope with the challenges posed by large numbers of unemployed workers and early retirees.[18]

A means-tested basic income guarantee (*dibao*) has emerged as an important form of transfer payments to the urban and rural poor. According to the Ministry of Civil Affairs, in 2007 this program provided assistance to 22.7 million urban and 34.5 million rural residents.[19] Unlike pensions and healthcare, the *dibao* is not insurance based but is paid directly from local government coffers. Because of this, the quality of administration and the levels of benefits vary widely across cities and counties. China's health care system has received a great deal of criticism from analysts and from the Chinese government. It essentially operates on a fee-for-service basis, and doctors and hospitals have strong incentives to enhance operating revenues from tests, drugs, and procedures.[20] The Chinese government announced plans in 2009 to introduce social insurance for health care to rural areas, to complement the expansion of rural health cooperatives.

China Compared

The preceding sketch of Chinese welfare policy, its shortcomings, and its positive developments may strike many observers of welfare policy development in East Asia as a familiar story. The subordination of social policy to growth objectives, or even the stance that rapid growth was *the* most important social welfare measure, is a theme found throughout discussions of welfare in the newly industrializing economies of East Asia.[21] In these accounts, the high-growth, minimal welfare provision eventually gave way to a kinder, gentler welfare policy in which an increasing number of citizens were eligible for various social insurance programs.[22] While this broad-brush account is accurate, it is important to point out several reasons why it would be less useful to compare Chinese welfare policy with those found among the East Asian economies.

Despite the obvious similarities between welfare policy in China and those of its Asian neighbors at earlier stages of development, comparing China with only East Asian cases can have substantial drawbacks. The East Asian cases were far more urbanized and had far higher per capita income levels than China does today or will any time in the foreseeable future. In addition, China's reforms have brought a rapid rise in income inequality, in

TABLE 5.1
Human development index, select countries, 1975–2004

	HDI, 1975 (ranking *n* = 102)	HDI, 1975 percentile	HDI, 2004 (ranking *n* = 177)	HDI, 2004 percentile
China	0.527 (61)	59.8%	0.768 (81)	45.8%
Indonesia	0.469 (69)	67.6	0.711 (108)	61.0
Brazil	0.647 (46)	45.1	0.792 (69)	39.0
South Africa	0.653 (45)	44.1	0.653 (121)	68.4
India	0.413 (82)	80.4	0.611 (126)	71.2
South Korea	0.712 (36)	35.3	0.912 (26)	14.7
Singapore	0.727 (33)	32.4	0.916 (25)	14.1

Source: United Nations Development Program, *Human Development Report 2006*, available at http://hdr.undp.org/en/reports/global/hdr2006/.

contrast to the East Asian developmental states that kept income inequality relatively stable. In part this outcome was obtained because of land reform in post–World War II Korea and Taiwan that reduced socioeconomic burdens on rural residents and prevented agrarian crises that occurred in other developing countries. Moreover, because of land reform, the political leadership in the East Asian cases never faced the challenges of agrarian crises and massive migration to cities that their counterparts in many other low- to middle-income countries have encountered.

Cross-national quantitative measures, such as the UNDP's Human Development Index (HDI), confirm the difficulties of placing China among the East Asian developmental states. Table 5.1 shows the HDI measures as well as the relative ranking for the three decades between 1975 and 2004 for South Korea, Singapore, China, Indonesia, Brazil, South Africa, and India (the UNDP does not calculate data for Taiwan). China in 2004 ranked among the middle range of the 177 countries in the HDI.[23] In relative terms, China has risen from its position in the 60th percentile in 1975 to the 46th percentile in 2004. South Korea and Singapore, by contrast, were near the top one-third percentile in terms of the HDI in the mid-1970s, and they saw large absolute and relative gains in the HDI measure over the next three decades. They (very likely along with Taiwan, if data were available) now rank among countries such as Portugal, Greece, and are not far behind Germany (at 21st). China and Indonesia saw significant absolute gains in their HDI ratings, moving from under 0.53 to over 0.71 over this time span, and Indonesia moved up slightly from the 67th percentile to the 61st. Brazil is now in the top 40th percentile, while India remains in the 70th percentile,

TABLE 5.2

Gini index and Gini index ranking, select countries, 2004

	Gini index, 2004	Gini index ranking, 2004 ($n = 126$)
China	44.7	92
Indonesia	34.3	40
Brazil	58.0	117
South Africa	57.8	115
India	32.5	29
South Korea	31.6	27
Singapore	42.5	81

Source: United Nations Development Program, *Human Development Report 2006*, available at http://hdr.undp.org/en/reports/global/hdr2006/.

advancing from the 80th percentile in 1975. South Africa's HDI measure has stagnated considerably, with the same HDI rating as in 1975, and it has fallen in relative terms from near the 45th percentile to near the 70th percentile. South Africa's HDI rating was at 0.74 in 1995, and it fell back to the mid-1970s level of 0.65 over the next decade.

While they have experienced different trajectories, the uneven developers remain afflicted with serious inequalities. The racial divides in South Africa, the rural–urban gap in China, and caste distinctions in India are among the most prominent. Table 5.2 uses the Gini coefficients (multiplied by 100) in the East Asian and developing country cases, as reported through the UNDP in 2004, to get at some of the intracountry variation in income levels. Here we see that China's Gini coefficient of 44.7 puts it at 92nd out of 126 countries with Gini coefficient data. China is closer to South Africa and Brazil, with their infamously high Gini coefficients of over 57. Indonesia and India, by contrast, have relatively low levels of income inequality. This fact does not rule out their consideration as "uneven developers." The salience and criticism of income inequalities as their economies have grown are a prominent part of the political debate in both countries. Regional inequalities in which disproportionate shares of the poor are concentrated in a few states or provinces are not readily detected in standard inequality measures.[24]

Measuring a government's commitment to welfare by looking at social expenditures poses numerous hazards, but this commonly cited statistic is worth mentioning here. For health spending, China is situated between Brazil and South Africa (over 3 percent of GDP) on the one hand and India and

TABLE 5.3

A typology of welfare systems among uneven developers

Political economy	Political goals of welfare policy	Welfare policy strategy	Modal forms	Main target of coverage	Outcome
Corporatist coalition (Brazil, South Africa)	Preempt threat from rural migrants	Incorporate rural sector, urban poor	Noncontributory pensions; some means-tested programs	"Universal" with unequal benefits	Persistent inequality and informality; high public expenditures
Socialist transitional (China)	Facilitate labor market liberalization, dilute opposition to mass layoffs	Compensate jobless labor market insiders; incorporate labor market outsiders	Social insurance; some social assistance	Urban enterprise workers, including migrants	Leveling of labor status hierarchies; low but increasing public expenditures
Fragmented representation (India, Indonesia)	Preserve support of core sector firms and unions	Local experiments and maintain status quo	Provident funds; local experiments in social assistance	Narrow, formal sector only	Preservation of labor status hierarchies; low public expenditures

Indonesia (1.1 to 1.2 percent of GDP) on the other. For education spending as a percentage of GDP, China's 2.2 percent is well above Indonesia but well below South Africa (5.4 percent) and Brazil (3.3 percent). According to World Bank data, China's expenditures on health care in 2002 were 2.0 percent of GDP, compared to an average of 2.7 percent for low- to middle-income countries and 1.5 percent for low-income countries. The average for the Asia Pacific region was 1.9 percent of GDP.[25]

These macrowelfare measures, especially the Human Development Index, offer a persuasive case for comparing China not with its East Asian peers but with the uneven developers. Among all five cases, ruling parties encountered pressures created by rapid growth. Regional and income inequalities grew, and rural-to-urban migration made such inequalities more salient. These pressures presented ruling parties with the political choice, but not the necessity, to extend some forms of welfare provision to rural areas and to the urban poor. Political choice, and welfare policy pathway, was conditioned on the interaction of the political coalition underlying the development strategy. The discussion in the sections that follow is summarized in Table 5.3.

South Africa

South African welfare policy reflects the legacies of both partisan political competition in the early twentieth century and policies of racial exclusion. In the 1920s, in response to strikes among immigrant white workers and political competition between the Labor Party and the National Party, a coalition government introduced noncontributory pensions and disability grants in 1928. These laws were designed to provide relief to the largely landless poor, designated as "colored" or white, who had been driven off their farms by the commercialization of agriculture.[26] But they also were a response to the perceived threat of the social mobility of black South Africans.[27] The South African government in 1944 passed a law to extend social insurance coverage to all white and colored citizens. The same law initiated social assistance payments to black South Africans in rural and urban areas.[28] According to Seekings, the primary driver of this path-breaking legislation was the wide extent of rural poverty in South Africa, and the inability of the rural poor to support themselves from agricultural production. By establishing a safety net for rural-to-urban migrants, the South African government alleviated labor shortages and kept wages down, thus enlisting the support of employers as allies in creating universal coverage for pensions and disabilities.[29]

A legacy of political competition, the enforcement of racial hierarchies, and the close coupling of welfare measures with employment have together led to perverse outcomes in terms of social policy in contemporary South Africa. Although faced with high unemployment (estimated at between 30 and 40 percent), South African government policy nonetheless premises most of its social assistance on full employment, so that only those who cannot work (because of age or disability) are eligible for assistance.[30] The unemployed receive nothing in the way of income support, although a basic income grant was considered and ultimately rejected in 2002.[31] Even the post-1994 African National Congress government has pushed job creation as the central thrust of its antipoverty programs and has sought to "educat[e] the poorest sections of the population to the idea that full citizenship revolves around individual responsibility, labor market participation and the avoidance of 'dependency' on public spending."[32]

In contrast to this policy of linking welfare programs to employment, all South Africans also have a noncontributory old-age pension funded from general tax revenues. Nearly 2 million South Africans receive this "social pension," which represents about 60 percent of social expenditures or 1.4 percent of GDP.[33] This program thus creates an important channel of income redistribution by transferring income taxes from high-income earners (usually white) to low-income earners (usually black).[34] According to Natrass, the social pension has helped to reduce South Africa's still very high measures of income inequality.[35] South Africa's pension benefits far exceed spending on other crucial areas, such as government AIDS prevention and treatment programs.[36] Seekings, drawing on the South African example, has argued that welfare legislation in developing countries is most likely to expand or reach universal coverage under conditions of "deagrarianization and democratization." As he puts it, "Competition for the votes of the poor, landless citizens leads to promises of redistributive welfare."[37] Such a pattern can also be identified in the evolution of welfare policy in Brazil.

Brazil

Like South Africa in the 1930s and 1940s, Brazil in the 1960s and 1970s underwent substantial expansions of welfare provision and coverage, largely in response to economic growth and the salience of rural poverty. Brazil's military regime expanded pensions to cover most of the population, including the rural sector and domestic servants, in the early 1970s.[38] Civil servants, the military, and public sector employees continued to receive lucrative benefits dating back to Brazil's industrialization in the early decades of the twentieth century, but by the late 1970s Brazil had achieved near-universal pension coverage.[39] The expansion of pension coverage under military rule took place in such a way that earlier groups and sectors retained generous benefit levels, while rural workers received flat-rate payments, and the growing number of informal sector workers in urban areas were out of the system altogether.

The renewal of democracy in Brazil in the late 1980s gave constitutional rights to welfare for rural and informal sector workers. In the early 1990s, the Brazilian government reduced retirement ages and introduced pensions to previously excluded workers in the agricultural, fishing and mining, and informal sectors. This was followed by a noncontributory pension for low-income urban residents. By the year 2000, Brazil spent about 1 percent of GDP on five million pensioners in three noncontributory programs.[40]

Despite the impressive expansion in these and other programs, and their enshrinement as constitutional rights, the distribution of benefits remained under the influence of clientelistic politicians who steered benefits to favored constituencies.[41]

The widely heralded Bolsa Familia program of the Lula administration actually began in the late 1990s at local levels and became a national program after 2002. By 2008, 11 million households or an estimated 50 million people received cash transfers under the condition that children remained enrolled in school and received regular health checkups and vaccinations. Government statistics reported in 2008 that incomes of the poor had risen 22 percent since 2003, which exceeded the estimated 5 percent growth rates of rich household incomes.[42]

The welfare policy paths of Brazil and South Africa illustrate an important if overlooked linkage found in most developing countries between labor market policies and welfare policies. Restrictive labor market policies—originating in corporatist politics or in outright exclusionary policies directed at certain groups—contribute to the growth of large informal sectors that absorb much of the labor force migrating from rural areas to cities. In these cases, the politically tempting option is to use welfare policy to thwart social unrest. A declaration of universal coverage for pensions based on citizenship can bolster the legitimacy of the incumbent regime. However, if pensions are tied to employment—and if benefits are based on contributions—then social policy becomes the hostage of labor policy. Brazil and South Africa have retained rigid labor laws that did little to reduce large informal sectors, whose workers and employers do not contribute to welfare financing, even though they are eligible for it. In South Africa, centralized collective bargaining and rigid labor laws mean that small and medium enterprises routinely evade registering their workers. An estimated 30 percent of jobs are informal, and possibly 90 percent of textile sector employment is informal.[43] In Brazil, the burden of 20 percent payroll taxes to finance pensions has been identified as a leading source of informal employment, put at over half of the workforce.[44] Inequality in welfare provision thus lies not in coverage—both countries have what amounts in principle to universal coverage—but in the levels of benefits across different groups. Following democratization, the ruling coalitions in Brazil and South Africa expanded welfare provisions, but these programs have done little to reduce income inequalities.

The Chinese Communist Party of the 2000s is facing the same dilemmas that the authoritarian regimes in Brazil and South Africa once encountered. Urbanization and industrialization have created pressures to extend welfare coverage to previously excluded categories of citizens. The Chinese leadership under Hu Jintao has repeatedly stressed its commitment to "scientific development" of sustainable growth and the expansion of welfare provision, especially to China's rural population. In taking steps to relieve a rural crisis, the Chinese government in the late 2000s faces a similar set of difficult choices encountered by governments in Brazil and South Africa after rapid increases in urbanization. Should rights to welfare be tied to employment or based on citizenship? If the latter, which policies would "lock in" existing inequalities, and which would create more redistributive effects to lessen inequality? China's relatively liberalized labor market and smaller informal sector in comparison with Brazil and South Africa would suggest the vital importance of unemployment payments and social assistance for the working poor. Yet, as already noted, welfare policy outcomes in China have tended toward a social insurance system that assumes that both workers and employers will contribute payroll taxes to local governments, who will then administer payments in accordance with central policies.

India

Unlike Brazil and South Africa, urbanization in India remains under 30 percent, and thus the political pressures created by rapid urbanization have been less intense in India relative to the other cases.[45] However, India's rapid growth since 1991 has generated much debate over the distribution of gains from growth. The widespread perception that reforms have benefited only the rich and have increased India's rural–urban inequality has given Indian politicians the incentives to pursue new social policies to cushion the effects of the market.[46]

Indian democracy and its electoral competition at national and local levels generate transfer payments at election time, but few incentives exist after elections for politicians to adopt major changes to national welfare legislation.[47] Kerala, the often-cited example of positive human development outcomes despite modest levels of income and economic growth rates, remains the exception in India's welfare profile. Several national labor commissions made up of respected political leaders have called for detailed policies that would bring coverage to the long-excluded informal and rural sectors, but commission findings have yet to be acted on.[48] Both formal sector unions and business associations have blocked proposed legislation to expand welfare provision or to liberalize labor regulations. The Congress government that came to power in 2004 announced its intention to invoke social protections for India's large informal sector, but it failed to produce any substantive welfare legislation, aside from the Rural Employment Guarantee Scheme.[49] Under this program, the rural poor can work for 100 days, thus linking welfare eligibility with employment. The program, however, fails to address the more difficult issues of building human capital.

The constraints on the development of welfare policy in India illustrate further the crucial nexus between labor market policy and social legislation. Laws adopted soon after independence in 1947 gave wide latitude for Indian employers, especially small and medium enterprises, to gain exemptions from compliance. In addition, programs such as the Employees' Pension Scheme are based on provident fund models—forced savings that accumulate for individual workers who then receive a lump-sum payment on retirement. Such programs are designed to minimize government expenditures. Today, estimates put less than 15 percent of India's labor force under the coverage of pensions and other social policies. The vast majority of workers are employed in the informal sector or in firms that are too small to cross the threshold of twenty employees for coverage under social policy legislation. Indian senior civil servants enjoy basically cost-free pensions and health care, while workers in the vast informal sector lack any coverage. In the middle are workers in the formal sector who participate in various social insurance programs.[50] As critics have pointed out, "The bottom line of the Indian experience with regard to labor market policies and social insurance is that despite a plethora of legislation, the economy has been able to achieve neither efficiency nor equity."[51]

Indonesia

Unlike India, and more closely resembling China, Indonesia experienced significant urbanization that saw the proportion of its urban sector rise from 19.3 percent in 1975 to 48.1 percent in 2005.[52] Yet, until the mid-2000s, the approach to welfare policy remained largely based on growth and economic development. Coverage under the welfare policy programs that did exist remained narrow, with benefits concentrated among civil servants and the public sector. Under Suharto, Indonesia established corporatist relations between large-scale firms and labor unions that precluded a political solution to broad welfare policy. Indonesia's rapid economic growth from the early 1970s to the late 1990s did little to resolve the problem of welfare provision to newly incorporated sectors. Estimates of pension coverage ranged from 10 to 15 percent of the labor force.[53] Consistent with this earlier estimate from the mid-1990s, a 2003 ILO study concluded that 10 percent of Indonesians were covered under pensions and 15 percent were covered under health insurance.[54] Indonesia's 1992 Social Security Law mandated coverage for firms having at least ten employees or monthly payrolls of at least 1 million rupiah. The broader coverage in the 1992 law yielded only limited compliance. Evasion by employees was estimated at about half of those who were legally obligated to provide coverage to their employees.[55]

In another departure from India, the logic of political competition since 1998 has generated national welfare legislation. The Indonesian legislature passed universal social security coverage in 2004, at the close of the Megawati administration. The law aimed to provide social protections to the informal sector, unemployed, and poor. The law called for a national agency to be established to administer the registration and contributions of Indonesian citizens. Opposition to the bill came from the Indonesian employers' federation and from the major labor unions, who objected to provisions that raised premiums paid by employers and workers. Both business and labor argued that the government should finance unemployment and antipoverty measures from the budget rather than from contributions by citizens.[56] Critics have noted that the Regional Autonomy Law of 2004 gave regional governments the responsibility to create social security policies and that conflicts between the regional law and the federal social security law were sure to occur.[57]

In addition to new social legislation, the Indonesian government passed a labor law in 2003. The legislation strengthened unions, required employers to seek official approval for firings, and mandated severance pay, even for voluntary departures.[58] The law also contained provisions for a relatively high minimum wage. The admittedly sound rationale for the high severance payments is that Indonesian workers have no other form of social protection, such as unemployment insurance, to rely on when they lose their jobs. But critics charge that the law introduced substantial labor market rigidities and did little to relieve unemployment, estimated at about 10 percent of Indonesia's workforce of about 106 million.[59]

Indonesia's welfare policy pathway underscores the importance of urbanization and political responses to inequality. Urbanization created pressures for welfare policy, but rapid growth allowed politicians to postpone such measures. Indonesia, like India, faced lower levels of inequality relative to Brazil and South Africa and, unlike China, managed to grow with relatively mild increases in inequality. Pressures to create new welfare policies in India and Indonesia were also relatively muted compared with Brazil or South Africa in earlier decades. Also like India, the relative autonomy of regions and local administrations in Indonesia meant that welfare measures could be crafted, if at all, to suit local conditions. In both cases the formal sector proved to be powerful opponents of welfare and social policy expansion at the national level. Indonesian politicians eventually used welfare policy to bolster regime legitimacy (in Indonesia's case, the fledgling democratic regime), and successfully overcame opposition to introduce universal rights to welfare. However, reforms did not include improved access for labor market outsiders to jobs in the formal sector. Indonesia's democratization and political competition created both stronger unions and stronger labor market regulations on employers.

Conclusion

The placement of China and its welfare policies among a set of "uneven developer" cases has brought considerable advantages over alternative strategies of comparison. Had we looked at China's welfare record only against East Asian cases, it might have been tempting to conclude that Chinese welfare policy is more or less at a stage where, for example, Taiwan or South Korea stood in the late 1950s or early 1960s as they turned to export-led industrialization. And we might have drawn the inference that, with further urbanization and industrialization, Chinese welfare policy would follow a path similar to those of its East Asian neighbors. Contemporary China would have stood out as exceptional among these cases for having had high levels of inequality accompany its growth, possibly because of policies that triggered rural migration. By the same token, had we placed China among the postsocialist cases, assuming that the politics underlying welfare policy in China was a subspecies of postsocialist retrenchment politics, we would have focused on the effects of the legacy costs of state socialism and the privatization of state enterprises. Here too China would have stood out as exceptional because the Russian and East European cases at least were relatively far more urbanized, and they offered much broader access to welfare rights before their political and economic transitions.

Using uneven developers as a comparison group has allowed us to identify two variables that were not present in either the East Asian or postsocialist cases yet were crucial for welfare policy expansion: demographic pressures from rural migration and the alignment of ruling parties with the interests of the "commanding heights" of the public or formal sector—including both employers and workers. Brazil and South Africa, which moved toward universal coverage, retained labor market rigidities that created large unemployment and informal sectors; Indonesia most recently has followed the same path. India has adopted neither universal coverage nor liberalized employment rules to reduce the size of the informal sector. China stands alone among the uneven developers for having adopted flexible employment legislation and welfare provisions that, on paper at least, grant workers in urban businesses the rights to social insurance coverage. And as the number of workers in such firms increases rapidly with urbanization, coverage has expanded on a relatively equal footing: one's rights to welfare provisions do not change across ownership sectors. This represents a dramatic change from the era of the planned economy and has worked to level somewhat the once entrenched labor market hierarchies.

From the perspective of ruling parties and their efforts to incorporate key constituencies through welfare policy, we have found that such incorporation takes place not just in democratic regimes but in authoritarian ones too. The Brazilian dictatorship of the 1960s and 1970s, the racially exclusive parties of South Africa in the 1930s and 1940s, and more recently in Indonesia's fledgling democracy, politicians have sought to use welfare policy as a way to bolster their legitimacy and to be seen as responsive to glaring social inequalities. Whether such policies actually alleviate poverty and inequality depends to a considerable extent on the orientation of employers and unions in the organized or formal sectors.

This analysis of large uneven developers has also identified an important constituency that can block or promote welfare policies. While the vast majority of welfare policy literature in capitalist economies rightly looks at the relative power of labor and business in influencing the results of political battles over welfare policies and social spending, our look at China and the uneven developers suggests that the political conflict over welfare policy may lie elsewhere. Large-scale public and formal sector firms, together with their unions and workforces, have a tendency to support the status quo of a stratified welfare regime and to oppose measures that would level the playing field by broadening welfare coverage. Small and medium enterprises are just as likely to oppose welfare provision if its design includes a heavy payroll tax, but research elsewhere has shown that small producers are likely to favor universal social insurance coverage if it is financed largely through income taxes.[60] This pattern of political conflict over welfare policy requires further scrutiny among uneven developers. A study of sixteen Latin American and East Asian cases found that "labor union strength" was associated with negative outcomes on human development measures.[61] Further research using detailed historical assessments of cases would be needed to confirm why strong labor organization in developing countries would be associated with policies biased in favor of the urban and formal sectors, at the expense of the rural and informal sectors.

When placed in the context of chapters elsewhere in this volume, the findings here provide further support for the skepticism that the political economy of contemporary China resembles that of the East Asian developmental state, past or present. Consistent with Kroeber's discussion of the unmet aspirations of Chinese leaders to model their economy and policies on those of the East Asian developmental states, my findings show that welfare policy in China has taken a different course, largely because of the much greater income inequalities and the different treatments of the rural and urban sectors. Furthermore, the stratified nature of welfare policies in China supports the discussion in Pearson's chapter of the Chinese economy as multitiered, with substantial differences in regulatory traits. In addition, while it is still difficult to see clear evidence of state officials in China seeking to coordinate their welfare and labor policies with organized (or otherwise) social forces, Pearson's concluding remarks on the need to watch closely for evidence of "concertation" are also relevant for the future of China's welfare regime. China's passage of revisions to the Labor Contract Law in 2007, the draft of which was made open for public comment, and its ongoing consideration of the draft Social Insurance Law demonstrate that, in the legislative process at least, Chinese officials are trying to solicit input from crucial constituencies such as employers and business organizations. Labor remains entirely excluded or at least entirely subservient to the CCP's monopoly on labor organization.

Finally, the findings here offer some qualification of the conventional assessment of China's reforms as gradual in nature. China's state sector restructuring and labor market reforms look gradual when placed against the former Soviet and East European cases of shock therapy. Yet, when compared with other large uneven developers, the same policies appear much more dramatic, in substance if not also in pace. The loss of 40 million state sector jobs in a seven-year period combined with an estimated 120 million rural migrants to urban areas have created labor market and social policy challenges for China that few politicians in developing countries would willingly embrace, as much as some of them profess the desire to follow the "Beijing consensus."

PART TWO

Interest Groups in an Authoritarian Context

Chapter Six

Fragmented Influence

Business Lobbying in China in Comparative Perspective

SCOTT KENNEDY

Pick a sector in China, and you will find companies lobbying. In 2000, Hangzhou's Geely Motors successfully lobbied to be allowed to be the country's first full-fledged domestic private automaker, breaking the dominance of state-owned and foreign producers. In 2006, TCL Chairman Li Dong-sheng used his post as a deputy to the National People's Congress (NPC) to issue a proposal demanding the government provide more support for the electronics industry so it could compete against foreign competition. In 2004, fifty-four multinationals jointly issued a research report to senior Chinese government agencies explaining how the unification of domestic and foreign corporate income tax rates, effectively raising their rates from 15 to 33 percent, would reduce China's attractiveness to foreign companies, and hence, harm its economic progress. In 2006, the Carlyle Group was thwarted from purchasing a majority stake in construction firm Xugong due to a media campaign by other domestic firms upset that they were not given the chance to acquire Xugong themselves. And, in 2005, the Shanxi government issued a policy banning small mines, but the Wenzhou entrepreneurs who owned many of these mines persuaded the Zhejiang government to issue a counterpolicy in early 2006 encouraging financing mechanisms to help the Wenzhou investors consolidate their mines to put them above the closure threshold.

What is so remarkable about these examples, all taken from a book on the explosion of lobbying in China, is that they seemingly could be about corporate political activity anywhere. As China has gone capitalist, capitalists have mobilized.[1] Think of the auto lobby stalling the raising of fuel economy standards in the United States or Japanese companies gaining the blessing of the Ministry of International Trade and Industry (MITI) to organize cartels. In China, the examples above are so commonplace as to put to rest the notion that Chinese companies care about making money, not politics. Whether in Washington, Tokyo, New Dehli, or Beijing, politics is business because regulations and policies directly affect the life chances of industry.

At the same time, if you ask most casual observers or even lobbyists themselves, they would assert that government–business relations in China are distinctive. The importance of connections, the prominence of state-owned enterprises, and the weakness of associations are seen as hallmarks of China's system.[2] In all of the preceding cases, the firms drew on their connections, and they lobbied directly, not through an industry association. So the question is: To what extent is lobbying in China just like in other countries, and to what extent is it unique?

To date we have little systematic evidence to know where China fits among other countries. There has been no systematic comparison of government–business relations in China with any other nation. Aside from the occasional anecdote, China has been compared to others only implicitly, by measuring Chinese reality against a range of ideal types drawn from experiences elsewhere, including pluralism, societal and state corporatism, and clientelism.[3] This strategy has regularly been adopted by others. Although there are exceptions, historically the vast majority of scholarship on lobbying more generally has also rarely been comparative.[4]

The purpose of the present discussion is to place China's government–business relations in explicit comparative perspective by comparing China with Japan, India, and Russia. The three were chosen for both the similarities and differences they have with the People's Republic. As "coordinated market economies," governments in all four of the countries have routinely intervened in their economies and have not rigorously fought to stop collusive, anticompetitive behavior on the part of firms.[5] In addition, all four are large countries (Japan is the world's 10th most populous country, with 127 million people, but only the 60th largest in terms of land area). But they also differ along a number of dimensions, including their political institutions (authoritarian versus democracy, federal versus unitary, presidential versus parliamentary), economic endowments, development strategies, ethnic group composition, and relative levels of economic development and distribution of wealth.

This comparative exercise is valuable not only to identify patterns of government–business relations but also to examine the factors that generate similarities and differences. Whereas there is some consensus about the patterns of government–business relations in many countries, there is still an unsettled discussion about the forces that shape these relationships. The question of why some interests form groups and engage in "collective action" is particularly thorny. Mancur Olson established the terms of the debate by arguing that smaller groups were more likely than larger ones to successfully cohere and defend their interests because free riding is harder in smaller groups.[6] Larger groups only overcome their collective action problem when involvement in the group yields distinct benefits for its members, hence raising the penalties of nonparticipation. Inspired by Olson—but not always agreeing with him on specifics—researchers have shown that an industry's economic characteristics, such as concentration level, patterns of firm ownership, and technological sophistication, are significant incentives in generating support for and against associational activity.[7]

In contrast to economic explanations, other scholars have long noted variation in patterns of government–business relations across countries, subscribing these differences to national political institutions. In this vein, some emphasize the state's broad preferences for how business is organized, while others stress how the structure of partisan politics affect collective action.[8] Recently, the discussion of political factors has moved beyond stable institutional parameters and stressed the specific efforts of political leaders to delegate regulatory authority and grant privileged policy-making access to certain associations, making it worthwhile for companies to actively participate in an association.[9]

By comparing four countries, we will be able to evaluate the extent to which economic and political factors shape how the business and political worlds intersect. In addition to examining the nature of collective action, the chapter also considers other important elements of government–business relations, including companies' lobbying strategies and policy coalitions on domestic and foreign economic issues.

This comparative exercise will demonstrate that government–business relations in China differ from that in all other three countries to some degree, particularly the extent to which lobbying is fragmented; yet it appears China is most distinct from its East Asian neighbor Japan, while it shares more in common with India and Russia. At the same time, there is extensive internal variation and change over time in China and the other three countries. These patterns and firms' relative influence are shaped by political factors such as the nature of political institutions and the attitude of ruling elites toward business as well as economic factors such as firm size, industry concentration, and the nature of sectors' integration into the global economy.

Fragmented Influence in China

As suggested at the beginning of the chapter, although the People's Republic of China (PRC) is a highly authoritarian country, Chinese companies and multinationals operating there have become deeply interested in public policy matters since the early 1990s. The move from plan to market and integration into international economic regimes such as the WTO has been accompanied by the adoption of thousands of new policies and regulations at the national and local levels that directly shape the life chances of business. Whereas industry used to wait until after regulations were issued to decide whether they would abide by or avoid them, it now typically seeks to shape the government's policy agenda as well as the content of laws and regulations *before* they are issued. State-owned enterprises (SOE), private companies, and foreign-invested firms are all in on the action. Policies related to taxes, foreign trade, technical standards, intellectual property rights, finance, advertising, labor, and competition have all been affected by industry. This may be surprising because the Chinese and foreign media typically only report the content of policies when they are issued. But media reports, articles, and interviews by the author with interested parties reveal that the real difficulty these days is in identifying industry policies that have not been shaped by lobbying.[10]

The manner in which industry makes its influence felt in the PRC is the product of both political and economic factors. The Chinese regime's desire to shape how it consults with industry has had a profound effect on business associations and the formal rules of the game, but there has been substantial variation in how companies from different sectors and of varying sizes and ownership forms have responded to these challenges.

CHINA'S POLITICAL ENVIRONMENT: INTENDED AND UNINTENTIONAL CONSEQUENCES

The country's association system bears the imprimatur of government preferences, which share some resemblance to state corporatism.[11] Associations in China can be divided between chambers of commerce, in which the members originally shared a common ownership form and industry-specific associations. In the former category are the All-China Federation of Industry and Commerce (ACFIC), the Self-Employed Laborers Association (SELA), the China Enterprise Confederation-China Enterprise Directors Association (CEC-CEDA), the China Association of Enterprises with Foreign Investment, and nationality-based chambers of commerce (such as the American Chamber of Commerce). As of 2010, there were 700 national industry associations and thousands of regional associations.

The great majority of industry associations in China are not completely independent. Many have been initiated by government authorities, not by their members. Associations in China are required to have a sponsoring government agency, which usually has a voice in how the association is operated.[12] The staff of associations often includes retired officials. And finally, some associations depend on government outlays to cover their expenses. There is some variation in associational autonomy (to be discussed in the following pages), but it is unusual to find a fully independent Chinese industry association.

Although trade groups are often not autonomous, they are not useless. Associations use their ties to the government to gain access to the policy debate. Associations without any autonomy have no incentive to represent their members, while fully autonomous ones often have difficulty gaining the trust of and access to officials necessary to help their members. Of the various chambers for domestic Chinese firms noted in the previous paragraph, the most influential is the ACFIC, which primarily represents large privately run companies.[13] The ACFIC, particularly at the national level, is far from independent. Despite elections for leaders, the Communist Party has some say over who is nominated and serves. But within the bounds of these constraints, the ACFIC pushes for the interests of private business. It advocated amending the constitution to add an article expressly protecting private property, something that was achieved in 2004, and it also supported the Property Rights Law adopted in 2007.

The government would prefer for associations to be the main conduit for industry consultation because it would foster orderly interaction that it perceives would benefit both sides. However, government intervention in associations limits their ability to aggressively represent their members; hence, companies often disdain them. The consequence of such intervention is not to eliminate industry's voice but to fragment it. As a Shanghai official told me, Chinese associations are like pedestrian road overpasses. Pedestrians in a hurry rarely climb the stairs and use the overpasses; instead, they cross the road at street level on their own.

The compromised autonomy of associations has led businesses to primarily lobby the Chinese government directly, one-on-one or in informal groups. This pattern is encouraged by the historic close ties that SOEs have had with the government. Because SOEs' leaders have often been appointed by the government or the Party, SOEs have had little difficulty in accessing supervisory agencies. The habit of direct contact has spread to private and foreign companies.

Interviews and recent survey data show that businesses most commonly lobby the ministries and agencies under the State Council because they draft most regulations important to business.[14] And so an electronics company, when facing a foreign business issue, will not only interact with the Ministry of Industry and Information Technology (MIIT) but will also likely interface with the Ministry of Commerce, the Customs Administration, and the National Development and Reform Commission (NDRC). As the National People's Congress's role in the lawmaking process has grown, so too has industry attention to it. Companies lobbied the NPC during deliberations of the revised Copyright Law and the Securities Law in the late 1990s and on recent laws regarding bankruptcy, fair competition, and labor rights. Attention to the NPC is aided by the fact that SOE managers and private entrepreneurs together account for one of the largest blocks of deputies in the NPC.[15]

Surprisingly, companies do not typically lobby the Communist Party on regular regulatory issues. Companies of all ownership stripes and sizes all responded in interviews that when they want to discuss an economic policy, they almost always seek out government offices, not Party organizations. This is partly explained by the fact that the Chinese Communist Party (CCP) has integrated itself so deeply into government agencies that there is no need for companies to actively seek out the Party; the Party is there, standing backstage. As several executives told me, the government and the Party may be a "distinction without a difference." On the other hand, it also appears that the Party is not the target of lobbying because it lacks the detailed policy apparatus and knowledge of government agencies. In addition, even though Party officials occupy government posts from top to bottom, these officials guard their government turf feverishly and do not want outside Party interference into their daily affairs. Company executives told me that even though they may know an official is a Party member, they determine who to lobby based on the officials' government responsibilities, not their Party job.

THE IMPACT OF ECONOMIC FACTORS

Although there are several elements of government–business ties that are common across industries, there are also several aspects of these ties that vary systematically. Chinese companies exist in a common political environment, but the economic contexts of industries and companies generate powerful signals to push companies to behave politically in different ways. Key industry factors include economies of scale, technological sophistication, industry concentration, importance of interbusiness cooperation, and the nature of integration into global markets. The most important company-specific factors are size and ownership.

The first aspect where variation exists is in the quality of business associations in different industries and regions. Although Chinese associations are typically less autonomous and influential than their counterparts in the United States and elsewhere, associations in some industries are clearly superior to those in others. Economic factors deserve much of the credit. For example, China's steel industry is led by a core group of large state-owned enterprises. These companies employ hundreds of thousands of workers, contribute a large portion of the tax revenue of their towns, and undergird many downstream industries. Add in the fact that SOEs are tethered to the state, and it is understandable why China's steel industry has had very weak industry associations. The China Iron & Steel Industry Association (CISA) was created in 1999, not at the behest of its members but as a consequence of the planned elimination of the government's metallurgy bureaucracy. CISA's offices are in the old ministry compound, and most of the association's leaders are former ministry officials. CISA has become more active, helping its largest members coordinate prices, pressing the Ministry of Commerce to more aggressively defend Chinese steel companies against unfair foreign competition, and, for one year, negotiating the annual import price for iron ore on behalf of the steel industry. However, China's steel executives have long been dissatisfied with CISA's efforts, and they more commonly lobby the central government directly without any coordination provided by CISA.[16]

The contrast with the software industry is not absolute, but it is stark. The software industry's smaller, private firms individually have small political voices, but they have a habit of cooperating on technical issues, which is eased by the fact that the industry is concentrated in Beijing, Shanghai, and the Pearl River delta. These economic characteristics translate into a more vibrant association system than in steel. China's software industry has more associations, many of which were initiated by their members and have played a significant role in helping their members. The China Software Industry Association (CSIA) has a strong official color, but there are over a dozen firm-initiated associations that focus on certain aspects of the industry, from business management software to protection of intellectual property rights and freeware. Some of the regional software associations also have more member support than the national association. Although technically focused on a specific aspect of software or a region of the country, these associations actually take on national issues that are also on the agenda of the national association, making the associations competitors with each other in some instances.

Regional associations also vary in quality largely due to the different economic conditions of the localities. The city of Wenzhou, in Zhejiang Province, has the best-developed associations of any locality in the country because Wenzhou's economy is composed almost entirely of small and medium-sized private firms who proactively organized associations across a range of industries to address their needs. These associations are deeply involved in interfacing with the government, providing services to their members, and representing the sectors in international trade disputes. Shenzhen,

China's most vibrant special economic zone located next to Hong Kong, also has several active trade associations. Similarly, Shanghai's association system has also improved during the past decade as the city's economy has shifted toward a larger percentage of private firms.

Economic factors play a role in other aspects of government–business relations. Although firms typically interact with the government directly, they differ in the *depth* of interaction they have. The largest firms in an industry have the deepest direct contact with officialdom. In the steel industry, that means large SOEs such as Baogang and Angang, which have no difficulty contacting vice ministers and ministers whenever necessary. In the software industry, by contrast, the private firm UFIDA and the American giant Microsoft interact as often with senior officials as does any state-owned firm. Given the importance of direct contact relative to associations, depth of interaction directly translates into greater policy influence.

Size also affects how aggressive companies are willing to be. Broadly speaking, officials expect to be treated with deference. Companies are not expected to push for policies that openly conflict with broad government preferences or the needs of the bureaucracies with which they interact. As such, firms try to present "win-win" policy proposals that benefit both themselves and the government—at least that is how they frame the proposals. However, many large companies are disdainful of official norms and are surprisingly aggressive in their dealings with bureaucrats. This certainly applies to Google, which in early 2010 directly challenged the government's authority, publicly accusing it of hacking into computer network and demanding that it discontinue censoring its China-based search engine, Google.cn. A small technology firm would never have considered being so brazen.

Finally, Chinese companies' policy positions have evolved as their economic interests have changed. The conventional wisdom is that SOEs are generally aligned with each other against private companies, while Chinese firms share common interests that consistently put them at loggerheads with foreign businesses. SOEs welcome their privileged access to bank loans and stock market listings, and private enterprises consistently are critical of this situation. However, on many issues the lines are not drawn so neatly. Instead, as companies become involved in business relationships with firms of differing ownership forms and nationalities, their policy preferences change accordingly. Since 1979, foreigners have invested over $700 billion in China, setting up over 250,000 companies. Chinese companies are part of global production networks in which their products and services are part of a value chain that includes firms from around the world. Hence, many Chinese companies oppose protectionist measures. A policy loss for their foreign partners is a loss for them as well. The result is that Chinese firms have become embedded in "transnational political alliances" (TPAs) whose logic is understandable only by recognizing the members' common business interests.[17]

Take fair trade policy. China is the most common target of antidumping investigations, but the People's Republic has also become the third most active initiator of cases against foreign firms supposedly dumping their goods in China. However, foreign firms have walked away with partial or complete victories in over 45 percent of the cases adjudicated by China's Ministry of Commerce because their Chinese customers regularly speak up on their behalf. Typical was a stainless steel case involving South Korean and Japanese firms. Some of China's largest home appliance manufacturers and automakers successfully lobbied against fully instituting punitive tariffs sought by domestic steel producers, including Baogang, arguing they required the higher-quality foreign steel to remain competitive. China's lone effort to date to institute safeguard measures against foreign steel was watered down and then abandoned in response to precisely the same pressures.[18]

China's political environment has generated a largely fragmented pattern of business lobbying, yet varying economic conditions across sectors and firms have led to differences in association development, depth and aggressiveness of lobbying, and the composition of policy coalitions. This overview provides the foundation for addressing two questions about where China fits in the comparative context: to what extent do government–business relations in China approach that of other capitalist countries, and how do political and economic factors shape lobbying in polities outside of China?

Another "Japan, Inc."?

Given China's rapid development over the past three decades, it is enticing to draw parallels between China and its East Asian neighbors. The close relationship between the Japanese government and business gave rise to the term *Japan, Inc.* The phrase has been adopted by some to describe the PRC, implying similar growth strategies and patterns of government–business relations.[19] However, as Kroeber and Frazier found in their respective chapters on industrial and social policies, a comparison of corporate political activity in the two countries yields more contrasts than similarities. China's political elite and Japan's long-time ruling Liberal Democratic Party (LDP) see business as their economic and political allies, and hence both interact extensively with industry. And in each country, the bureaucracy is the primary target of industry attention on policy matters.[20] Yet across a range of issues—industry organization, direct interaction, and the political posture of business— Japanese industry's political role and influence seem far more institutionalized than what transpires in China.

The most glaring difference between the two countries is the nature and significance of business associations. In both countries there is little overlap in associations' jurisdiction, and former officials have regularly assumed leadership positions in associations.[21] This similarity masks some major differences. While occasionally hiring former officials or LDP members, Japanese associations are genuinely independent and represent their members' interests. They are also far more significant in every measure than those in China. Japanese associations take on self-regulatory functions, setting standards for performance and accrediting members' products and services. Associations engage in extensive policy consultations with the government. Totally absent in China, Japanese associations regularly become involved in election campaigns, donating to favored candidates.

Japan's most important industry group is Keidanren, the Japanese Federation of Economic Organizations. In 2000, it had just over 1,000 corporate and 119 industry association members. As James Babb writes, "For most of the postwar period, the Keidanren has been unassailable as the main voice of big business in Japan."[22] Keidanren is a genuine "peak" association. It can claim to authoritatively represent industry in discussions with the government. Keidanren maintains over sixty committees on policy and social issues, each of which is headed by a leading figure in Japanese industry. Until the mid-1990s, it coordinated campaign contributions of its members.[23] China's nearest competitor, the ACFIC, cannot begin to claim Keidanren's organizational virtuosity or clout. The result of these differences is that whereas direct lobbying predominates in China (except in certain sectors and regions), it is a complement to organized advocacy in Japan.

Direct contact between industry and the bureaucracy is common in both countries, and in both China and Japan companies often hire former officials to lubricate interaction. Former officials can gain access to their former colleagues and provide information about the policy process. At the same time, this practice is more institutionalized in Japan. Japanese bureaucrats nearing retirement age are regularly hired by the companies they previously regulated, what is know as *amakudari* (descent from heaven). Bureaucrats most often go to work for medium and large companies who are just below the most competitive firms in their sectors. According to a former MITI official interviewed by the author in Tokyo, young Japanese officials who leave government to go work in business are derided as "dropouts," making the practice quite rare. Multinationals in Japan also regularly hire former officials. Calder argues that the practice has an equalizing effect on policy influence. Leading firms in a sector more easily have political access and do not need to hire former officials.[24] By contrast, there is no uniform hiring pattern in China. State-owned enterprises do not "hire" former officials so much as have officials appointed by the government (or Party) to run their companies.[25] Among private and foreign companies, younger officials are often hired away depending on the financial inducement provided by the company, and interview sources say that this practice is not frowned on by their colleagues who remain behind. To some extent these efforts may "level the playing field," but it is the leading private and foreign firms that obtain the best-placed former officials.

There are also differences in the degree to which industry can take an aggressive posture toward officialdom. The Japanese are known for being nonconfrontational and indirect, and some sources suggest that Japanese industry usually does not directly pressure the government, and they phrase their particular "special interests in terms of the national good," something we have seen in China.[26] However, it appears that Japanese industry is more demanding than their Chinese counterparts. Japanese companies can be strongly partisan, attacking some politicians while supporting others. In 1989 Nissan chairman Takeshi Ishihara called for the resignation of Prime Minister Takeshita, a move unimaginable in China.[27] Since at least the early 1990s, Keidanren has been a vociferous advocate for deregulation. The stridency of its positions has been stronger than that of the ACFIC in its work to extend legal protection to the Chinese private sector. In the mid-1990s Keidanren, *Nikkei* newspapers, and others were outspoken advocates for a more progressive law for nonprofit organizations, a goal achieved with its passage in 1998.[28] By contrast, the ACFIC and other domestic Chinese business groups have only politely pushed for revising China's regulations governing social organizations; perhaps as a result, change has been slower and primarily at the local level. The largest Chinese companies appear only willing to be more aggressive on issues most closely connected to their firms and not on society-wide problems.

If there is an area where China looks more liberal than Japan, it is with regard to the composition of policy coalitions. The traditional divisions of state-owned versus private and Chinese versus foreign have gradually been supplanted by more interest-based coalitions as Chinese industry has integrated into global production networks. In Japan, although a sizeable part of industry has called for deregulation in ways consistent with foreign preferences, they have been slower to get their way. Protectionist walls in Japan still seem quite high, suggesting that most of Japanese industry do not have their heart in genuine liberalization.[29] Foreign companies are more likely to obtain lobbying help from their Chinese partners regarding protectionist problems than they are from their Japanese counterparts.

Why do Japan and China have such different patterns of government–business relations? Japan's democratic political system appears to be central to any analysis. Less intervention in associations, business involvement in elections, and industry's willingness to aggressively defend its interests are the consequences of this institutional difference. The government has also encouraged organized industry activity, serving as a support to industry associations, Keidanren, and other chambers of commerce. As significant as these political factors assuredly are, Japan's economic context may also help explain its experience. Tilton argues that one reason Japanese associations in the aluminum, cement, petrochemical, and steel sectors were able to effectively organize cartels for a sustained period is the high firm concentration in these sectors.[30] By contrast, Chinese associations' efforts to organize cartels in the late 1990s in the face of falling prices floundered because of the low industry concentration across the Chinese economy.[31] While not explaining the vast differences in organizational vibrancy between the two countries, this raises the question of the need to further examine how effective Japanese associations are across different sectors. In addition, it seems even clearer that the varying policy coalitions in China and Japan are the result of different levels of foreign direct investment in the two countries. There are simply fewer domestic Japanese allies of foreign business than there are in China. As Japan's economy gradually opens up, one should expect to see these patterns change in ways more similar to that in China.

A Pluralizing India: China Has Fallen Behind

Compared to broader differences with Japan, government-business relations in China and India have been moving along similar paths. However, the distance between China and India appears to be growing, not because China is retreating but because India is reforming its government–business relations system more rapidly. India began its economic reforms in 1991, over a decade after China started; and progress has in general been more halting and less comprehensive, leading one scholar to assert that much of the pre-1991 regime was still intact and that India has yet to become fully capitalist.[32] Despite this, the limited data that exist suggest that government-business relations in India have changed substantially compared to when reforms started fifteen years ago. As a result, we can see a fuller blooming of a pluralist pattern of government–business ties in India than China. But at the same time, we see both political and economic sources behind India's trajectory consistent with the variations visible in China.

THE ERA OF THE "PERMIT, LICENSE, QUOTA RAJ"

Through the 1980s government–business relations in India shared similarities with those aspects in China that were the product of a planned economy with extensive bureaucratic intervention. Following independence, India implemented an economic system that mixed elements of nationalism and socialism. High barriers to foreign trade and investment were erected, the state took over a large part of the economy, and the bureaucracy set about establishing detailed rules for every aspect of business. The result was that a company's success depended first and foremost on obtaining approvals from what became known as the "permit, license, quota raj." Companies paid little attention to broad regulatory issues and much more energy on developing personal connections (*sefarish*) with bureaucratic patrons, the equivalent of *guanxi* in China.[33] As a result, the Indian economy became beset by corruption, and crony capitalism became entrenched. The 1970s became dominated by "briefcase politics," in which the price of a bureaucrat's help was measured in the number of suitcases of cash one had to provide. Large business houses established "industrial embassies" in the capital of New Delhi to facilitate this interaction.[34]

Business associations in India date at least to the 1920s, under influence from the British example. However, in an era of crony capitalism, associations served the interests of their largest members; they were quite reactive and were mainly involved in helping individual members overcome bureaucratic obstacles.[35] During the state of emergency declared by Indira Gandhi in the mid-1970s, she unsuccessfully tried to institute a system of state corporatism, by banning independent groups, encouraging "national forums" for dominant sectors, and creating peak organizations to regulate labor–management relations. But these efforts were short lived and ended with her electoral defeat in 1977.[36] Government–business relations returned to their previous state.

THE MOVE TOWARD PLURALISM

Since 1991, though, lobbying in India has changed dramatically. India's leading chamber of commerce may not be as powerful as Keidanren, but it is more independent and influential than China's ACFIC. India's original general chamber, the Assocham, was founded in 1920 as a "gentleman's club of merchants" and has represented professional family businesses and foreign industry, with a western regional slant, centered in Mumbai (Bombay). Assocham has suffered from membership squabbles due to divisions of caste, family, region, and its emphasis on public sector development.[37] The Federation of Indian Chambers of Commerce and Industry (FICCI), founded in 1972, has been a representative for more traditional family-owned businesses. It has a regional bias toward the country's North and East and also has been allied with the Congress Party. Like Assocham, internal splits hurt its effectiveness in the 1970s and 1980s.

With the Congress Party being thrown out of office in the wake of the 1989 economic crisis and India in need of major economic reform, into the breech stepped the Confederation of Indian Industry (CII). Rajiv Gandhi supported the group and likely was the inspiration behind the group's shift in 1992 from being an association of engineers to a full-fledged multisectoral chamber of commerce. "CII used these early political and bureaucratic contacts within the central bureaucracy to build regular—both formal and informal—relationships with key elements within the state."[38] Led by its secretary general, Tarun Das, CII took advantage of this opportunity to surpass FICCI and Assocham to become the country's leading voice for business.

CII has developed a professional secretariat of 300 employees who have an excellent relationship with every level of the Indian bureaucracy.[39] Just as with associations in China and Japan, CII stresses "quiet diplomacy," emphasizing the common interests between its members and the government's own goals. "The process involves frequent informal personal contacts, providing up-to-date information, avoidance of public criticism, and working to help bureaucrats achieve their policy objectives without asking for quid pro quo."[40] As a result, CII has shaped numerous government policies since the early 1990s, beginning with revisions to the 1992 Foreign Exchange Regulation Act. In a change from pre-1991 standard practices, CII "self-consciously abjures distributive and particularistic needs of its individual members."[41] This helps keep the group united and focused on its members' common interests.

Lobbying has evolved in other ways as well. CII's rise is also distinctive because it did so in direct competition with its two older rivals. There is occasional competition between industry associations in China, but never in such an overt way. Since the early 1990s, there has also been a flowering of sectoral trade associations that vigorously represent their members. And a nascent professional lobbying industry has emerged, supported by former officials who work for domestic and multinational firms.[42]

India's liberalization is the product of political elites' initiative, the incentives to reform political behavior as a result of the greater prominence of broader regulations (as opposed to specific implementation), the pressures of a more competitive economic environment, and the ingenuity of new association leaders. Sinha emphasizes the leading role of Rajiv Gandhi in encouraging associational innovation; Kochanek stresses the changing economic environment that gave incentives to lobby differently; and Pedersen focuses on the growing numbers of people in society benefitting from liberalization who have pushed forward India's "quiet revolution."[43] There is something to each of these positions. It is clear that political leaders were critical in getting things started and providing regulatory certainty for this new pattern; but social actors—companies and associations—have been central to sustaining the changes because of their receptive response, which was far from preordained. In fact, many groups have fought against liberalization.

Economics may also explain some of the variation we have seen within India. Associations may in general be more active, but those that have received the most attention by scholars have been in emerging industries. Just as in China, there has been a flowering of associational activity in the software industry.[44] The National Association of Software and Service Companies (NASSCOM) was founded in 1988 and has developed just as rapidly as India's software sector. It has successfully lobbied for providing software companies tax breaks, lowering import duties, reducing regulatory hurdles, improving intellectual property rights (IPR) protection, and keeping overseas markets open to outsourcing. Although there have been a few firms who have criticized NASSCOM and withdrawn, the association has benefitted from representing small firms who individually lack the power to influence state policy; at the same time, a relatively small number of software companies compose a majority of the industry, reducing their collective action problem. By 2005, NASSCOM represented over 95 percent of India's software industry.

By contrast, India's bio-tech industry has had more difficulty organizing politically.[45] The All-India Biotech Association was founded in 1994 as the industry began to take off. Yet, as the industry became more fragmented in terms of product areas and interests, it became harder to organize the industry as a whole. Subsequently, the association splintered in two, and a third association also emerged. One of them, the Association of Biotechnology-Led Enterprises, made its headquarters in Bangalore because most biotech manufacturing is in southern India.

Evolving economic conditions also explain shifting policy coalitions of India. As the software and other intellectual property-based industries have grown, so has their influence, and in ways consistent with foreign producers. The Indian music industry has cooperated with foreign labels to improve intellectual property rights protection in India.[46] In the retail sector, where there are less transnational business ties, local traders are more unified against foreign interests. Hence, small shop owners and their associations have vigorously opposed allowing Wal-Mart and other global retailers to operate in India.[47]

In sum, the greater autonomy and assertiveness of India's chief chamber of commerce and some industry associations have been helped by Indian politics—specific support by a leading political figure, the federal system, and legal protections for societal organizations. At the same time, the broad trend of liberalization and the nature of certain industries also rounds out the picture of why there are also some similarities between the two Asian giants.

Russia: A Chinese Turn?

If government-business relations in China are less organized than in Japan and less pluralistic than in India, how then does China compare to the world's other large postcommunist state, Russia? A comparison presents startling contrasts and surprising similarities. Russia's jump to democracy in the early 1990s was accompanied by radical economic reform, including privatization of much of state assets. During the 1990s, government–business relations in Russia diverged from China's in the sheer depth and breadth of power held by leading business leaders, known collectively as "the oligarchs."[48] Yet, since his accession to power in 2000, Putin has reigned in industry's political influence, arresting oligarchs and sponsoring politically loyal business associations. In Russia there is an even stronger tilt toward direct lobbying, but, as in China, there is a gradual shift afoot to greater involvement in business associations.

THE ERA OF CHAOTIC CAPITALISM

In the 1990s, Russian business captured the state and took most of its assets for themselves, turning once poor apparatchiks and petty entrepreneurs into instant tycoons. However, it would be less appropriate to call this transfer of wealth "stealing" than to call it "accepting gifts." Boris Yeltsin's first prime minister, Yegor Gaidar, initially tried to hold back business. During the first few months in office, he banned meetings with businesspeople.[49] But Yeltsin and Gaidar's replacement, Viktor Chernomyrdin, willingly handed over state assets in exchange for the oligarchs' political support.[50] Leaders intentionally created a vacuum of authority that the businesses filled, creating the conditions for what Lane calls "chaotic capitalism," or what Hutchcroft terms "booty capitalism."[51] Although a handful of the sons and daughters of China's political elite, known as "princelings," occupy positions of authority in business and government, they have nowhere near the economic and political clout of Russia's business tycoons.

As in China, the oligarchs applied most of their influence directly. They focused on lobbying the Kremlin and the government bureaucracy, but they also funded election campaigns of Duma candidates and provided bribes to Duma members once in office in exchange for making their preferred regulatory changes.[52] Company leaders also did not shy away from running for office. In 1995, 40 percent of Duma deputies were company owners or managers, a much higher percentage than in China.[53] A survey of 500 firms in 2000 showed that personal direct lobbying was the most common avenue of interfacing with the government.[54] The most powerful lobbies were sectors dominated by just a few privatized or state owned firms. For example, Gazprom, the natural gas monopoly, successfully lobbied against requiring open access to its pipelines and against caps on energy prices.[55]

Business leaders typically did not exert their influence collectively. The initial optimism some scholars displayed toward associations was not realized during the Yeltsin era.[56] Many sectoral associations were formed, but, as Rutland says, they had "an air of unreality," with only a virtual existence on paper.[57] Many of the earliest associations were created by former bureaucrats, while others were "pocket associations" founded by a company to promote its narrow interests.[58] Those that did gain sway did so by engaging in rent seeking.[59] In the late 1990s, according to one survey, only 15 percent of Russian firms belonged to an association.[60] The dominance of direct ties and weak associations reflects the political climate as well as the economic clout individual companies had that made them see associations as irrelevant.

The most prominent chamber of commerce, the Russian Union of Industrialists and Entrepreneurs (RUIE), did have its moments of influence as a representative of the "red directors," that is, managers of state-owned factories. RUIE, which originated in 1990 as the Scientific and Technical Union, lobbied successfully in 1992 for wage and price controls, foreign investment restrictions, cheap energy, and subsidized credit for its members. In the mid-1990s, RUIE participated in the drafting of bills in the Duma. But, until 1998, it was largely ineffectual because it was split between pro- and anti-reform groups. When the oligarchs finally joined RUIE en masse in 1998, they turned it into their puppet, as it lobbied on their behalf for tax breaks, liberalized currency transactions, and land reform.[61] But its moment in the spotlight was short lived.

THE PUTIN ERA

When Putin took over, he set about taking back power from the oligarchs. He had the state resume control of some of its companies, claiming the original privatization was performed illegally. And he arrested others, the most important being Mikhail Khodorkovsky, the head of Yukos. When he was detained in 2003, very few of the other oligarchs spoke up on his behalf. Any cooperation they exhibited in the late 1990s has vanished.[62] Many who had Duma seats were forced out.[63] There still may be some influential Russian business leaders, but there does not appear to be the atmosphere of cooperation between government and business that exists in China.

Putin also shook up the association system, with some surprising consequences. He may have had the Chinese experience in mind with hope of creating only politically loyal organizations. On the one hand, he weakened RUIE and instead promoted two other more politically reliable chambers of commerce. The Russian Chamber of Commerce and Industry (RCCI), which has 169 association members, originated under the Ministry of Trade as the Chamber of Commerce and Industry of the Soviet Union. Putin had former foreign minister Yevgennii Primakov elected as its president in 2001.[64] Reminiscent of China's CEC-CEDA, Rutland calls the RCCI "a moribund organization with roots in the Soviet era, but that could now be activated as a tame business lobby to do the Kremlin's bidding."[65] In addition, the Kremlin in 2001 created the United Entrepreneurs' Organizations of Russia (OPORA) as a chamber directed at small and medium-sized businesses. Even though China's ACFIC has limited autonomy, it appears to be more active than any of the Russian chambers of commerce.

As the Kremlin tightened the reins on the oligarchs and chambers of commerce, there has been a slow but visible emergence of industry associations. There are no comprehensive statistics, but one Russian source estimates there may be 5,000 industry associations.[66] Duvanova finds that trade associations seem to be catching on in sectors in which small private entrepreneurs are threatened by rapacious bureaucrats who engage in extortion to provide basic stability to their markets.[67] She cites the case of small private firms who created the Guild for Audio-Video Trade Development to bring stability to a market threatened with both rampant piracy and overzealous officials handing out exorbitant fines. On the other hand, Pyle, who completed three surveys of companies and industry associations, arguing for a clearer economic logic, found that restructured firms and those involved in greater international trade are more likely to be involved in associations, a finding not unlike what is occurring in China.[68] Larger firms (58 percent) are more likely than smaller companies (21 percent) to be members. Many apparently join not to receive special favors but because of the market-enhancing services the associations provide, such as worker training, opportunities for international trade, collateral for bank loans, and employee training. Under Putin there exist some "developmental" associations that are more common in Japan and India and operate in certain sectors and regions in China.[69]

Conclusion

China's great leap toward capitalism has pushed Chinese firms to be more attentive to public policy. In the context of China's own political history, industry's policy influence has risen substantially over the past two decades. No longer are economic regulations and laws the obvious reflection of political elite or bureaucratic preferences. Large companies, Chinese and foreign, occasionally set the policy agenda, and they regularly contribute policy suggestions.

That said, situating China comparatively helps us more clearly see in relative terms how Chinese industry interacts with the government and the extent of its influence. China is distinctive, but government–business relations there could be made out of a composite of elements of Japan, India, and Russia. China's associations are less developed than those in Japan and India, but in certain sectors and regions they are more mature than many Russian associations. Limits on associations mean that most Chinese companies, to borrow a phrase from the Mao era, usually "walk on one leg" and interact individually with officialdom, which is also common in Japan. Although direct lobbying exists in all four countries, it more fully complements collective action in Japan and India than in China or Russia. This distinction is reinforced by a recent survey of the worldwide government affairs executives of American multinationals. As Table 6.1 shows, although Americans believe that their employees are their companies' most effective advocates, a substantially higher minority believe that associations in Japan and India are quite important to their efforts than in China or Russia.

TABLE 6.1
Who lobbies effectively?

	Companies' employees most effective (%)	Industry associations most effective (%)
China	78	3
Japan	49	16
India	54	11
Russia	28	3

Source: Brian P. Hawkinson, Marin A. Randall, and Jennifer E. Poos, *International Government Relations: Benchmarking Report* (Washington, DC: Public Affairs Council, June 2007), 16–18.

Although Russian and Chinese associations still have relatively limited influence, particularly in Russia, Russia's oligarchs (at least prior to Putin) seem to have been individually powerful and certainly more attuned to electoral politics and the legislature than Chinese business. On banking and finance issues the old battle lines of state-owned versus private and Chinese versus foreign still apply in China, but coalitions that cross ownership and nationality boundaries are common in many other issue areas. This does not yet seem to be the case in Japan, while India seems to be trending in the same direction.[70]

This review shows that both political and economic factors help shape a country's political economy. The political leadership's attitude toward collective action matters immensely, and this is not easily captured in a government's regime type. Russia is, after all, officially a democracy. At the same time, political institutions and elite preferences provide a context, but they do not guarantee how industry will respond. That may also depend on the characteristics of their firms and their industries. Chinese companies in certain sectors are more prone to associations than other firms, while Chinese companies more fully integrated into global markets share policy preferences with their foreign partners. Economic factors to some extent shape lobbying in the other countries as well.

In addition to pointing to the need to be attentive to political and economic forces that affect government–business relations, the analysis also highlights the benefit of acknowledging and analyzing the variation that exists within each of the four countries. The literature on comparative capitalism tends to emphasize variation between states, but there is far less attention to explaining systematic variation within countries. Just as Pearson found in examining regulation in China and elsewhere, countries may have not one political economy but multiple political economies, plural.

Although suggestive, these findings are tentative. The amount of academic research on business's role in policy making in developing countries is quite limited. There is a small but growing number of single-country analyses but far fewer comparative studies. Hence, we face severe problems in terms of standards of measurement as well as simply lacking information on certain subjects. In particular, there is a growing stock of research on chambers of commerce, which tends to highlight the significance of political factors; but there is far less systematic research on industry associations and sectoral politics that compares multiple industries within a country or a single sector across several countries. There is also insufficient research on the tactics of individual company lobbying and how it compares to the behavior of associations. Such studies could help us clarify how political and economic factors yield diverse patterns of lobbying that exist in China and other countries.

Chapter Seven

Comparing China's Capitalists
Neither Democratic Nor Exceptional

KELLEE S. TSAI

The stunning expansion of China's private sector since the late 1970s has inspired political scientists to speculate that economic development and the ensuing rise of China's capitalists portend a transition to democracy. By 2007, there were 34 million private businesses, accounting for 40 percent of the GDP and 70 percent of fixed-asset investment.[1] Chinese entrepreneurs have become statistically consequential, yet they lack the right to elect political leaders who will defend their material interests. Various observers thus expect that China's growing population of capitalists will push for democracy to protect their private property rights. For example, Guo Xiaoqin suggests, "An emerging powerful entrepreneurial class could gradually and ultimately become the main engine of China's reform economy and a constituency independent from state power that demands a strong voice in the political process."[2] Zheng Yongnian similarly predicts, "Chinese business classes are likely to play a role that their European counterparts did in the past. Capitalism is generating a Chinese bourgeoisie. It is a class with teeth."[3]

From the vantage point of this volume's comparative analytic agenda, these types of predictions commit the opposite fallacy of Chinese exceptionalism—namely, assuming the universal validity of modernization theory and the teleological expectations of democracy associated with it. Even though various large-scale quantitative analyses have established a correlation between high levels of economic development and democracy, these triumphalist accounts make little effort to justify implicit comparisons between today's Chinese capitalists and the eighteenth-century British bourgeoisie or American revolutionaries who demanded democracy in the spirit of "no taxation without representation."[4] If pressed, proponents of the idea that capitalist development presages democratization in China point to the more recent and regionally proximate examples of Taiwan and South Korea where democratic transitions followed only a few decades of rapid economic growth.[5] In this view, it is only a matter of time and further economic growth before China joins the ranks of democracies in Asia.

While acknowledging that democratic transitions have occurred in rapidly growing countries due to a wide range of factors—including foreign intervention, the rise of civil society and social movements, shifts in elite politics, and mobilization by labor or capital—this chapter focuses on the specific hypothesis that private entrepreneurs provide the basis for a democratic transition in China. In so doing, I examine the existing literature on democratization and institutional change, present findings from an original national survey of private entrepreneurs, and draw comparative insights from other transitional and developing countries. Empirically, my research finds little evidence to support the view that China's private sector bears democratic potential, which is consistent with the conclusions drawn by other studies of the country's private economy.[6] Analytically, the case of China's capitalists has both theory-disconfirming and theory-building implications for the comparative objectives of this volume.

First, contrary to the most simplistic, yet most popular, interpretation of modernization theory, capitalists are not inherently prodemocratic as a class. Like their counterparts in various Latin American, Asian, and European countries, China's business owners are sociologically, economically, and regionally diverse and, thus, deal with the government in different ways. The causal basis of this observation resonates with the points made in the chapters by Margaret Pearson, Mark Frazier, and Scott Kennedy, respectively, about the absence of a single model of political economy in China, the persistence of regional imbalances and inequalities, and the differing economic conditions of Chinese businesses. These realities are antithetical to capitalist class formation, much less class-based agitation for democracy.[7]

Second, this chapter uses the case of China's capitalists as an opportunity for concept formation. Although China's private entrepreneurs are not clamoring for political change, they have had a structural impact on Chinese politics—but not in the manner that structural theories of democratization would expect.[8] In the course of their day-to-day interactions, entrepreneurs are changing the country's formal political institutions to reflect their needs and interests. Major reforms in China's formal institutions have enhanced the private sector's political legitimacy and economic security—and yet these macrolevel institutional reforms have occurred in the absence of political mobilization by business owners. Regardless of whether China experiences a democratic transition, examining the actual political influence of China's private sector presents political scientists with a revealing case of endogenous institutional change. Specifically, business owners have fundamentally altered the formal political landscape through what I call "adaptive informal institutions," meaning the informal coping strategies created by local economic and state actors to bypass regulatory restrictions. As will be shown, over time, these adaptive informal institutions have paved the way for reformers to change China's most important formal political institutions in a manner that protects private capital. The comparative implication of this claim is that, even in an authoritarian regime, informal interactions among state and nonstate actors have the causal potential to change formal, state-level institutions. The issue of whether this causal potential for institutional transformation is realized depends on the political context of individual countries. Under certain circumstances, the popularity of adaptive informal institutions can expand the political opportunity for reform-oriented elites to enact significant changes in formal institutions in a manner that legitimizes their hitherto controversial proposals.

The chapter proceeds as follows. The first section outlines the theoretical context for the issues under consideration. Whether structural or voluntarist in orientation, few scholars actually propound a simple linear model of political development based on an overgeneralization of Barrington Moore's famous quotation, "no bourgeois, no democracy."[9] Hence, the more interesting analytical question is how major transformations in China's formal institutions could have occurred endogenously and in the absence of regime change. Building on theories of institutional development, I propose that adaptive informal institutions play an important mediating role in explaining the influence of informal practices on formal institutions. The second section presents evidence from my national survey of China's private entrepreneurs, which demonstrates the limits of class formation and mobilization among contemporary business owners. Studies of entrepreneurs from other transitional economies reveal that China's business owners are not unique in this respect. At the same time, we will see that entrepreneurial agency at the grassroots level has had a structural impact on China's most important political institutions: the Chinese Communist Party now admits capitalists, and the People's Republic of China (PRC) Constitution now protects private property rights. Ultimately, the private sector's political influence has unfolded in an indirect and incremental manner. Again, this dynamic can also be seen in other contexts where formal channels for political participation remain restricted.

The (Misplaced) Sources of Democratic Expectations

The comparative democratization literature presents at least two causal sequences that connect private sector development with democratic transition.[10] First, from a structural perspective, capitalists may become a prodemocratic class. Second, from a voluntarist perspective, reform-oriented political elites may collaborate with capitalists to undermine authoritarian rule. Neither approach predicts democratization in China and other late industrializing countries in a determinate manner.

First, given that China has experienced rapid growth rates under marketizing conditions, the structural, class-based explanation is the typical framework invoked by observers who anticipate democratic development in China.[11] Yet capitalists have demonstrated neither consistent opposition to authoritarian regimes nor consistent support for democratic ones in twentieth-century regime transitions. As Eva Bellin has argued, the political preferences of capitalists in late industrializing countries hinge on their degree of state dependence for the protection of their material interests and the extent to which capitalists fear that mass political empowerment would have destabilizing consequences.[12] Capitalists are not likely to support democracy if they are highly dependent on the state and fearful about the disruptive potential of democratization, and vice versa. This is best illustrated by the situation of capitalists in Suharto's Indonesia, where business elites (concentrated in the ethnic Chinese minority) depended on the state for access to credit and licenses and never represented a force for democracy.[13] The cases of Brazil and South Korea also illustrate this contention: in both countries, industrialists supported bureaucratic-authoritarian regimes during periods of economic growth and only gradually came to support regime transition after other segments of society had already mobilized for democracy.[14]

Second, if capitalist elites were to partake in a voluntarist version of democratic transition, their participation would be motivated, at a minimum, by exclusion from the current political regime and a loss of confidence in the ability of the current regime to protect its material interests.[15] However, business elites have not been active in either initiating or consolidating democratic transitions in the third wave democracies. It seems that the strongest statement one can make about the role of the Latin American bourgeoisie is that they have not blocked transitions to democracy.[16] Business elites were similarly quiescent in the South European transitions. The cases of Argentina and Spain show that, even when industrialists are dissatisfied with an authoritarian regime, it does not mean that they will collaborate with other elites in facilitating a transition to democracy.[17]

In brief, the association of capitalist development with democracy involves complex processes that extend beyond the mere emergence of private entrepreneurs—as a class and/or as an elitist vanguard.[18] Indeed, both my own research in China and studies of entrepreneurs in late industrializing countries show that business owners are not prone to engage in collective action, much less demand democracy. Yet, in China and elsewhere, the private sector has thrived, and once unthinkable changes have occurred in the country's most fundamental political institutions. How did this occur in the absence of popular mobilization, regime change, or external shocks?[19]

Explaining Endogenous Institutional Change

The typological concepts of "sequencing," "layering," and "conversion" in historical institutionalism all draw on the internal logic of formal institutions to explain the endogenous origins of institutional change. I propose that focusing on informal institutions may clarify the causal mechanisms in these accounts of institutional development.

PATH DEPENDENCE AND SEQUENCING

Although the sequencing approach to institutional development typically emphasizes self-reinforcing dynamics, path dependence does not preclude change over time. In particular, Paul Pierson distinguishes between "self-reinforcing event sequences" and "nonreinforcing event sequences" in path dependent arguments.[20] A common expression of a self-reinforcing event sequence is when certain political actors consolidate power early on and end up promoting institutions that enable them to maintain their authority.[21] On the other hand, in "nonreinforcing event sequences," or what James Mahoney calls "reactive sequences," certain events occur in reaction to earlier events, which then propel subsequent ones on an alternative trajectory.[22]

The concept of reactive sequences is fruitful for showing that short of regime transition, considerable changes could occur within the apparent limits of the existing political system.[23] The issue of when reinforcing processes are likely to shift to reactive ones is addressed by the notions of institutional layering and conversion, discussed next.

INSTITUTIONAL LAYERING AND CONVERSION

The second category of explanations for endogenous institutional change emphasizes institutional layering and complexity as a product of multiple sources of human action. "Layering" refers to the fact that most institutional environments comprise a variety of institutions that may be inconsistent with one another. The reality of multilayered institutional contexts thus limits the degree of coherence that particular formal institutions (for example, the U.S. Congress) may have at any given point in time.[24] As for the potential timing of endogenous institutional change, Robert Lieberman hypothesizes that "significant extraordinary political change" is more likely when there is "friction among multiple political orders."[25] And the "causal mechanism linking structural friction and political change is the reformulation of the incentives and opportunities for individual political action that friction produces."[26] Due to this friction among various institutional layers, actors may establish adaptive patterns that are simultaneously new, yet familiar.

A related phenomenon is what Kathleen Thelen calls "institutional conversion," meaning the use of existing institutions for new or alternative purposes.[27] This perspective recognizes that even when the formal attributes of institutions remain in place, their substantive roles may change quite dramatically. Moreover, Thelen's analysis demonstrates that "more subtle and smaller scale changes in 'settled' rather than 'unsettled' times are also worthy of our attention, as, over time, they can cumulate into significant institutional transformation."[28] The case of reform-era China provides many examples of how institutional conversion can result from endogenous processes of economic and social change during normal times.[29]

In sum, the sequencing, layering, and conversion approaches provide a basis for explaining the coexistence of regime continuity amid various institutional changes. The next section builds on these insights by showing how the analysis of informal institutions may elucidate the potential for flexibility in formal institutions.

THE FORMAL ORIGINS OF ADAPTIVE INFORMAL INSTITUTIONS

My argument brackets what Douglass North calls the "deep-seated cultural inheritance" underlying informal institutions and starts with the blank slate of formal institutions, which I define as rules, regulations, policies, and procedures that are promulgated and meant to be enforced by entities and agents generally recognized as being official.[30] Furthermore, formal institutions are both constraining and enabling. Although formal institutions limit the range of officially permissible behavior, multilayered institutional environments also provide opportunities for actors to adjust, ignore, or evade discrete portions of formal institutions. Initially, these adaptive responses may appear to be idiosyncratic or isolated. However, when the adaptive strategies become regularized patterns of interaction that violate or transcend the scope of formal institutions, they constitute what I call "adaptive informal institutions." Unlike informal institutions writ large, *adaptive* informal institutions refer to regularized patterns of interaction that emerge in reaction to constraints and opportunities in the formal institutional environment. Differentiating between long-standing informal practices (for example, culture) and those that appear in the context of new opportunities enables us to focus on a subset of informal coping strategies that derive from shorter-term considerations of convenience, efficiency, and possibility. This is the first part of the proposed causal sequence in explaining endogenous institutional development.

The second part concerns what happens after adaptive informal institutions emerge. At the most basic level, the spread of adaptive informal institutions may undermine the legitimacy of formal institutions. The relevance of institutions, whether formal or informal, depends on their capacity to guide human perceptions and practices. But do the enforcers of formal institutions ignore, incorporate, or discipline the actors sustaining adaptive informal institutions? The answer to this question is historically and nationally contingent. When adaptive informal institutions constitute flagrant forms of criminal activity, they are likely to elicit the attention of law enforcement entities. But if the latter are party to the offending activities, then efforts to curb the activities are unlikely to be effective. In contrast, adaptive informal institutions that merely stretch the limits of formal institutions or create new patterns of interaction not explicitly governed by formal institutions may survive for some length of time. And in some cases, adaptive informal institutions may become so widespread that the actors with authority to reform formal institutions choose to incorporate the practices popularized by adaptive informal institutions. Political elites and decision makers may decide to exercise their authority—within the context of their official positions—to reform formal institutions. Formalization of adaptive informal institutions could occur without jeopardizing the survival of preexisting formal institutions.

The next section illustrates this logic by presenting data on China's private sector, with supporting examples from other contexts. Evidence is lacking for claiming that private entrepreneurs constitute the basis for either the structural or voluntarist paths to democratization. In navigating various political and regulatory restrictions, however, entrepreneurs have had a structural impact on political institutions in China and elsewhere.

China's Private Entrepreneurs: Fragmented, but Influential

From 2002 to 2003 I conducted a national survey of private entrepreneurs as part of a broader project to assess the political implications of private sector development in China.[31] This section highlights a few findings to assess the plausibility of popular hypotheses about the democratic potential of private entrepreneurs.

LACK OF CAPITALIST CLASS FORMATION

Support for the structural hypothesis requires, at a minimum, evidence of class formation among private entrepreneurs.[32] Class formation would then provide the basis for collective action in defense of class interests. However, the current generation of China's business owners has widely divergent identities, interests, and coping strategies. Differences in entrepreneurs' employment backgrounds, political networks, size of business, and local political economic conditions all contribute to class fragmentation rather than class formation.

Because most contemporary entrepreneurs have different employment backgrounds, the vast majority of business owners do not identify themselves as capitalists. During field interviews, many business owners preferred to describe themselves as teachers, farmers, workers, or even cadres rather than as "entrepreneurs" (*qiyejia*). This limited sense of identity is due to the relative youth of China's private sector. As shown in Table 7.1, substantial inter- and intragenerational differences in occupational history exist within the private sector; the diversity of private entrepreneurs' previous work experience is

TABLE 7.1

Employment background of entrepreneurs, spouses, and parents, 2002

Occupation	Self	Spouse	Parents
Professional, skilled personnel	11.3%	6.4%	4.9%
Government/administrative officer/cadre	4.0	4.9	7.9
Enterprise manager	15.7	5.7	7.2
Administrative staff	7.2	8.0	4.2
Ordinary worker	17.8	20.7	18.7
Commercial/sales personnel	8.7	9.5	4.4
Farmer	20.3	21.5	42.7
Soldier	1.9	0.2	0.8
Other	7.7	7.8	4.1
No occupation	5.3	15.3	5.1
	100%	100%	100%
Valid responses	1,465	1,148	1,133

Type of Work Unit			
Party/government organization	5.4%	4.5%	6.6%
State-owned enterprise	22.4	15.5	23.0
Collective enterprise	19.4	9.5	12.4
Foreign enterprise	0.8	1.1	0.1
Private enterprise	10.3	19.8	2.6
Individual business	10.8	11.1	3.4
Rural household or collective	21.9	20.8	45.2
Other	3.3	5.8	3.2
No unit	5.7	11.8	3.6
	100%	100%	100%
Valid responses	1,453	1,132	1,114

mirrored by the diversity in employment backgrounds of their parents and spouses.

Studies of so-called New Russians have similarly found a reluctance by its members to self-identify with the label. Harley Balzar observes, "New Russians are hardly a single group," as they include professionals, former *nomenklatura*, criminals, and young entrepreneurs.[33] At the same time, a 2003–2004 survey of Russian entrepreneurs found that the proportion of relatives running businesses is higher among entrepreneurs than nonentrepreneurs, which suggests a family diffusion effect in entrepreneurship within a span of twenty years in Russia.[34] Even though China's entrepreneurs continue to come from all walks of life, the same researchers have observed a comparable dynamic in China.[35]

While diversity in previous occupation does not preclude class formation, my survey also found that China's entrepreneurs have varying "interests," as indicated by the types of problems that they encounter in the course of doing business and the extent to which they believe certain policy issues require improvement. In particular, entrepreneurs previously employed by the state are more likely than those without state employment backgrounds to complain about having access to bank loans, securing land for production, high taxes and fees, the local allocation of collective funds, and employee stability (Table 7.2). Former state employees are also more likely to express a need for improvement in a wide range of policy areas, including protection of private property rights, intellectual property rights, public opinion of the private sector, tax policy, credit policy, macroeconomic management, more equitable treatment of private businesses, fighting corruption, and improving the provision of public utilities, education, and the social security system. This higher level of discontent reflects the fact that former state employees are accustomed to receiving more services from the government than farmers and other rural citizens.

Studies of private sector development in transitional economies have identified a similar degree of internal fragmentation among private entrepreneurs. For example, in their analysis of entrepreneurship in former socialist countries in Central and Eastern Europe, David Smallbone and Friederike Welter distinguish among small businesses, informal operations, and "nomenklatura" enterprises run by former state employees.[36] In a manner that mirrors my observations of China's private sector, they find that the socialist-era identities of entrepreneurs fundamentally shape their social and

TABLE 7.2

Experiences and attitudes of entrepreneurs with state employment backgrounds: independent samples *t*-test

Encountered Problems with:	Mean(a)		
	No state employment	Former state employee	*t*
Access to bank loans	2.26	2.09	4.53**
Securing production site	2.68	2.56	3.56**
Utilities	2.81	2.77	1.12
Attracting skilled staff	2.62	2.56	1.90
Taxes	2.61	2.55	1.99*
Fees	2.53	2.37	4.37**
Allocation of collective funds	2.57	2.45	3.30**
Government services	2.60	2.54	1.63
Employee stability	2.74	2.66	2.54**
Safety of self/family	2.89	2.88	0.47
Need improvement in:			
Protection of property rights	0.69	0.78	−3.66**
Protection of intellectual property rights	0.62	0.76	−5.25**
Public opinion of entrepreneurs	0.65	0.78	−4.57**
Tax policy	0.82	0.90	−4.14**
Credit policy	0.81	0.88	−3.20**
Macroeconomic controls	0.57	0.67	−3.66**
Management of private business	0.76	0.82	−2.54**
Household registration system	0.57	0.60	−1.21
Equal treatment of different business types	0.76	0.85	−4.19**
Eliminating corruption	0.91	0.95	−3.12**
Political system reform	0.67	0.72	−1.65
Public utilities	0.75	0.80	−2.10*
Education system	0.80	0.85	−2.61**
Social security system	0.85	0.92	−4.30**

*Significant at the $p < 0.05$ level.

**Significant at the $p < 0.01$ level.

For the first set of issues, the responses were measured on a scale of 1 to 3 such that 1 indicated "large problem" and 3 indicated "not a problem." For the second set of issues, dummy variables were used such that 0 indicated "no need for improvement" and 1 indicated "need for improvement."

business networks and, thus, their relative access to key resources such as bank loans.[37]

As the chapters by Frazier, Kennedy, and Pearson also emphasize, attending to differences in China's regional and sectoral conditions is essential for understanding the segmented variation in political economic outcomes. In my larger study, I identified five local developmental patterns: (1) the Wenzhou model, which is based on small-scale private enterprises; (2) the Sunan model, which used to privilege collective enterprises but now emphasizes foreign investment and larger private businesses; (3) the South China model, which depends on foreign direct investment; (4) the state-dominated model, which inherited a large state sector from the Mao and early reform eras; and (5) the pattern of limited development, which faces a range of geographic and economic challenges.[38] These developmental patterns affect the operating conditions experienced by business owners and therefore the manner and extent to which they seek redress for perceived problems. Table 7.3 shows that private entrepreneurs operating in the Wenzhou model localities have much fewer grievances than their counterparts in other developmental patterns. Table 7.4 shows that entrepreneurs in the Wenzhou model area are also the least likely to use "assertive means" of dispute resolution, but, on the whole, they are much more likely to solicit assistance from business associations. This latter finding is consistent with Kennedy's observation in the preceding chapter about business associations in Wenzhou being particularly active and influential.[39] The local variation that I found in entrepreneurs' use of different means for solving problems also resonates with the sectorally-differentiated influence of business associations identified in Kennedy's chapter.

TABLE 7.3
Local variation in entrepreneurial perception of problems

Developmental pattern	Wenzhou model	Sunan model	South China model	State-dominated model	Limited development pattern	Sample average
Have disputes with local government	14.4%	24.1%	10.8%	27.9%	16.1%	22.7%
Have serious capital constraints	28.4	71.8	62.3	78.8	73.2	69.6
Problems with land for production site	13.8	27.5	39.9	43.8	32.3	34.4
Problems with utilities	3.0	8.0	35.1	19.6	25.8	19.3
Problems with taxes	8.4	32.2	59.5	45.0	34.7	37.8
Problems with fees	11.4	44.1	59.5	58.4	39.5	47.7
Problems with government services	3.6	34.9	45.6	48.1	47.6	39.0
Ranking of developmental type by level of complaints*	5	4	2	1	3	n.a.

*1 indicates that the respondents in that developmental type have the highest overall level of complaints, while 5 indicates the lowest overall level of complaints.

TABLE 7.4

Means of addressing problems by developmental pattern, 2002
(percentage of respondents who indicated using these means either "sometimes"
or "frequently")

Developmental pattern	Wenzhou model	Sunan model	South China model	State-dominated model	Limited development pattern	Sample average
Express opinion directly to political leaders	4.8%	25.3%	16.4%	27.3%	16.9%	22.4%
Solicit assistance from those with influence on political leaders	11.4	27.3	12.1	30.4	6.5	23.8
Express opinion through mass organizations	24.7	7.9	6.4	15.5	10.5	13.0
Express opinion through NPC delegates	0.6	7.0	2.9	5.9	5.6	5.4
Express opinion through CPPCC members	0.6	5.9	5.7	9.5	4.8	6.7
Express opinion through entrepreneurs associations (ILA, PEA, UFIC)	27.7	17.8	7.8	17.3	10.5	17.2
Write letters to relevant government agencies	0.6	5.4	5.0	5.8	9.7	5.4
Report to official organizations accepting inquiries or complaints	0.6	5.2	5.0	2.0	0.8	3.0
Seek organizations to arbitrate the dispute	0.0	3.4	1.4	2.7	0.8	2.3
Appeal to courts	1.2	9.7	3.5	9.4	6.5	7.8
Percentage of assertive entrepreneurs*	0.6	9.0	4.8	4.8	8.8	5.5

*The survey asked respondents, "When you encounter disputes, how do you normally resolve the matter? (Please rank the following eight choices.)" Those who selected "appeal to government or higher authorities," "appeal to courts," or "resolve through news media" as their typical first course of action constitute "assertive entrepreneurs" in my typology of entrepreneurs' coping strategies. Note that these percentages are calculated directly from the survey and do not take into account the estimated 15 percent of unregistered entrepreneurs. When the latter are taken into account the raw percentages from the survey are reduced by 15 percent.

In short, these types of findings call into question the extent to which business owners from all walks of life, operating in different political economic environments, currently constitute a coherent class with the capacity to engage in collective action in defense of "class" interests.[40]

ABSENCE OF PRODEMOCRATIC ELITES

Given the limits of class formation among private entrepreneurs in general, do wealthy entrepreneurs who are Communist Party members, or "red capitalists," exhibit signs of partaking in a voluntarist path toward democratization in China? In Dickson's 1999 and 2005 surveys of entrepreneurial elites and local officials, large-scale business owners are far more politically cautious than local officials.[41] By the same token, my survey found that business owners who are more politically active—that is, those who are leaders and members of formal political organizations—face better operating conditions and have fewer grievances than ordinary entrepreneurs.[42] Table 7.5 shows that both political members and political elites are more likely to be older, to have entered the private sector earlier, and to run businesses that are more profitable and have more employees. With respect to capitalization issues, red capitalists are also more likely than other business owners to have access to formal bank loans and private loans, as well as investment by groups of shareholders, the township government, government agencies, and even investors from abroad. On the whole, political members and elites are also less likely to encounter disputes with consumers.[13] Given their membership in formal political institutions, it makes sense that they are also more likely to express their opinions directly to political leaders, use the court system, and use other formal political institutions to reflect their views to higher-level officials.[44] Yet, compared to most entrepreneurs, political members and elites have fewer grievances and are less likely to be concerned about various policy issues; the main areas that they indicate a need for improvement are protection of intellectual property rights, public opinion of private entrepreneurs, and equitable treatment of different types of enterprises.

Overall, the majority of red capitalists exhibit "loyally acceptant" coping strategies, meaning that they generally express their concerns in a manner that seeks to reform (or merely implement) certain rules and regulations rather than to overthrow the government.[45] Even though capitalist elites possess the material resources and, increasingly, the political access to promote regime transition, they show no signs of doing so at this point. A similar dynamic may be observed among the so-called bourgeoisie or new business elite in Vietnam. Martin Gainsborough explains, "While this elite is new in terms of its business interests, it is in fact rather old in terms of its political ties."[46] As a result, like the portion of China's red capitalists who were born out of party-state patronage, Vietnam's business elites seem much more supportive of the authoritarian status quo than interested in calling for political liberalization.

TABLE 7.5

Attributes of members and elites of formal political institutions:
t-test comparison of means

General attributes	Nonpolitical members	Political members	Political elites
Birth year	1963	1956**	1956**
Year business started	1995	1992**	1992**
Gross Sales in 2001 (10,000 *yuan*)	334	1,147,651*	252,045
Net Sales in 2001 (10,000 *yuan*)	29	183**	195**
Number of employees	44	222**	222**

Credit and investment conditions			
Use of bank loans	0.4763	0.6107**	0.6145**
Ease of access to bank loans	2.24	2.34**	2.40**
Private loans outstanding	0.2795	0.4393**	0.4358**
Investment by group of shareholders	0.0257	0.0679**	0.1006**
Investment by township government/ neighborhood committee	0.0024	0.0179**	0.0168**
Investment by government agency/military/ law enforcement, etc.	0.0032	0.0107**	0.0112**
Investment from abroad	0.0040	0.0143**	0.0223**

Nature of disputes encountered			
With suppliers	0.5149	0.4893	0.4637
With buyers	0.6201	0.5893	0.6089
With employees	0.1245	0.1179	0.1173
With consumers	0.4193	0.2893**	0.3017**
With local government agencies and/or officials	0.2169	0.2714**	0.2682**
With local residents or other local organizations	0.1494	0.2000**	0.2067**
With news media	0.0145	0.0214	0.0223

Policy concerns			
Need for improvement in property rights	0.7068	0.7214	0.7095
Need for improvement in intellectual property rights	0.6410	0.7000*	0.6983**
Need for improvement in public opinion and propaganda	0.6739	0.7464**	0.7486**
Need for improvement in tax policy	0.8386	0.8429	0.8380
Need for improvement in credit policy	0.8345	0.8286	0.8324
Need for improvement in macroeconomic regulation and policy	0.5904	0.6357	0.6313*
Need for improvement in regulation of business	0.7871	0.7500	0.7430*
Need for improvement in household registration system	0.5735	0.5714	0.5531
Need for improvement in equality of treatment in enterprises	0.7695	0.8500**	0.8436**
Need for improvement in eliminating corruption	0.9285	0.8857**	0.8827**
Need for improvement in reform in the political system	0.6803	0.7000	0.6816
Need for improvement in public utilities	0.7582	0.7607	0.7318
Need for improvement in education system	0.8177	0.7821**	0.7654**
Need for improvement in social security system	0.8643	0.8750	0.8715

TABLE 7.5 *(continued)*
Attributes of members and elites of formal political institutions:
t-test comparison of means

Forms of Dispute Resolution Used	Nonpolitical members	Political members	Political elites
Negotiate and compromise as much as possible, and then let the issue resolve itself	0.8273	0.8321	0.8380
Appeal to local government or higher authorities	0.2490	0.2786*	0.2682
Appeal to court	0.2378	0.2929**	0.2682
Mediation through relatives and/or friends	0.2161	0.2161**	0.1955
Resolve through society and social relations	0.4410	0.4357	0.4860
Resolve through news media	0.0153	0.0143	0.0168
Feel powerless	0.1382	0.1536	0.1397
Express opinion directly to political leaders	0.5165	0.7500**	0.7318**
Ask for help from those with influence over political leaders	0.5454	0.5607	0.5419
Reflect opinion through mass rally groups	0.3470	0.4071**	0.3911
Reflect opinion through NPC delegates	0.1863	0.3214**	0.2793**
Reflect opinion through CPPCC members	0.1904	0.3679**	0.3184**
Reflect opinion to higher authorities via business associations	0.4161	0.5357*	0.5084
Write letters to the relevant government department	0.2129	0.2607**	0.2514
Write letters to the media	0.1703	0.1429*	0.1173**
Report to organizations accepting inquiries	0.1663	0.1750	0.1508
Look for organizations to arbitrate the dispute	0.2120	0.2286	0.1955
Meet with higher authorities for help	0.2546	0.3643**	0.3017
Refuse to be bribed	0.1622	0.1500	0.1453

**Indicates .01 level of significance; *indicates .05 level of significance.

The Informal Influence of Private Entrepreneurs

Although there is minimal indication of class formation among private entrepreneurs, and capitalist elites remain politically quiescent, remarkable changes have occurred in China's political institutions and official ideology. These changes have elevated the status of private entrepreneurs in official discourse from embodying the evil "rat tail of capitalism" during the Cultural Revolution to representing the country's "most advanced productive forces" during the early 2000s. In addition to the complete reversal in ideology, the political influence of the private sector is reflected by its growing representation in formal political organizations: by the end of 2006, over 3.6 million Party members (about 5 percent of the members) were working in the private sector, and, at the Tenth National People's Congress in 2006, over 200 of the delegates were private entrepreneurs.[47] How can these political and institutional transformations be explained?

I propose that adaptive informal institutions at the local level have contributed substantially to shaping the substance of major institutional changes concerning the private sector. While central state-level policies have provided an increasingly permissive environment for private commerce, local economic and political actors have interpreted these policies in a highly selective manner and, in the process, created a wide range of adaptive operating strategies that depart from the original scope and spirit of formal regulations. With widespread repetition, these coping strategies evolve into adaptive informal institutions, which in turn may inspire reactive change on the part of political elites with vested interests in bolstering the legitimacy and efficacy of formal institutions. For illustrative purposes, consider the temporal gaps between the actual practices and formal policies that sanctioned larger private businesses, allowed capitalists to join the Communist Party, and enhanced constitutional protection of the private economy.

THE PATH TO PRIVATE ENTERPRISE

Throughout the 1980s and most of the 1990s, private entrepreneurs experienced not only a social stigma for being profit oriented but also political persecution. There was political uncertainty about the trajectory of economic reform, and private entrepreneurs were publicly criticized during the national campaigns against "spiritual pollution" in 1983–1984 and against "bourgeois liberalization" in 1987. At the local level, entrepreneurs were subjected to arbitrary treatment by tax collectors and harassment by other bureaucrats. In contrast, state and collective enterprises received favorable treatment relative to private ones in terms of tax breaks, bank loans, and use of land. Those were the operating realities that business owners faced.

Why, then, were entrepreneurs willing to enter and stay in business? One way for entrepreneurs to avoid social and political ostracism was to "wear a red hat" by registering private enterprises as collective ones. This adaptive strategy was so widespread that "wearing a red hat" became (and remains) a common term in everyday discourse. The practice became institutionalized as a standard, albeit informal, operating practice for private entrepreneurs. Yet the actual process through which this occurred was not simply the case of entrepreneurs deceiving local bureaucrats; instead, the actions of agents were collaborative and strategic. Most local cadres knew exactly what they were doing when they accepted a registration fee from a local proprietor to run a collective enterprise. Hundreds of thousands of both state and non-state actors were complicit agents in popularizing the red hat phenomenon. By the time that central-level elites realized so many collectives were really private enterprises, it was futile to insist that the scale of the private sector be limited to household producing units with fewer than eight employees. In the 1988 revision of the PRC Constitution, a key paragraph in Article 11 finally recognized the private sector as "a complement to the socialist economy," which provided the legal basis for allowing "private enterprises" (*siying qiye*) with more than eight employees to operate.

The practice of wearing a red hat is an example of how an adaptive informal institution contributed to institutional conversion of a formal regulation, the collective registration status. Instead of displacing the collective sector, red hat enterprises represented an additional form of collective enterprise; this innovative practice expanded the institutional space for private businesses to operate in, and then generated the political possibility for creating a more fitting registration status for larger private enterprises. Specifically, the economic success and widespread use of this adaptive informal institution provided reformers with the requisite evidence that expanding the scope of the private sector would enhance China's productive forces during the initial stage of socialism. In the absence of red hat enterprises, reformers would have faced more entrenched political opposition to liberalizing China's then nascent private economy. Ultimately, the adaptive informal institution of wearing a red hat not only influenced the legalization of private enterprises with more than eight employees but also provided the basis for subsequent institutional changes in the CCP and state constitutions.

THE CHINESE COMMUNIST PARTY'S INCORPORATION OF CAPITALISTS

The first generation of profit-oriented business operators in post-Mao China generally came from two different backgrounds. The group of "individual entrepreneurs" (*getihu*) was comprised of street peddlers and small retail business owners who were marginalized during the socialist period and did not have the benefits of state employment. At the other extreme were cadre entrepreneurs and red capitalists who used their privileged political status to run businesses indirectly or help others run red hat operations. Even though CCP members were not allowed to operate private businesses, throughout the 1980s and 1990s many were already active participants in the nonstate sector. Indeed, official surveys reveal an increasing proportion of self-identified CCP members among private entrepreneurs over time, such that only 7 percent of business owners admitted to being Party members in 1991, but by 2003 over one-third admitted to being private entrepreneurs.[48] It is likely that the earlier official figures underestimate the true proportion of Party members in the private sector. For many years, the uneasy coexistence between China's official socialist ideology and reality of private sector development accounts for the simultaneous growth of business owners among Party members—and the underreporting of Party members in official surveys of private entrepreneurs.[49]

On the occasion of the CCP's eightieth anniversary on July 1, 2001, General Secretary Jiang Zemin gave a landmark speech widely interpreted as inviting private entrepreneurs to join the Party. The rationale was weaved into Jiang's "Theory of the Three Represents," which made the controversial recommendation that the Party should represent "the most advanced forces of production, the most advanced cultural forces, and the interests of the overwhelming majority of people." The CCP had launched a mass media campaign publicizing the "Three Represents" leading up to the anniversary; then the July 1 speech, followed by the Sixteenth Party Congress in late 2002, clarified the implication of the "theory," that is, that the CCP should not discriminate against private entrepreneurs and should in fact embrace them because they are contributing (the most) to China's economic development.

Given that a number of the Party's old guard disapproved of this sharp ideological turn, it is remarkable that the CCP agreed to reverse its former ideological depiction of capitalists as exploitative "class enemies." As Bruce Dickson and Joseph Fewsmith have suggested, however, allowing private entrepreneurs into the Party was a strategic decision to incorporate a growing and increasingly wealthy portion of Chinese society.[50] While this strategic interpretation of the Party's decision makes sense, I would add that the underlying causal mechanisms leading to this decision were rooted in the growing power of the informal rules of the game that had evolved over the first two decades of economic reform. Party members were already active in the private sector well before private entrepreneurs were formally permitted to join the Party. All of the informal coping strategies that both state and nonstate actors had reproduced in their daily interactions took on an institutional reality of their own, thereby challenging national leaders to adapt preexisting formal institutions to assimilate these hitherto informal practices. The cumulative effect of this dynamic can also be seen in revisions to the PRC constitution that have become increasingly favorable toward the private sector.

PRIVATE SECTOR–FRIENDLY REVISIONS
TO THE PRC CONSTITUTION

Of the various constitutional changes that have occurred since 1982, the first two revisions represent reactive formalization of local practices and realities. First, formal recognition of the private sector in 1988 clearly trailed ground-level practices. Second, the 1999 revisions changed a key passage in Article 11 to say that private businesses "are major components of the socialist market economy." The revisions further indicated that the PRC is a "socialist country ruled by law." These changes signaled a more legitimate and secure status for the private sector. By this time, "privatization" or "restructuring" (*gaizhi*) of TVEs had already been occurring for five years and the selling off of small and medium SOEs, announced at the Fifteenth Party Congress in 1997, was gaining momentum.

Meanwhile, the most recent revision puts forth an ambitious objective that was inspired by the two adaptive informal institutions previously discussed—wearing a red hat and the proliferation of red capitalists. In 2004, Article 11 was revised to indicate that the state "protects the lawful rights and interests of the private sector of the economy, including individual and private businesses." And Article 13 introduced, "The lawful private property of citizens shall not be encroached upon." Meanwhile, the "Theory of the Three Represents" was incorporated into state ideology alongside "Marxism, Leninism, Mao Zedong Thought" and the "Theories of Deng Xiaoping."

Unlike the first two amendments already discussed, however, the constitutional stipulation that private property rights would be protected should be viewed as an objective rather than post hoc recognition of ground-level realities. Formal protection of private property rights ultimately requires strengthening the institutions that support the rule of law.[51] In the interim, various adaptive informal institutions will continue to serve as self-enforcing substitutes for property rights—a phenomenon that has been observed in numerous contexts both within and beyond China.[52]

Although the series of constitutional revisions relating to the private sector appears to be a linear progression of increasing official recognition and legal protection of its interests, there was nothing automatic or predetermined about the development of various formal institutions to support the private sector. The process of institutional development has been highly contested and incremental—and, as I have suggested, an outgrowth of adaptive informal practices at the local level. Moreover, examples abound of adaptive informal institutions that remain quasi-legal or simply illegal because they have yet to influence broader reforms. The examples already given were positive cases of (unintended) policy influence because the adaptive practices resonated with the agendas of economic reformers. Space constraints prevent delineation of all the adaptive informal institutions that the central party-state has attempted to eradicate rather than incorporate.[53] Suffice it to say that the combination of elite politics and the nature of central–local relations at any given point in time are critical in determining whether adaptive informal institutions are ignored, formalized, or banned at the national level.

Comparative Implications

Despite the popular association of capitalist development with democracy, a closer examination of the democratization literature reveals that, more often than not, capitalists support incumbent authoritarian governments. Often the overarching reason is quite simple: business elites may depend on the state for a range of institutional and material resources. Analysis of survey data from China shows that the reasons for private entrepreneurs' political quiescence also include differences in social and political backgrounds as well as diversity in local political economic conditions. These key differences inhibit the prospects for capitalist class formation and, therefore, the prospects for class-based mobilization for democracy.

Yet the case of China's capitalists also demonstrates that unformed classes can nonetheless have a structural impact on politics. Theoretically, this chapter proposes that adaptive informal institutions may play an important role in endogenous accounts of institutional change. Specifically, adaptive informal institutions emerge out of the collaborative coping strategies of state and nonstate actors when they find formal institutions too constraining. Over time, reform-oriented elites may leverage the popularity and/or effectiveness of adaptive informal institutions to build political support for major transformations in formal institutions. This reactive sequence of institutional change can occur even in authoritarian contexts where political institutions are not necessarily expected to be responsive to grassroots interactions, and where nonstate actors are typically prohibited from forming autonomous organizations to articulate group interests.

While my argument originates from research conducted in China, it is apparent that adaptive informal practices also emerge in other contexts where there is a disjuncture between formal institutions and the possibilities envisioned by local "entrepreneurs" (in the broadest sense of the word). From registering the Soviet Union's first independent oil company as a nongovernmental organization to using land use rights as collateral for private bank loans in Vietnam, local economic and political actors have devised a variety of creative means to circumvent and stretch the boundaries of formal institutions.[54] Furthermore, these local innovations are not merely acts of criminality or self-contained "weapons of the weak."[55] In the course of their daily interactions with one another and with local staff of the state, entrepreneurs have had a structural impact on the direction of formal institutional reforms. In the case of China, private entrepreneurs as a group have not demanded protection of their property rights or for membership in the Chinese Communist Party. Instead, people from different social backgrounds have entered the private sector as a self-help strategy to enhance their material welfare, and, in the process, that have appeared to party-state elites as an increasingly important constituency. Beyond China, the collapse of collective farming in Vietnam, "spontaneous privatization" in Hungary, and legalization of private security services in Russia have also been traced to informal everyday practices that became widespread and commanded the attention of national authorities who then sanctioned the informal activities ex post facto.[56]

The methodological implication of this argument is that day-to-day modes of interaction at the grassroots level warrant our attention. Although the approach outlined here does not make deterministic predictions about when and if formal institutions will incorporate various informal practices, it is apparent that adaptive informal institutions nonetheless mediate, and sometimes subvert, the substance and spirit of formal institutions. This dynamic of informal adaptation can serve as an endogenous source of formal institutional change when key elites believe that the demonstration effect of these adaptations supports their reform agendas. As such, the analytic implication of this claim is that major political and institutional transformations are possible in the absence of regime change. Hence, rather than speculating about the prospects for democracy in China and other authoritarian regimes, it would be more fruitful to examine the extent to which informal interactions and adaptive informal institutions are undermining or contributing to the country's political resilience. Perhaps comparativists who do not specialize in China might find the concept of adaptive informal institutions worthy of engaging.

Chapter Eight

When Are Banks Sold to Foreigners?
An Examination of the Politics of Selling Banks in Mexico, Korea, and China

VICTOR SHIH

In January 2006, the Ministry of Foreign Affairs (MOFA) in Beijing received a letter from former President George H. W. Bush. In the letter, Bush urged the Chinese government to approve an impending deal in which the Chinese government would sell 85-percent share ownership of a troubled Chinese bank to a consortium led by Citibank. In addition to praising Citibank and the other foreign member of the consortium, the Carlyle Group, Bush also intimated that a successful acquisition would be "beneficial to the comprehensive development of Sino–US relations."[1] Undoubtedly, this letter quickly made its way to Zhongnanhai, where the Politburo Standing Committee discussed its content. The letter was then sent to the China Banking Regulatory Commission (CBRC), the bureaucratic entity formally charged with approving this deal, along with a set of instructions from the leadership. In March 2006, the content of the letter was leaked to the official press by the government. Instead of facilitating the deal, the leaked letter made it virtually impossible to approve the deal because it would appear that the Chinese government was caving in to foreign pressure. Soon afterward, the CBRC announced that the deal would not be approved as it stood because Citibank had asked for a higher share of the bank than was allowed under Chinese regulations at the time.[2] In the end, Citibank had to abandon the Carlyle Group as its partner and submit a much more modest bid to gain 20 percent control over Guangdong Development Bank, in line with existing regulations.

The amazing aspect of this incident is that a letter needed to be sent through such formalized channels in the first place. Instead of intimate gatherings where Citibank officials pitched the sale to members of the Politburo or golf outings with senior technocrats, Citibank needed to mobilize someone with the stature of Bush, who in turn only had the option of sending a letter through the proper channels. Although some foreign investment banks have had success gaining access to the political elite, they often took place in formal settings or during inspection trips. This contrasts sharply with the cozy relationship between domestic private capital and the state in Mexico and Korea and, in the case of Mexico, seemingly intimate relations between foreign capital and the state.[3]

At first glance, the explanation of why foreign banks have had such a tough time acquiring Chinese financial institutions seems straightforward. Sales of state banks or domestically owned private banks often took place in the aftermath of financial crises that depleted the banking system of capital. Illiquidity forced the beleaguered state to bring in foreign capital to restructure the banks, often allowing foreign banks to gain controlling stakes. In recent years, multinational financial institutions (MNFIs) acquired major banks in Mexico, Brazil, Argentina, and Korea in the aftermath of financial crises. However, an examination of the pattern of bank restructuring in Mexico, Korea, and China suggests that there is at most a loose correlation between liquidity need and successful foreign acquisition of domestic banks. Both Mexico and Korea spent enormous amount of public funds to recapitalize banks before selling to either domestic private interests or MNFIs. None of these cases exhibited a clear pattern of fire-sales to cash-rich MNFIs.

A Framework

This paper explains the variation in MNFI success in acquiring controlling stakes in financial institutions in Mexico, Korea, and China by focusing on the role of *domestic* private capital in the bank restructuring process. Even in cases where MNFIs gained controlling stakes in domestic banks, the role of domestic capital is likely crucial. Without active lobbying by powerful domestic interests, MNFIs would have a difficult time succeeding, even in a place like Mexico, where the United States looms large in the political landscape.

Two characteristics of domestic private capital emerge as key explanatory variables. First, it matters whether representatives of private capital make up the political selectorate. By selectorate, I mean "the set of people whose endowments include the qualities or characteristics institutionally required to choose the government's leadership."[4] As discussed in the following pages, domestic private capital constituted a powerful member of the selectorate because of the financial resources it could mobilize to support political actors. Many works on the East Asian developmental state already focus on the informational aspect of the business-government relationship because information exchange is seen as the bedrock of successful government policies.[5] In the literature on China, Kennedy's work likewise shows that both private and state business conglomerates have regular contacts with government officials for information exchange.[6] Although information may cause government bureaucrats to modify policies, businesses have little leverage with which to change the entire course of government action without the ability to influence elite selection.

Second, the concentration of bank ownership in private hands plays an important role. Because the large-scale sale of domestic banks to foreign investors ultimately constitutes a radical policy change, it requires concentrated private owners to solve the collective action problem and to actively lobby the government.[7] For example, the concentration in bank ownership in Mexico gave owners incentive to lobby the government first to recapitalize the banks and then to grant permission to sell them to MNFIs at high prices. In contrast, relatively low concentration of bank ownership or concentrated ownership in the state's hands would lead to inaction as bank owners would have little incentive to solve the collective action problem to push for recapitalization and sales. In Korea, although *chaebols* were politically powerful, they were highly diversified and held only small stakes in banks, thus giving them only weak incentive of selling to foreigners for a high cash premium.

As one can see in Table 8.1, the more important variable is the ability to influence elite selection. Where the political selection process is insulated, bank ownership structure has little impact because the state would carry on according to its own interests, which most often implies maintaining banks under state ownership. We witness this pattern in many authoritarian developmental states, including Taiwan in the 1970s, Iran, and China today. Although the concentration of private bank ownership varied somewhat among

TABLE 8.1

The impact of elite selection and bank ownership structure
on bank sale outcomes

	Insulated elite selection	Private capital participation in elite selection
Concentrated private bank ownership	Continual domestic ownership—??	High incentive and ability to sell to foreign entities—Mexico
Diffused or low private bank ownership	Continual domestic ownership—Taiwan in the 1970s, Iran and China today	The state dominates restructuring, limited sale—Korea

the three cases, all three regimes kept a tight grip on banks even through economic hardship.[8]

Where private capital is a member of the selectorate, the concentration of bank ownership exerts a much more substantial influence. If bank ownership is concentrated, the benefits of government policies accrue to a few individuals who own financial or industrial conglomerates, giving them high incentive to either singly or collectively influence government policies. Concentration of ownership also allows domestic private capital to exert more powerful political influence through concerted action. Strong motivation and higher political influence empower domestic private capital to shape banking policies, including permitting the sale of key national banks to foreign investors. However, if bank ownership is diluted with a multitude of private and state actors owning numerous small banks or small shares of a few major banks—as was the case in Korea—MNFIs also face a daunting obstacle. Although banks are privately owned and business interests are strong, it is much more difficult for MNFIs to make an alliance of mutual interest with domestic conglomerates because they have only low stakes in the banks. Given that, domestic capital would rather lobby the government for bailouts of the banks, followed by bank bailouts of the business conglomerates. They have little to gain if banks were sold to MNFIs for a high cash premium because banks would no longer continue the flow of preferential credit to domestic conglomerates.

In examining capital's role in the elite selectorate and bank ownership structure, it becomes clear that the two dimensions are not completely orthogonal to each other. When a developing state such as China is insulated from societal political pressure, it typically can maintain control over the banking sector through state ownership. Where the political process is subject to influence by nonstate interests, however, the concentration of bank ownership is often a product of other historical institutional factors.[9] Thus, although the concentration of bank ownership is tied to the political process, these two characteristics are not the same.

Alternative Hypotheses

The conventional explanation of varying policy outcomes in developing countries centers on the autonomy of the bureaucracy. According to this argument, the more economic bureaucrats are insulated from politics, the more they are able to ward off rent-seeking influence and make growth-promoting policies.[10] With respect to banking policies, if the insulated technocracy believes that private control over banks would lead to higher bank efficiency, they could quickly privatize banks through competitive bidding. They would not first nationalize banks and use tax payers' money to recapitalize these banks before selling them. More recent research reveals that bureaucrats in all three countries were subject to considerable intervention by the political leadership.[11] As I show in three cases, it is not the degree of political intervention that separates these three cases but the source of political intervention. In the case of China, the political elite intervened in the decisions of technocrats to fight off or appease political pressure emanating from within the regime. In the case of Mexico and South Korea, domestic private capital played a heavy role in exerting political pressure.

As already mentioned, liquidity needs in the aftermath of financial crises seem to be the most obvious explanation of selling domestic banks to foreign investors.[12] The classic case of this pattern is Argentina, which privatized a sleuth of provincial banks to MNFIs in the aftermath of the 1995 crisis.[13] In the case of China, due to its enormous foreign exchange reserve and relatively healthy fiscal position, it is able to recapitalize banks with relative ease, almost eliminating its need of foreign capital.[14] A close examination of banking policy in Mexico after the 1994 Tequila Crisis and in Korea after the Asian Financial Crisis, however, reveals that these governments did not hold a "fire sale" of domestic banks to foreigners to meet liquidity needs. Rather, the government first expended enormous amount of public money to write off nonperforming loans and to recapitalize troubled banks before selling banks to domestic capital and MNFIs.

One alternative hypothesis is that the United States historically exerted greater influence over Mexico and Korea than over China, giving U.S. MNFIs greater access to the political elite in these countries. While there is some indication of this in the Mexican case, MNFIs still ran into enormous difficulties without the help of domestic capital. For example, when the Mexican deposit insurance agency repaid Citibank ahead of schedule, causing a reduced profit of $300 million, Citibank's Robert Rubin, the former secretary of treasury who engineered a major U.S. bailout of Mexico in 1994, could not reach top-level officials for days.[15] In contrast, with the help of domestic capital, Citibank was able to acquire Banamex in a matter of weeks.

Mexico

Despite severe bank liquidity problems, MNFIs did not acquire Mexican banks at rock-bottom prices in the aftermath of the Tequila Crisis in 1994. Rather, these banks were acquired after enormous public money was spent to recapitalize them. Without a doubt, the main beneficiaries of the sale of Mexican banks were a small group of domestic financiers, who were highly motivated to lobby for public bailouts and were at the same time crucial actors in the Mexican political system.

The postwar Mexican financial system underwent several rounds of liquidity crises due to a prolonged Partido Revolucionario Institucional (PRI) strategy to use state fiscal and financial resources to buy political support from politically threatening groups, including the urban poor, domestic capital, and the urban middle class.[16] Up to the late 1970s, the PRI had balanced the interests of the urban poor and those of the major conglomerates, but, with the increasing ease of capital flight, the PRI regime began to pay closer attention to the demands of domestic capital.[17] Although the de la Madrid administration did not reverse bank nationalization implemented at the end of the Portillo administration, the PRI compensated increasingly organized domestic capital with high-yield government bonds and control over brokerages, the combination of which guaranteed the buyers of government bonds—the newly privatized brokerages—high margins.[18]

Into the Salinas administration, increasing electoral threats from rival parties forced the PRI to privatize the banks to raise cash to implement a generous redistribution program to appease the urban poor, who had voted for the opposition in the 1988 election.[19] The privatization was unusually transparent for a developing country, beginning with the evaluation of bank value by international consulting firms to establish base-line prices of these banks.[20] Nonetheless, only domestic capital was allowed to bid, and some thirty or so domestic outfits, mostly cash-rich brokerage houses, bid on eighteen state banks, which held almost all deposits in Mexico.[21] Contrary to the portrait of insider privatization, private capital bid aggressively, resulting in a large windfall for the PRI. Banamex and Bancomer, the two largest banks in Mexico at the time, drew winning bids of around $2 billion each.[22] PRI then compensated aggressive bidders with protectionist policies to limit foreign competition, which drove up domestic interest rates and bank profit.[23]

After the privatization, the new owners of the top five banks in Mexico controlled a large share of the banking market, and, due to the auction process, their ownership of these banks was also highly concentrated. Newly energized with enormous bank assets and easy access to foreign capital, these newly privatized banks went on a borrowing binge to take advantage of the relatively low international interest rates. When international capital lost confidence in Mexico in 1994, the country was plunged into a financial crisis involving rapid devaluation, high inflation, and recession. Despite a $20 billion credit from the United States, the meltdown continued as interest rates shot upward.[24] Ordinary Mexicans suddenly found themselves owing much more than they had borrowed originally, thus driving up the default rate to over 33 percent.[25] Instead of forcing bankrupt Mexican banks to sell stakes to MNFIs, the government set up an expensive scheme to recapitalize the banks. To be sure, during the crisis, few but the most daring foreign investors would have willingly invested money in Mexican banks, but low prices might have enticed some investors.

In June 1995, the Bank Deposit Protection Fund (Fobaproa—its acronym in Spanish) swapped bank nonperforming loans (NPLs) for Fobaproa bonds that were backed by the government but paid no yield. Within months, twelve banks swapped their nonperforming loans for some 67 billion pesos worth of Fobaproa bonds, instantly converting nonperforming assets into "performing" assets.[26] After the swap, an additional relief was granted to the banks. Instead of being forced to recover NPLs within a time frame on behalf of the Fobaproa, banks themselves decided when to recover the nonperforming loans, in effect allowing them to decide when to realize the book losses of the NPLs. This became an enormous problem for Fobaproa in subsequent years because banks essentially had no incentive to realize the losses and did little to recover NPLs on behalf of Fobaproa.[27]

After the Tequila Crisis, the ceiling on foreign ownership of banks was raised for smaller banks, and Spanish and American MNFIs came in aggressively to acquire domestic banks. Because of the extensive bailout program, domestic capital was able to sell banks at a much higher price to MNFIs. For example, before Citibank agreed to pay $200 million for Banco Confia, Grupo Abaco, the owner of Confia, persuaded Fobaproa to take over some three-quarters of Confia's loan portfolio and give Confia Fobaproa bonds. Unlike the other swaps, where the bank and Fobaproa shared the book losses of NPLs, Fobaproa was persuaded to take the entire loss itself.[28] As a result, Citibank's offer price of $200 million was only slightly less than the $212 million that Grupo Abaco paid for Confia in 1991.[29]

In 1998, President Zedillo, who oversaw a legislature dominated by the opposition, pushed for an even more costly scheme to bail out privately owned banks. In 1998, there was roughly $18 billion worth of Fobaproa notes held by Mexican banks. Instead of zero coupon bonds, Zedillo wanted to convert these notes into interest-bearing treasuries. Although there was technical merit to this scheme, such as increasing liquidity in the banking system, this scheme would have quickly increased the deficit from 28 percent of GDP to 42 percent of GDP.[30] Despite an initial fury of outcry from the public and from opposition legislators, PRI and opposition Partido Acción Nacional (PAN), both of which received extensive business support, formed a coalition to convert much of the Fobaproa notes into treasuries.[31]

After this enormous public bailout, Mexican banks became prime real estate for MNFIs acquisitions. The race to conquer the Mexican banking market culminated to Citibank's $12.5 billion purchase of Banamex in 2001. In total contrast to the tortuous path of selling banks to foreigners in China, the deal was struck in five weeks.[32] While Robert Rubin, former secretary of the treasury and vice-chairman of Citigroup, might have helped push the deal along, pressure from domestic capital was likely the decisive factor in paving the way for the Banamex deal. For one, the Banamex deal made major shareholders fabulously rich. Over one-third of the $12.5 billion sale ended up in the pockets of three individuals: Alfredo Harp, Roberto Hernandez, and Jose G. Aguilera. Hernandez, the largest shareholder, received 0.38 percent ownership of Citigroup, as well as nearly $1 billion.[33] This constitutes a nearly sixfold return for Hernandez and company as the group of financiers originally paid only $2.3 billion for the bank in 1991.[34]

What explains the pattern of Mexican banking policy, which involves costly public bailout before selling to MNFIs for relatively high prices? First, economic nationalism fails to explain the trajectory of banking policies because much of the banking sector ended up in the hands of the MNFIs anyway. Looking beyond ideational explanations, domestic capital has long been important players in the political arena. The Monterrey financiers helped found the opposition PAN in order to threaten PRI dominance, which in effect forced PRI to implement more procapital policies.[35] Moreover, Mexico had a tightly knitted elite who came from a selected group of families and attended a handful of private schools and universities. This further increased the density of communication and mutual influence between the government and business elite.[36] Furthermore, after the Salinas privatization gave control of banks to a handful of domestic financial groups, the owners of these banks had high incentive to influence government policies to maximize the profit of these entities. They lobbied for liberalization of international financial flow to take advantage of the arbitrage, and, when the financial crisis descended on Mexico, they lobbied for public bailouts so as to minimize losses, if not to make a fabulous profit at the public's expense.

Although the influence of MNFIs doubtless facilitated the sale of domestic banks, available evidence suggests that foreign influence did not approach the importance of domestic pressure. In 2000, the Mexican government repaid $2.5 billion in converted Fobaproa notes held by Banco Confia, costing Citibank some $300 million in lost interest. Citibank's Vice-Chairman Robert Rubin, who had engineered a U.S. bailout of the Mexican government in 1995, was soon on the phone trying to reach top Mexican officials. However, he reportedly spent days calling old contacts with little success.[37] In contrast, after Banamex chairman Hernandez approached Citibank about a possible sale, he guided the deal through Mexico's complex political terrain and bureaucratic red tape. In addition to arranging meetings between Citibank management and top Mexican officials, Hernandez also persuaded his old college roommate, President Fox, to give public endorsement of the deal.[38] The deal, the biggest in Mexican history, was completed within five weeks. Without highly motivated and influential domestic capital, the sale of domestic banks to MNFIs would have been much more difficult.

Korea

Although MNFIs initially succeeded in purchasing Korean financial institutions due to postcrisis IMF pressure, the Korean government's attitude against MNFIs soon hardened, and the government clearly revealed a preference for domestic ownership of banks. The *chaebols'* enormous clout in politics throughout postwar era, as well as their low stakes in Korean banks before the crisis, likely made MNFI acquisition of domestic banks extremely difficult.

In the aftermath of his successful coup, Park Chung-hee made a show of fighting corruption by arresting the heads of large *chaebols* and by nationalizing all four of Korea's private banks.[39] Thus began an era of government directed credit to promote industrial polices.[40] Moreover, state directed credit gave rise to a crony capitalism in which *chaebols* benefited from soft loans from the government and, in return, gave cash kickbacks to Park's political machinery and to his personal trove.[41] In addition to domestic loans, the Park government also gave connected *chaebols* government guarantees to foreign loans. Given the spread between international and domestic interest rates, *chaebols* with loan guarantees made an automatic profit from the spread, which encouraged accelerated foreign borrowing by these *chaebols*.[42] Not surprisingly, high foreign borrowing eventually led to a debt crisis where many highly leveraged firms were on the verge of defaulting on their foreign loans. Initially, the government prevented an attack on the won by preemptively devaluating the won, which further increased dollar-dominated debt owed by *chaebols*.[43] In response to the growing crisis, Park simultaneously placed a moratorium on all loans, converted many short-term loans to either long-term loans or equity ownership of the firms, and blocked capital account convertibility.[44] This introduced an era of highly repressed financial allocation for the remainder of the 1970s. However, the government ensured that connected *chaebols* received enormous amount of state loans for the heavy and chemical industry (HCI) drive, thus intensifying *chaebol* reliance on state resources and concurrently state dependency on *chaebols* to generate growth and employment.[45]

In the Chun Doo-hwan administration, banks were slowly privatized, but each *chaebol* could hold at most only an 8 percent share in a bank. Furthermore, the Office of Banking Supervision regulated how much banks could lend to large *chaebols*.[46] In the short and medium run, *chaebol* financing was limited by the latter policy, which forced expanding firms to seek financing through alternative channels: the capital market, nonbank financial institutions (NBFIs), and foreign credit. By 1990, NBFIs accounted for roughly the same share of corporate financing as banks.[47] Because there were no regulations on *chaebol* ownership of NBFIs, the conglomerates soon formed numerous NBFIs to organize finance for the groups. Coupled with loose regulations on borrowing from abroad, these NBFIs borrowed heavily from abroad on behalf of the *chaebols*, planting the seeds for the Asian Financial Crisis (AFC).[48] A longer-term implication of Chun's banking policies is that influential *chaebols* could not acquire large stakes in major banks, which, after the Asian Financial Crisis, gave them much weaker incentive than Mexican financiers to seek the sale of Korean banks to cash-rich MNFIs.

In the fall of 1997, the currencies of Asian countries toppled in succession, and Korea was forced to float the won in December.[49] The devaluation of the won immediately created massive liquidity problems in the system. Highly leveraged NBFIs, many of which were owned by the *chaebols*, saw a sudden surge of their dollar-denominated debt in won terms. Thus, they were unable to provide financing to *chaebols*, which by that time had a debt-equity ratio of 519 percent, compared with an average of 154 percent in the United States.[50] This in turn caused a massive wave of defaults, creating high numbers of nonperforming loans and illiquidity in many of the major banks in Korea.

As in 1972, the government intervened massively to stabilize the financial system. However, because the Korean government received IMF facilities to prevent a further devaluation of the won, it also had to make a show of complying with IMF demands during the bailout. The 1998 bailout of Korean financial institutions totaled some 123 trillion won, or roughly $123 billion.[51] Of this, $48 billion was used for bank recapitalization, while $42 billion was earmarked for buying NPLs from distressed banks. Finally, another $19 billion was used for deposit insurance claims.[52] To finance this costly undertaking, the government issued $104 billion in bonds through Korea Deposit Insurance Corporation (KDIC) and Korea Asset Management Corporation (KAMCO).[53] This was well over 10 percent of Korea's GDP in 1998.

Unlike Mexico, however, big businesses pressured the government to bail out banks not so much to restore the value of the banks but to ensure the flow of credit to *chaebols*. To be sure, the Korean government forced many *chaebols* to undergo "work out" programs in which banks imposed conditions on distressed debtors before restructuring loans or extending more liquidity.[54] Nonetheless, massive government bailout of the banks greatly decreased banks' incentives to put pressure on *chaebols* to truly restructure, which meant that many "work out" programs amounted to little more than debt forgiveness.[55] With relatively low ownership of banks, *chaebols* did not seem to care that some eight banks were nationalized by the government, as long as banks received enough liquidity with which to bail out the troubled *chaebols*. They also did not press the government to sell Korean banks to MNFIs after the recapitalization of these banks. If anything, they probably opposed it because foreign ownership would end the cozy relationship between banks and business conglomerates.

However, because Korea had to make a show of complying with IMF conditionality, the government sold substantial stakes of some six national-level banks in the aftermath of the crisis. However, absolute majority share was sold in only one case (Korea First Bank) to U.S.-based private equity firm Newbridge Capital.[56] When HSBC asked for controlling stake of Seoul Bank, however, the government rejected the deal, opting for continual state control over the bank.[57] After the sale of KFB to Newbridge, the Korean government, under pressure from the public and from the *chaebols*, halted the sale of banks to MNFIs. In order to escape IMF conditionality, Korea repaid its IMF loans early in 2000.[58] Subsequently, the government committed an additional $40 billion into bank restructuring.[59]

Instead of selling restructured banks to MNFIs at a high premium, the government either began to place banks under permanent state ownership or engineered their sales to large domestic financial conglomerates. The Ministry of Finance and Economy, now operating under President Kim Dae-jung, pushed for a banking act that would eliminate the limit for Korean business groups to hold bank shares if they were classified as "specialized financial groups."[60] After this law passed in 2002, both domestic and foreign financial conglomerates could bid on banks, and the first test case was that of Seoul Bank. Both U.S.-based Lonestar Capital and Hana Bank, a domestic bank with minority foreign shareholders, bid on Seoul Bank, but government regulators expectedly gave Hana control over Seoul Bank, even though Lonestar offered more up-front cash than Hana did.[61] The tide against MNFIs turned further when the government pressured Kookmin Bank, a bank where Goldman Sachs had acquired controlling stakes, to merge with government controlled Housing Credit Bank, making Goldman Sachs the second largest shareholder of the new entity behind the government.[62]

Similar to the case of Mexico, large *chaebols* constituted important members of the selectorate for much of the postwar period.[63] In exchange for government financial and fiscal subsidies, domestic capital provided campaign financing and bribes.[64] Even under the Park dictatorship, his party, the Democratic Republican Party, spent some $43 million annually while some $40 million was spent to buy votes in the 1967 election alone.[65] Without corporate sponsorship, such extravagant spending would have been impossible, and Park would have been under greater political threat.

With the introduction of democracy in Korea, money politics became even more important as politicians scrambled to raise sufficient funds to win competitive elections. The 1992 National Assembly election, for example, cost an estimated $5.1 billion, whereas the 1981 election cost between $266 and $400 million.[66] Between 1994 and 1998, Samsung in all likelihood contributed over $1 billion to politicians, while Hyundai and LG both gave well above $500 million each.[67] Besides *chaebols'* enormous impact on campaign finance, there was frequent social and policy interaction between business leaders and officials. This "embeddedness" stemmed partly from the common practice of parachute appointment in the Korean bureaucracy, which placed early bureaucratic retirees in various *chaebols*.[68]

As a result of their political contributions and their dense interaction with officials, *chaebols* influenced financial policies throughout Korea's postwar history. For example, when President Kim Young-sam set up a commission on financial reform, the *chaebols* sent their representatives and blocked stricter regulatory measures over merchant banks and NBFIs.[69] Although the precise channels through which *chaebols* exerted influence on postcrisis banking policies remain unclear, past experience strongly suggests that they had a hand in the generous government bailout and hardening attitude against foreign acquisitions. As in Mexico, the influence of private conglomerates can clearly be felt in the political arena. However, due to low *chaebol* ownership of major banks and, concurrently, diverse *chaebol* holdings across several sectors, their main goal after the crisis was to use public resources to continue the flow of soft loans to the conglomerates, rather boosting the sale price of Korean banks.

China

In contrast to Korea and Mexico, nonstate private conglomerates had no political leverage over the senior leadership in China. Although there is disagreement over the composition of the selectorate in China, elite selection remains much more insulated from the influence of private capital compared with Mexico or Korea. Unless one is a member of the central committee, one can exert little direct influence on the selection of top leaders in China.[70] Even large state conglomerates have weak incentive and ability to influence elite decision. Thus, MNFIs seeking to gain controlling stakes in Chinese banks can find no powerful allies that can influence an outcome.

Although there was no apparent banking crisis in China in the aftermath of the Asian Financial Crisis, the Chinese banking system, which was composed of a few major state-owned banks, had long exceeded the threshold for technical insolvency by 1997.[71] Non-performing loan ratio was estimated at 40 percent, equivalent to over 50 percent of GDP at that time.[72] Taking the opportunity of the AFC, Premier Zhu Rongji played up the possibility of a financial crisis in China and orchestrated an impressive bailout of Chinese banks. Taking a cue from Korea, Zhu formed state-owned asset management companies (AMCs) to take over some $205 billion (¥1.4 trillion) in NPLs from the Big Four Chinese banks. Similar to both the Korean and the Mexico bailouts, the AMCs issued government backed notes in the same amount to the banks, instantly transforming NPLs into performing assets.[73] Although China did not face an attack on the renminbi (RMB) due to its relatively strict capital control, minutes of the PBOC Monetary Committee reveal that top policy makers were worried about the integrity of the RMB in the midst of the AFC.[74] Thus, rapid sale of Chinese banks in the aftermath of the AFC was not completely inconceivable from a liquidity standpoint.

Despite the enormous bailout in 1998, Chinese banks were still in poor shape at the end of Zhu's tenure in 2003. By that time, however, China's foreign exchange reserve had grown severalfold, and the new leadership found a new way with which to bailout the major state banks: injections from the foreign exchange reserve. Within months of taking power, the Wen Jiabao Administration announced that the government would inject $45 billion from the foreign exchange reserve to China Construction Bank and the Bank of China, the two state banks in the best condition.[75] A further $15 billion was later injected into the Industry and Commerce Bank of China, in combination with a $15 billion allocation from the treasury.[76] In exchange for these funds, equity in the three banks was shifted to the Central Huijin Company, a state-owned holding company jointly run by the central bank and the Ministry of Finance (MOF).[77]

After over $200 billion in bailout, the technocrats pushed for listing the healthiest state banks in the international equity market to increase discipline in these banks. However, Chinese policy makers never contemplated ceding control over these banks either to the stock market or to MNFIs. While Chinese technocrats realized that limited cooperation with MNFIs was necessary to drum up interest in the IPOs, they made it clear from the beginning that MNFI ownership of Chinese banks would be tightly regulated. Under regulations at the time, no foreign bank could own more than 20 percent of a Chinese bank, and combined foreign ownership of a Chinese bank was restricted to below 25 percent. Although Newbridge Capital obtained de facto control over Shenzhen Development Bank (SDB) in 2003 by becoming the largest shareholder, SDB remained a relatively minor lender, and the Chinese government showed no sign of allowing another such bid to succeed. Even after the successful listing in Hong Kong, Temasek and Bank of America, the two strategic partners of China Construction Bank (CCB), held less than 15 percent of CCB shares. Besides these major cases, MNFIs have managed to acquire small stakes in a handful of small regional banks.

In December 2005, a consortium led by Citibank shocked the Chinese financial world by placing a bold $3 billion bid for some 85 percent of Guangdong Development Bank shares. The Guangdong Development Bank (GDB) had been a troubled midsize regional bank that even State Council technocrats realized required inventive methods of recapitalization.[78] With the encouragement of both the Guangdong Provincial Government and some central bureaucrats, Citibank placed a bid that well surpassed the existing limit on foreign ownership. Although the consortium included both foreign and Chinese entities, the bid called for 40 percent ownership by Citibank and 9.9 percent ownership by the Carlyle Group, which sums to an unprecedented 49.9 percent foreign ownership.[79] Aware of the unusual nature of the bid,

Citibank strategically invited a major Chinese state conglomerate to join the consortium, presumably to provide some political clout, and, as mentioned at the beginning of this chapter, it asked former President Bush to write a letter to the Chinese government.

Although the China Banking Regulatory Commission (CBRC) gave preliminary approval in early 2006, the regulatory process bogged down at the annual meeting of the National People's Congress (NPC), where NPC delegates voiced complaints that bank assets were sold to foreigners "too cheaply."[80] When asked about the GDB deal at a March 12 NPC press conference, Premier Wen answered that the state should continue to hold majority control in the process of "commercial banking reform."[81] His wording indicated government unwillingness to cede majority control to foreign hands even for a bank like GDB. In official banking lexicon, "state-owned commercial banks" (*guoyoushangye yinhang*) refers to the Big Four state banks, while "commercial banks" (*shangye yinhang*) refers to all commercial banks in China. Soon after Wen's comments, the Bush letter was leaked, and the CBRC circulated a memo stating that the government would not alter the rule governing foreign ownership in the case of GDB, in effect rejecting Citibank's bid.[82]

The regulatory hurdle compelled Citibank to completely restructure the bid, including dropping the Carlyle Group from its list of partners and recruiting even more state-owned conglomerates to take part in the consortium. Most important, Citibank bank reduced its share ownership from the original 40 percent to 20 percent, which was allowed by existing regulations.[83] In the end, regulatory compliance rather than a letter from George Bush allowed Citibank to lead a consortium of mostly Chinese state-owned companies to take over 85.6 percent of Guangdong Development Bank.

If examined in isolation, an outside observer may conclude that Chinese unwillingness to cede control over domestic banks stems from its enormous store of foreign exchange and its rapidly growing economy. With so much money, China had little need to place banks on the auction block. However, a comparison with banking policies in Mexico and Korea reveals that money was by no means the decisive factor. In the case of China, government elite had little incentive to sell domestic banks to MNFIs. First, senior officials in the Party had a strong incentive to maintain control over the banking system in order to channel loans toward various political and policy demands.[84] Instead of benefiting specific industrial or financial conglomerates, Chinese financial policies were mainly designed to benefit broad swaths of either state industrial or, increasingly, agricultural interests in order to bolster the "administrative accomplishments" of the leading technocrats. Furthermore, whether the selectorate was the Central Committee or just the Politburo, control over the banking sector allowed top leaders to buy political support by disbursing preferential credit. Bank managers and bureaucrats who oversaw the banks were junior officials in the Party hierarchy and must obey the wishes of the Standing Committee. Although they influenced the agenda by providing information and policy alternatives, they had little direct leverage over senior officials. Being outside of the Party hierarchy, private capital in China had minimal influence over leadership selection, especially compared with their powerful counterparts in Mexico and Korea.

Furthermore, although MNFIs often partnered with state owned financial institutions or large state-owned enterprises in their bids for Chinese banks, their Chinese partners at most had weak incentive to lobby for the sales, especially if the deals called for surpassing existing regulations. State-owned enterprises relied on the central government for a host of other subsidies in order to survive. They were thus reluctant to outright dispute the wishes of the State Council. Beyond that, MNFIs had no political leverage against the Chinese government since they remained completely outside of the political system.

Conclusion

It is obviously not a novelty to use domestic selectorate or the concentration of bank ownership to explain policy outcomes. Combining the two, however, yields some counterintuitive explanations about a country's willingness to sell banks to MNFIs. First, while large domestic capital in Mexico and Korea has a say over policies because they are members of the selectorate, private capital is excluded from the elite selection process in China. Thus, there is a sharp contrast between the composition of the selectorate in China and in Mexico and Korea, where voters, labor organizations, and domestic capital loom large in the elite selection process. Although domestic Chinese capital is increasingly able to make its voice heard through lobbying, as detailed in Chapter 6 by Kennedy, its exclusion from the selectorate renders its voice weaker than counterparts in the other two countries. As a result, banking policies diverge further away from the ideal policies of domestic private capital in China than in the other two cases.

To the extent that industrial or financial interests are represented in the selectorate through Central Committee membership, they represent state-owned entities with much weaker profit incentive than their private counter-parts in Mexico and Korea. Instead, they are motivated by a mix of perfor-mance and political incentives. Moreover, in order for SOEs to do well they need a host of government subsidies and preferential policies.[85] Although some CEOs of large state conglomerates are members of the Central Com-mittee, the position hardly affords them political leverage vis-à-vis the se-nior leadership, who decide on their appointment in the first place. At most, they have access to the senior leadership and can lobby for a deal. However, this access is a far cry from the direct leverage that *grupos* and *chaebols* can exert on the political leadership in Mexico and Korea. Thus, even if MNFIs partnered with large state conglomerates in their bids for Chinese banks, the Chinese partners have weak incentive—and even weaker ability—with which to influence elite decisions. The framework suggested by this paper predicts that this situation will not change until the elite selection process opens up to the influence of nongovernmental interests. To be sure, such a change would fundamentally alter state-society relations. Because open po-litical competition requires funds, the opening of the political process will likely introduce private capital as an influential member of the selectorate.

Among countries where financial interests took part in the political pro-cess, the concentration of bank ownership explained the varying outcomes in the sale of banks to MNFIs. Because bank ownership was concentrated in Mexico, owners had strong incentive to lobby for massive government bailouts in the aftermath of a financial crisis with the goal of restoring the values of the banks and possibly selling them to MNFIs for high prices. In contrast, because major conglomerates only had small stakes in Korean banks, they lobbied for government bailouts for an entirely different rea-son, to continue the flow of easy credit to large industrial conglomerates. Thus, although there was great political pressure for bank bailouts in Korea, there was much weaker impetus for selling banks to MNFIs. Rather than economic nationalism, the difficulty of foreign entry into China and Korea stemmed from two entirely different reasons. In the case of Korea, *chaebol* opposition probably played an important part. In the case of China, the con-tinual dominance of the Party hierarchy, both in the higher reaches of the government and in the largest banks and industrial conglomerates, excluded outside actors from the political process.

Beyond banking policy, the combination of selectorate and industrial structure might explain policy outcomes in a wide range of areas, especially in examining privatization and regulatory policies. This framework needs to be fully fleshed out and tested on a wider range of cases. In the mean time, MNFIs should not be surprised if Chinese technocrats do not bend to the will of well-financed foreign capital. Their main job is to appease their political superiors, and, until that fact changes, directly influencing Chinese policies will remain a difficult proposition for outsiders.

CONCLUSION

Chapter Nine

Placing China in Comparison
An Outsider's Perspective

GREGORY J. KASZA

As Scott Kennedy writes in the introduction to this volume, most research on China's political economy, and in fact, on Chinese politics in general, ostensibly takes the form of the national study, not comparative politics. China is hardly unique in this respect. Most nationals of any country study its politics because it is their politics, a vital part of their lives, not because they aspire to develop general scholarly theories. And, for a variety of reasons, even most foreign scholars of a given political system seem to limit themselves to single-country case studies. Like scholarship on U.S. politics, however, research on China suffers more from this "one-country area" syndrome than most others, for reasons that are easy to surmise.

First, when Chinese area studies programs took root in U.S. academia in the mid-twentieth century, they were initially anchored in the three humanities fields of language, literature, and history. Most scholars in these fields produced (and continue to produce) noncomparative research, and they trained their students accordingly. Reinforcing this trend was the fact that many of the founders of modern Chinese studies in the West were the children of missionaries or people who otherwise came by their exposure to China prior to undertaking academic vocations. Consequently, many approached their disciplines with the goal of expanding their knowledge of China, rather than approaching the study of China to develop the interests of their disciplines.

Second, thanks to the extraordinary richness of premodern Chinese civilization, it has attracted extensive scholarly interest, and this, too, helped to establish a pattern of narrowly focused research. Given traditional China's limited interaction with other parts of the world, scholars of classical Chinese painting or Confucian philosophy, for instance, naturally focused all of their attention on China.

Third, China experts are now numerous enough to operate as a self-governing epistemic community. This community offers specialized programs of study in universities, manages its own journals, provides a sizable readership for specialized research, and establishes standards of competent scholarship. Because nonspecialists are rarely called on to referee scholarly manuscripts on China, success in Chinese studies depends on the approval of others within this community.

Fourth, it takes many years to master the Chinese language, leaving little time for China experts to study other languages, and this impedes in-depth research on other parts of the world. Moreover, although Chinese is an official language in Singapore and Taiwan and spoken by a fair number of people in parts of Southeast Asia, there is no other country approaching the political importance of mainland China where Chinese is the predominant tongue. Scholars who have mastered English, Spanish, or Arabic have complete linguistic access to a dozen or more countries where they might conduct research, but such is not the case for those who work in Chinese.

Fifth, thanks to China's importance in world affairs and to Taiwan's development into a wealthy nation, both the U.S. and Taiwanese governments, as well as foundations, have generously funded specialized research on China.

Sixth, before the 1980s, Chinese scholars had little access to research materials on other countries and few opportunities to do research abroad. Even today there are few foreign social scientists teaching in Chinese universities. Thus, even those Chinese scholars with comparative inclinations have confronted great obstacles to doing comparative research.

And lastly, like India and the United States, China is a country of much internal diversity. This diversity encourages scholars to do within-nation comparisons in order to grasp China's complexity, but it tends to discourage cross-national comparisons. As several chapters of this volume attest, it is challenging for scholars to cope with China's internal variations, and these variations make it hard to formulate general characterizations of China that might facilitate comparisons with other countries. This is especially true in the current period of dramatic change, when even the most carefully documented generalizations often prove short lived. Thus, China's internal diversity invites within-nation comparisons but inhibits cross-national research.

For all these reasons, China, like the United States, has been something of a worst case for comparative political research. The isolation of Chinese studies is reflected in the unique vocabulary that not only contemporary historians but also social scientists have used to portray Chinese politics. Terms such as the Middle Kingdom, the Great Leap Forward, *guanxi*, and the Four Modernizations are unique to China. They seemingly have little or no comparative reach, and their prevalence reflects the paucity of comparative research on China, a disregard for the comparative glossary of social science, and a deep-seated conviction that Chinese politics constitutes a unique and autonomous reality.

To be sure, this characterization of the field as a whole does not apply to every China scholar, but it will suffice to explain the raison d'être of this volume, which marks an exciting new trajectory in the study of Chinese political economy. This is the first time that a sizable group of social scientists, all of them established experts on China, have joined together in an effort to stretch their field of research in a comparative direction. Their scholarship offers new insights into many aspects of contemporary China. Even more importantly, their contributions provide us with an opportunity to review the comparative frameworks that China experts currently find most promising and to identify potentially advantageous avenues of comparison that have yet to be exploited.

Because there are endless possibilities for comparison, China scholars who would explore comparative perspectives must first answer the critical question posed in this volume by Mark Frazier: Compared to what? Which other countries present the most insightful comparative reference points, and why? Which comparisons have scholars developed with profit thus far, and which remain unexamined? The selection of cases to compare inevitably sets the parameters of the research and shapes the analysis that will result. Each comparison brings a different perspective to bear on the phenomenon under study, shedding light on some aspects of the subject matter while removing others from view. The choice of comparative cases and an acute awareness of the implications of that choice are thus essential to good comparative research.

Judging from the contributions to this volume, there are currently three prominent comparative frameworks for the study of China's political economy. The first compares China to the East Asian developmental states, namely, Japan, South Korea, and Taiwan; the second compares China with Russia; and the third places China alongside other large developing countries such as India, Brazil, and Mexico. The logic behind each of these frameworks deserves careful scrutiny.

The comparison of China with the so-called East Asian developmental states is fairly recent. Indeed, yet another reason for the lack of comparative research on modern Chinese politics is that East Asia has not constituted a coherent political region during much of the last half century, and thus comparative studies of countries within the region have been few. In most fields of scholarship on contemporary society, East Asia has been a loose conglomeration of one-country areas, quite different in this respect from Latin America, Western Europe, or the Middle East. China's remarkable growth rates over the last two decades have altered this situation by inviting comparisons with Japan, the Republic of Korea, and Taiwan. The suspicion that China may be using one or more of its East Asian neighbors as models for various aspects of its developmental program further recommends this comparative framework.

The contributors to this volume disagree as to whether China belongs to the class of developmental states. Margaret Pearson finds striking similarities between China and the East Asian developmental states. Pearson underscores the persistent power of government in the economy, an affinity for large enterprise groups, and lingering restraints on market competition as features common to China, Japan, South Korea, and Taiwan. Arthur Kroeber, however, finds that adverse conditions have frustrated China's desire to emulate the developmental states. He judges China's central government to be considerably weaker than some other scholars contend, and he stresses that the global shift toward economic liberalization and the high degree of foreign participation in China's economy have caused it to diverge from the standard East Asian developmental model. Frazier reinforces Kroeber's position when he notes that China's industrialization is causing higher levels of income inequality than occurred in the East Asian developmental states, and Victor Shih likewise underscores the differences in the influence of big business in South Korea and China in his study of the decision to allow foreign ownership of banks.

Clearly there is a need for more research on China within this comparative framework. It might begin with a more detailed examination of China's emulation of foreign models than anyone has yet conducted. Several contributors to this volume remark in passing that China has used the East Asian developmental model as a reference for its own economic strategy, but this is a theme worthy of in-depth study. Exactly how do Chinese policy makers and business people assess the significance of the Japanese, South Korean, and Taiwanese experiences for their own economic development? How complete or accurate is their comprehension of those experiences? Do they base their assessments on their exposure to Japanese, South Korean, and Taiwanese companies operating in China today, or do they study the history of the economic development of neighboring states? If the latter, which periods of the economic history of Japan, South Korea, and Taiwan do the Chinese examine for lessons? In regard to comparisons with the developmental states, one must ask not only "compared to what?" but also "compared to when?"

Of course, the study of China's emulation of foreign models should transcend the context of the East Asian developmental states alone. Other developmental patterns have undoubtedly attracted the attention of Chinese economic actors, and one would like to know how they weigh the relevance of East Asian precedents compared to models elsewhere. A better understanding of China's emulation of foreign patterns will open the door to a new wave of comparative research projects. The likely impact of foreign models on China's economic course today means that comparative research will serve even those scholars whose only objective is to understand China. If China's reality is linked to foreign models, then those models must form part of research on China.

The comparison of China's system of communism-in-transition with Russia's postcommunist system rests on their more-or-less common starting point as Leninist states and their recent movements in more liberal directions. Andrew Wedeman features this comparison in his research. He sees China's partial, gradual transition as having produced better results in terms of economic growth and social stability than Russia's big-bang approach to politicoeconomic change, and he cites the greater degree of institutional continuity in China as a key to this outcome. His analysis brings to mind Samuel P. Huntington's famous contention in *Political Order in Changing Societies* that the building of stable institutions and authority should take precedence over democratization in developing societies.[1]

While the comparison of Russia and China is a natural one, thus far there have been few comparisons of China with the newly independent states of Eastern Europe, with other states to emerge from the former Soviet Union, or with Vietnam.[2] Because these countries share transitional or postcommunist regimes with China and Russia, this would appear to be an auspicious avenue for future research. Viewing China against the full range of postcommunist reform trajectories should facilitate a more nuanced analysis than that to emerge from the two-country comparison alone. Thus far comparative research on China has failed to engage the diversity of postcommunist states.

Because China is the world's largest country, the temptation to compare it to other large countries seems irresistible. Indeed, none of our contributors opted to compare China to any country of less than several tens of millions of inhabitants, and the populations of most of the referent countries exceed a hundred million. In several cases, the decision to compare large countries was self-conscious. Frazier chose to compare China's welfare system to those of other big countries (Brazil, South Africa, India, and Indonesia) due to the great sectoral and urban/rural disparities likely to characterize the welfare systems of large developing states. Kennedy chooses the comparative cases of Japan, India, and Russia partly because large size complicates the task of monitoring officials over large territories. In other chapters, the choice to compare large countries was based on criteria unrelated to size per se, as in Shih's comparison of the banking policies of China and Mexico.

There are some obvious reasons why it might make sense to compare China's politicoeconomic system to those of other large countries. In addition to Frazier's rationale related to the presence of marked within-nation differences, countries with large domestic markets clearly enjoy developmental options unavailable to most small states. Furthermore, when a country's size makes it a major player in regional or global geopolitics, as China's size obviously does, a different set of international factors may sway its economic development more than would be true of smaller countries. Still, in most cases it is probably unwise to limit comparisons of China to other large countries unless there are reasons other than size alone for doing so.

There may be ample logic underlying comparisons of China with smaller countries. For instance, China's high degree of dependency on exports and foreign direct investment would seem to be more typical of small countries than large. And, for many objects of comparison, such as labor-management relations, women in the workforce, or the collaboration of business and universities in conducting basic research, a country's size may be irrelevant.

One reason that China scholars tend to limit themselves to large-country comparisons may be that their units of analysis are almost always national in scope. It is the auto industry of *China*, the welfare system of *China*, the news media of *China*, and so forth that are the subjects of interest. This is somewhat surprising because (as already noted) the research of many of our contributors underscores the great diversity of these very phenomena within China itself. In future one might hope to see more research that compares China to other countries by employing subnational units of comparison.[3] Once the object of study becomes one factory or stock exchange, one city or region, or one foreign-owned enterprise or bank in each of several countries, the range of appropriate cases will expand far beyond countries of similar size.

Besides countries of small size, another subset of countries rarely encountered in these comparisons was the advanced industrial states of the West. Other than Pearson's inclusion of France in her comparison of regulatory systems, our contributors offered only the briefest references to Western states. Granted, many China scholars are likely to experience a visceral reaction against the idea that China is following Western precedents of state building, democratization, or capitalism. The West often dominated comparative research in the past, and this arouses an instinctive fear that comparisons with the West might compromise the integrity of China's historical experience, dressing it in ill-fitting concepts and theories devised elsewhere.

This fear is unwarranted. There is no reason that comparisons of China and the Western states need misrepresent China. The purpose of comparative research is not just to catalog similarities but to identify and explain differences. Indeed, every chapter of this book enlightens in large measure by exploring differences between China and other countries. Comparative research sharpens a scholar's eyesight not only by putting similar characteristics in relief but also by documenting the differences between states. The best way to liberate Chinese studies from the powerful theoretical apparatus of Western-based social science is to probe both the similarities and differences between China and the likes of Germany, the United States, Sweden, and France. This may also be the best way to make the Chinese experience speak to that theoretical apparatus, altering its terms to accommodate a wider reality. Paradoxically, it is impossible to make a persuasive case for

Chinese uniqueness without doing comparative research, though such research will inevitably reveal some unexpected similarities as well.[4]

Experts on any one part of the world are bound to wonder if comparative research is worth the trouble. It inevitably appears risky to write about countries that one does not know in detail but only through secondary research, an experience I have had as a Japan specialist who occasionally incorporates China in his work.[5] But the truth is that, despite the ostensible isolation of most case studies, there is no escaping comparative judgments in social science. A scholar who writes that China is a large country, a rapidly developing country, or a country with a high level of foreign investment is implicitly comparing these traits of China to the traits of other countries. A noncomparative social science would have to be a social science without adjectives, an empty exercise. All of us judge what we see against comparative reference points. The real question is whether to allow those reference points to creep into our judgments through the back door, unspecified and unexamined, or to incorporate them as objects of research. The former strategy is far more risky than the latter. When unstudied comparisons enter by the back door, the comparative reference points will often be vague, superficial, or mistaken and lead to erroneous judgments concerning the country of primary interest.

Let me offer a brief illustration. It is common to read in studies of Chinese politics that 99 percent of all defendants brought to trial in China are convicted.[6] When I first read this, my immediate thought was that China's court system must be barbaric, giving the accused no chance to mount an effective defense. The implicit, almost unconscious, comparative reference point in the back of my mind was the U.S. court system, which, I imagined, must produce a much higher number of acquittals. Because I have never studied the U.S. system of justice, this impression was rooted in little more than court dramas I had seen on American television. Sometime later, I was paging through a book of statistics on Japan and discovered that of 986,914 sentences passed by Japanese courts in 2001, there were 986,224 convictions, 644 cases dismissed, and only 46 acquittals.[7] Knowing that Japan's criminal justice system works against defendants in some ways that the U.S. system does not (for example, Japanese police can detain and question suspects for up to a week without bringing formal charges, and defense lawyers have less access to their clients), I began to wonder if both the Japanese and Chinese systems were unfairly loaded against the defendant. Out of curiosity, I consulted the website of the U.S. Department of Justice and found that in a sample of 56,146 felony cases filed in the U.S. during 2002, 85 percent of those that went to trial resulted in convictions.[8] The lessons of this anecdote should be obvious:

- We inevitably absorb new information about the politics of one country by comparing it to what we already know or think we know about the politics of other countries. (In the Japan field, the primary comparative reference point is usually some foggy image of American or Western democracy.)
- If the comparative reference points are left unstudied, they can easily produce faulty analysis. It may well be that Chinese or Japanese courts offer defendants fewer opportunities to defend themselves than courts elsewhere, but conviction rates alone clearly do not warrant that conclusion. It is possible that prosecutors everywhere are disinclined to take cases to trial unless they are fairly certain that they have the evidence to convict.
- The only way to decipher correctly the data we encounter about any polity is to incorporate a comparative dimension into our research, so that we engage in a deliberate and accurate manner those ubiquitous comparative reference points that inevitably sway our thinking. It would require some careful comparative study to reach reliable conclusions regarding the current state of Chinese criminal justice.

The essays in this volume offer a more promising template for research on Chinese politics and political economy than the solitary case studies that have hitherto dominated the field. They exemplify the benefits to be gained from comparative scholarship on China while also pointing the way toward further comparative work that will include a broader range of postcommunist and Western states, smaller countries, and comparisons of subnational units. No scholar can find safety any more by focusing his or her attention on a dot on the wall, even if that dot is as large and important a country as China. In the age of globalization, all the dots are connected, and the only way to comprehend their meaning is to do comparative research.

Notes

NOTES TO CHAPTER ONE

1. For important discussions of research methods, including the comparative approach, see Charles Ragin, *The Comparative Method: Moving Beyond Qualitative and Quantitative Strategies* (Berkeley: University of California Press, 1987); David Collier, "The Comparative Method: Two Decades of Change," in Rustow and Erickson, eds., *Comparative Political Dynamics* (New York: Harper Collins, 1990), 7–31; and John Gerring, "What Is a Case Study and What Is It Good for?" *American Political Science Review* 98:2 (May 2004), 341–354.

2. This approach is epitomized by Roderick MacFarquhar, author of the trilogy, *The Origins of the Cultural Revolution* (New York: Columbia University Press, 1974, 1983, and 1997). Also see Frederick C. Tiewes, *Politics and Purges in China*, second edition (Armonk, NY: M. E. Sharpe, 1993); Joseph Fewsmith, *Dilemmas of Reform in China: Political Conflict and Economic Debate* (Armonk, NY: M. E. Sharpe, 1994); and Andrew J. Nathan, *Chinese Democracy* (Berkeley: University of California Press, 1985).

3. James D. Seymour, *China's Satellite Parties* (Armonk, NY: M. E. Sharpe, 1987); Dali L. Yang, *Remaking the Chinese Leviathan: Market Transition and the Politics of Governance in China* (Stanford: Stanford University Press, 2004).

4. Harry Harding, *Organizing China: The Problem of Bureaucracy, 1949–1976* (Stanford, CA: Stanford University Press, 1981); Kenneth Lieberthal and Michel Oksenberg, *Policymaking in China: Leaders, Structures, and Processes* (Princeton, NJ: Princeton University Press, 1988); David Bachman, *Bureaucracy, Economy, and Leadership in China: The Institutional Origins of the Great Leap Forward* (Cambridge, UK: Cambridge University Press, 1991); Richard Baum, *Burying Mao: Chinese Politics in the Age of Deng Xiaoping* (Princeton, NJ: Princeton University Press, 1994); Cheng Li, "University Networks and the Rise of Qinghua Graduates in China's Leadership," *Australian Journal of Chinese Affairs*, 32 (July 1994), 1–30; and Murray Scot Tanner, *The Politics of Lawmaking in China: Institutions, Processes, and Democratic Prospects* (Oxford, UK: Clarendon Press, 1998).

5. Susan L. Shirk, *The Political Logic of Economic Reform in China* (Berkeley: University of California Press, 1993); Fubing Su and Dali L. Yang, "Political Institutions, Provincial Interests, and Resource Allocation in Reformist China," *Journal of Contemporary China* 24 (July 2000), 215–230; Yumin Sheng, "Central-Provincial Relations at the CCP Central Committees: Institutions, Measurement and Empirical Trends, 1978–2002," *China Quarterly*, 182 (June 2005), 338–355.

6. Kevin J. O'Brien and Lianjiang Li, *Rightful Resistance in Rural China* (Cambridge, UK: Cambridge University Press, 2006).

7. Elizabeth J. Perry, *Rebels and Revolutionaries in North China, 1845–1945* (Stanford, CA: Stanford University Press, 1980). Also see her *Challenging the Mandate of Heaven: Social Protest and State Power in China* (Armonk, NY: M. E. Sharpe, 2002); and Elizabeth Remick, "The Significance of Variation in Local States: The Case of Twentieth Century China," *Comparative Politics* 34:4 (July 2002), 399–418.

8. Gordon White, Jude Howell, and Shang Xiaoyuan, *In Search of Civil Society: Market Reform and Social Change in Contemporary China* (Oxford, UK: Clarendon Press, 1996); Susan H. Whiting, *Power and Wealth in Rural China: The Political Economy of Institutional Change* (Cambridge, UK: Cambridge University Press, 2001); Kellee Tsai, *Back-Alley Banking: Private Entrepreneurs in China* (Ithaca, NY: Cornell University Press, 2002); William Hurst, "Understanding Contentious Collective Action by Chinese Laid-Off Workers: The Importance of Regional Political Economy," *Studies in Comparative International Development* 39:2 (Summer 2004), 94–120; Sangbum Shin, "Economic Globalization and the Environment in China: A Comparative Case Study of Shenyang and Dalian," *Journal of Economic Development* 13:3 (2004), 263–294; and Andrew C. Mertha, *The Politics of Piracy: Intellectual Property in Contemporary China* (Ithaca, NY: Cornell University Press, 2005).

9. Edward S. Steinfeld, *Forging Reform in China: The Fate of State-Owned Industry* (Cambridge, UK: Cambridge University Press, 1998); Doug Guthrie, *Dragon in a Three-Piece Suit: The Emergence of Capitalism in China* (Princeton, NJ: Princeton University Press, 1999).

10. Margaret M. Pearson, *China's New Business Elite* (Berkeley: University of California Press, 1997); and Scott Kennedy, *The Business of Lobbying in China* (Cambridge, MA: Harvard University Press, 2005).

11. Tianjian Shi, *Political Participation in Beijing* (Cambridge, MA: Harvard University Press, 1997); Jie Chen, *Popular Political Support in Contemporary China* (Stanford, CA: Stanford University Press, 2004); and Wenfang Tang, *Public Opinion and Political Change in China* (Stanford, CA: Stanford University Press, 2005).

12. For one study on the economic benefits of joining the Chinese Communist Party, see Bruce J. Dickson and Maria Rost Rublee, "Membership Has Its Privileges: The Socioeconomic Characteristics of Communist Party Members in Urban China," *Comparative Political Studies*, 33:1 (February 2000), 87–112.

13. Melanie Manion, *Retirement of Revolutionaries in China* (Princeton, NJ: Princeton University Press, 1993); Yang Zhong, *Local Government and Politics in China: Challenges from Below* (Armonk, NY: M. E. Sharpe, 2003); Andrew Wedeman, "Anticorruption Campaigns and the Intensification of Corruption," *Journal of Contemporary China* 14:42 (February 2005), 93–116; and Victor Shih, *Factions and Finance in China: Elite Conflict and Inflation* (Cambridge, UK: Cambridge University Press, 2007).

14. Donald Treadgold, ed., *Soviet and Chinese Communism: Similarities and Differences* (Seattle: University of Washington Press, 1967); Chalmers Johnson, ed., *Change in Communist Systems* (Stanford, CA: Stanford University Press, 1970); and Lucian W. Pye, *The Spirit of Chinese Politics* (Cambridge, MA: Harvard University Press, 1966).

15. Harry Harding, *China's Second Revolution: Reform after Mao* (Washington, DC: Brookings Institution, 1987); Mary E. Gallagher, *Contagious Capitalism: Globalization and the Politics of Labor in China* (Princeton, NJ: Princeton University Press, 2005).

16. Gordon White, ed., *Developmental States in East Asia* (New York: St. Martin's Press, 1988); Robert P. Miller, ed., *The Development of Civil Society in Communist Systems* (Sydney: Allen & Unwin, 1992); Barrett L. McCormick and Jonathan Unger, eds., *China after Socialism: In the Footsteps of Eastern Europe or East Asia?* (Armonk, NY: M. E. Sharpe, 1996); Juan D. Lindau and Timothy Cheek, eds., *Market Economics and Political Change: Comparing China and Mexico* (Lanham, MD: Rowman & Littlefield, 1998); Kjeld Erik Brodsgaard and Susan Young, eds., *State Capacity in East Asia: China, Taiwan, Vietnam, and Japan* (New York: Oxford University Press, 2001); Edward Friedman and Bruce Gilley, *Asia's Giants: Comparing China and India* (New York: Palgrave Macmillan, 2005); and Saadia M. Pekkanen and Kellee Tsai, eds., *Japan and China in the World Political Economy* (London: Routledge, 2006).

17. Minxin Pei, *From Reform to Revolution: The Demise of Communism in China and the Soviet Union* (Cambridge, MA: Harvard University Press, 1994); Yanqi Tong, *Transitions from State Socialism: Economic and Political Change in Hungary and China* (Lanham, MD: Rowman & Littlefield, 1997); Bruce J. Dickson, *Democratization in China and Taiwan* (Oxford, UK: Oxford University Press, 1997); Yan Sun, *Corruption and Market in Contemporary China* (Ithaca, NY: Cornell University Press, 2004); Kellee S. Tsai, "Imperfect Substitutes: The Local Political Economy of Informal Finance and Microfinance in Rural China and India," *World Development*, 32:9 (September 2004), 1487–1507; Yanqi Tong, "Environmental Movements in Transitional Societies: A Comparative Study of Taiwan and China," *Journal of Comparative Politics*, 37:2 (January 2005), 167–188; Andrew C. Mertha and William R. Lowry, "Unbuilt Dams: Seminal Events and Policy Change in China, Australia, and the United States," *Journal of Comparative Politics*, 39:1 (October 2006), 1–20; Randall Peerenboom, *China Modernizes: Threat to the West or Model for the Rest?*

(Oxford, UK: Oxford University Press, 2007); Shiping Hua, *Chinese Utopianism: A Comparative Study of Reformist Thought with Japan and Russia, 1898–1997* (Stanford, CA: Stanford University Press, 2009); Shalendra D. Sharma, *China and India in the Age of Globalization* (Cambridge, UK: Cambridge University Press, 2009); Dorothy J. Solinger, *States' Gains, Labor's Losses: China, France, and Mexico Choose Global Liaisons, 1980–2000* (Ithaca, NY: Cornell University Press, 2009); and Yan Sun and Michael Johnston, "Does Democracy Check Corruption? Insights from China and India," *Comparative Politics* 42:2 (January 2010).

18. Kenneth Lieberthal, *Governing China: From Revolution through Reform*, second edition (New York: W. W. Norton, 2004); Tony Saich, *Governance and Politics of China*, second edition (London: Palgrave MacMillan, 2004); and June Teufel Dreyer, *China's Political System: Modernization and Tradition*, seventh edition (New York: Pearson Longman, 2010).

19. Harry Harding, "From China, with Disdain: New Trends in the Study of China," *Asian Survey* 22:10 (October 1982), 934–958; Nina P. Halpern, "Studies of Chinese Politics," in David Shambaugh, ed., *American Studies of Contemporary China* (Armonk, NY: M. E. Sharpe, 1993), 120–137; Elizabeth J. Perry, "Trends in the Study of Chinese Politics: State–Society Relations," *China Quarterly*, 139 (September 1994), 704–713; Avery Goldstein, "Trends in the Study of Political Elites and Institutions in the PRC," *China Quarterly*, 139 (September 1994), 714–730; Peter R. Moody Jr., "Trends in the Study of Chinese Political Culture," *China Quarterly*, 139 (September 1994), 731–740; Lowell Dittmer and William J. Hurst, "Analysis in Limbo: Contemporary Chinese Politics Amid the Maturation of Reform," *Issues & Studies* 38:4 and 39:1 (December 2002/March 2003), 11–48; and Lynn T. White III, "Chinese Political Studies: Overview of the State of the Field," *Journal of Chinese Political Science*, 3 (Winter 2009), 229–251.

20. Richard Baum, "Studies of Chinese Politics in the United States," in Robert Ash, David Shambaugh, and Seiichiro Takagi, eds., *China Watching: Perspectives from Europe, Japan and the United States* (London: Routledge, 2007), 147–168.

21. Harry Harding, "The Study of Chinese Politics: Toward a Third Generation of Scholarship," *World Politics* 36:2 (January 1984), 284–307. The only other defense of comparison that was located is Andrew J. Nathan, "Is Chinese Culture Distinctive?" *Journal of Asian Studies* 52:4 (November 1993), 923–936.

22. John King Fairbank, *The United States and China* (Cambridge, MA: Harvard University Press, 1949), 7–8.

23. John King Fairbank, "The People's Middle Kingdom," *Foreign Affairs* 44:4 (July 1966), 574–586; Ross Terrill, ed., *The China Difference* (New York: Harper & Row, 1979); Harrison E. Salisbury, *The New Emperors: China in the Era of Mao and Deng* (Boston: Little, Brown, & Co., 1992); and Martin Jacques, *When China Rules the World: The End of the Western World and the Birth of a New Global Order* (New York: Penguin Press, 2009), 233–271.

24. There has been a flowering of historical political economy research which compares China with Europe, Japan, and elsewhere. The most noteworthy is Pomeranz's explicitly comparative analysis of why Great Britain did and China did not experience an industrial revolution in the nineteenth century. Kenneth Pomeranz, *The Great Divergence: China, Europe, and the Making of the Modern World Economy* (Princeton, NJ: Princeton University Press, 2000). Other significant recent works that are part of this discussion include R. Bin Wong, *China Transformed: Historical Change and the Limits of European Experience* (Ithaca, NY: Cornell University Press, 1997); and Sucheta Mazumdar, *Sugar and Society in China: Peasants, Technology, and the World Market* (Cambridge, MA: Harvard University Press, 1998).

25. Halpern, "Studies of Chinese Politics."

26. For an explanation, see Wang Yu, "Our Way: Building Socialism with Chinese Characteristics," *Political Affairs Magazine*, January 2004, retrieved on May 10, 2006 from www.politicalaffairs.net/article/view/36/1/1/. Also see Xu Yi, *Zhongguo tese lun* (On Chinese characteristics) (Economic Science Press, 2004); and H. Lyman Miller, *Science and Dissent in Post-Mao China: The Politics of Knowledge* (Seattle: University of Washington Press, 1996), 31–60.

27. This author tracked the frequency of the use of the term *Middle Kingdom* in the American media from 1988 to 2006 using the Factiva database owned by Dow Jones, Inc., accessed on April 7, 2007. The appearance of the term jumped dramatically in 1989 as a result of the spring 1989 protests and subsequent crackdown and again in 1996–1997 following the rise of tensions between the United States and China as a result of the former granting a visa to Lee Teng-hui and the subsequent Chinese displays of force.

28. Gregory J. Kasza, *One World of Welfare: Japan in Comparative Perspective* (Ithaca, NY: Cornell University Press, 2007). What country is most commonly the outlier among advanced industrialized countries on almost every measure? The United States, not Japan.

29. Valerie J. Bunce, *Subversive Institutions: The Design and the Collapse of Socialism and the State* (Cambridge, UK: Cambridge University Press, 1999). For an insightful critique of this research agenda, see Paul Kubicek, "Post-Communist Political Studies: Ten Years Later, Twenty Years Behind?" *Post-Communist Political Studies* 33, 3 (September 2000), 295–309.

30. Grzegorz W. Kolodko, *From Shock to Therapy: The Political Economy of Postsocialist Transformation* (Oxford, UK: Oxford University Press, 2000).

31. Pei, *From Reform to Revolution*; Tong, *Transitions from State Socialism*; Barry Naughton, *Growing Out of the Plan: Chinese Economic Reform, 1978–1993* (Cambridge, UK: Cambridge University Press, 1996); and Fang Cai, Zhou Li, and Justin Lin, *The China Miracle: Development Strategy and Economic Reform* (Hong Kong: Chinese University Press, 2003).

32. Minxin Pei, *China's Trapped Transition: The Limits of Developmental Autocracy* (Cambridge, MA: Harvard University Press, 2006). Pei's second book directly challenges the findings of his first book (1994), which painted a more optimistic view of China's gradualist approach compared to the more chaotic conditions that prevailed in Russia in the early 1990s as a result of shock therapy and the sudden demise of the Soviet Union.

33. Vladimir Popov, "Shock Therapy versus Gradualism Reconsidered: Lessons from Transition Economies after 15 Years of Reforms," *Comparative Economic Studies* 49:1 (March 2007), 1–31.

34. Ronald Dore, William Lazonick, and Mary O'Sullivan, "Varieties of Capitalism in the Twentieth Century," *Oxford Review of Economic Policy* 15:4 (1999), 102–120; Peter A. Hall and David Soskice, eds., *Varieties of Capitalism: The Institutional Foundations of Comparative Advantage* (Oxford, UK: Oxford University Press, 2001); and Wolfgang Streeck and Kozo Yamamura, *The Origins of Non-Liberal Capitalism* (Ithaca, NY: Cornell University Press, 2001). For several cogent critiques of this approach, see *Socioeconomic Review*, 3:3 (September 2005).

35. White, *Developmental States in East Asia*; Greg Mastel, *The Rise of the Chinese Economy: The Middle Kingdom Emerges* (Armonk, NY: M. E. Sharpe, 1997); Russell Smyth, "Should China Be Promoting Large-Scale Enterprises and Enterprise Groups?" *World Development* 28:4 (April 2000), 721–737; Ming Xia, *The Dual Developmental State: Development Strategy and Institutional Arrangements for China's Transition* (Aldershot, UK: Ashgate, 2000); Jorgen Delman, "Cool Thinking? The Role of the State in Shaping China's Dairy Sector and Its Knowledge System," *China Information*, 17:2 (2003), 1–35; Ted C. Fishman, *China, Inc.: How the Rise of the Next Superpower Challenges America and the World* (New York: Scribner, 2005); Xiaoming Huang, *The Rise and Fall of the East Asian Growth System, 1951–2000: Institutional Competitiveness and Rapid Economic Growth* (London: RoutledgeCurzon, 2005); and Anita Chan and Jonathan Unger, "A Chinese State Enterprise Under Reforms: What Model of Capitalism?" *China Journal*, 61 (July 2009), 1–26.

36. Minxin Pei, "Will China Become Another Indonesia?" *Foreign Policy*, 116 (Fall 1999), 94–109; George Gilboy and Eric Heginbotham, "The Latin Americanization of China?" *Current History*, September 2004, 256–261; and Victor Shih, "Development, the Second Time Around: The Political Logic of Developing Western China," *Journal of East Asian Studies*, 4:3 (September–December 2004), 427–451.

37. An important wide-ranging contribution that is not comparative is Christopher A. McNally, ed., *China's Emergent Political Economy: Capitalism in the Dragon's Lair* (New York: Routledge, 2008). An exception is Peerenboom, *China Modernizes*, but he strictly compares economic outcomes and does not delve into economic policies or regulatory approaches.

38. For the original perspective, see Chalmers Johnson, *MITI and the Japanese Miracle: The Growth of Industrial Policy, 1925–1975* (Stanford, CA: Stanford Univer-

sity Press, 1982); Robert Wade, *Governing the Market: Economic Theory and the Role of Government in East Asian Industrialization* (Princeton, NJ: Princeton University Press, 1990); Meredith Woo Cumings, ed., *The Developmental State* (Ithaca, NY: Cornell University Press, 1999). For critiques, see Richard K. Samuels, *The Business of the Japanese State: Energy Markets in Comparative and Historical Perspective* (Ithaca, NY: Cornell University Press, 1987); Phillip Oppenheim, *Japan without Blinders: Coming to Terms with Japan's Economic Success* (Tokyo: Kodansha America, 1992), 121–149; Michael Hobday, *Innovation in East Asia: The Challenge to Japan* (Aldershot, UK: Edward Elgar, 1995); Scott Callon, *Divided Sun: MITI and the Breakdown of Japanese High-Tech Industrial Policy 1975–1993* (Stanford, CA: Stanford University Press, 1995); Gregory W. Noble, *Collective Action in East Asia: How Ruling Parties Shape Industrial Policy* (Ithaca, NY: Cornell University Press, 1999); and Steven K. Vogel, *Japan Remodeled: How Government and Industry Are Reforming Japanese Capitalism* (Ithaca, NY: Cornell University Press, 2006).

39. Gordon Redding, *The Spirit of Chinese Capitalism* (New York: de Gruyter, 1990).

40. Timothy M. Shaw and Shaun Breslin, *China and the Global Political Economy* (London: Palgrave Macmillan, 2007). Also see Shaun Breslin, "Capitalism with Chinese Characteristics: The Public, the Private, and the International," Murdoch University Asia Research Centre, *Working Paper* no. 104 (June 2004); and Gustav Ranis, "Capitalism with Special Chinese Characteristics," *YaleGlobal Online*, June 19, 2007, available at http://yaleglobal.yale.edu.

41. Yasheng Huang, *Capitalism with Chinese Characteristics: Entrepreneurship and the State* (Cambridge, UK: Cambridge University Press, 2008). Also see Arthur Sweetman and Jun Zhang, eds., *Economic Transitions with Chinese Characteristics, Vol. 1: Thirty Years of Reform and Opening Up* (Montreal: McGill-Queen's University Press, 2009); and *Vol. 2: Social Change during Thirty Years of Reform* (Montreal: McGill-Queen's University Press, 2009).

42. Joshua Cooper Ramo, *The Beijing Consensus* (New York: Foreign Policy Centre, May 2004); Peerenboom, *China Modernizes*.

43. Suisheng Zhao, Philip Hsu, and Yu-Shan Wu, eds., *In Search of China's Development Model: Beyond the Beijing Consensus* (New York: Routledge, 2011).

44. More recent scholarship fitting with this approach has recognized variation in China and engaged in comparison, though primarily of the ideal type–to–ideal type variety. See Gordon Redding and Michael A. Witt, *The Future of Chinese Capitalism* (Oxford, UK: Oxford University Press, 2008).

45. Scott Kennedy, "The Myth of the Beijing Consensus," *Journal of Contemporary China*, 19:64 (June 2010).

46. David Lane, "What Kind of Capitalism for Russia? A Comparative Analysis," *Communist and Post-Communist Studies* 33:4 (December 2000), 485–504; Leo McCann, "Globalisation and Post-Socialist Development: The Tatarstan Variety of Capitalism," *Post-Communist Economies* 16:3 (September 2004), 349–362.

47. Gordon White, *Riding the Tiger: The Politics of Economic Reform in Post-Mao China* (Stanford, CA: Stanford University Press, 1993).

48. Richard Baum and Alexei Shevchenko, "The 'State of the State'," in Merle Goldman and Roderick MacFarquhar, eds., *The Paradox of China's Post-Mao Reforms* (Cambridge, MA: Harvard University Press, 1999), 333–360; Jean Oi, *Rural China Takes Off: Institutional Foundations of Economic Reform* (Berkeley: University of California Press, 1999); and Bruce J. Dickson, "Cooptation and Corporatism in China: The Logic of Party Adaptation," *Political Science Quarterly* 115:4 (Winter 2000–2001), 517–540.

49. Dorothy Solinger, "Urban Entrepreneurs and the State: The Merger of State and Society," in Arthur Lewis Rosenbaum, ed., *State and Society in China: The Consequences of Reform* (Boulder, CO: Westview Press, 1992), 121–141; David L. Wank, *Commodifying Communism: Business, Trust, and Politics in a Chinese City* (Cambridge, UK: Cambridge University Press, 1999).

50. Heath B. Chamberlain, "Civil Society with Chinese Characteristics?" *China Journal*, 39 (January 1998), 69–81; Pearson, *China's New Business Elite*; and Kennedy, *The Business of Lobbying in China*.

51. Kasza, *One World of Welfare*; Gregory J. Kasza, *The Conscription Society: Administered Mass Organizations* (New Haven, CT: Yale University Press, 1995).

52. Barbara Geddes, "How the Cases You Choose Affect the Answers You Get: Selection Bias in Comparative Politics," *Political Analysis* 2:1 (1990), 131–150.

NOTES TO CHAPTER TWO

1. This literature, which now nearly dominates the study of comparative capitalism, was initiated with the publication of Peter A. Hall and David Soskice, *Varieties of Capitalism: The Institutional Foundations of Comparative Advantage* (Oxford, UK: Oxford University Press, 2001). Related volumes include: Vivien A. Schmidt, *The Futures of European Capitalism* (Oxford, UK: Oxford University Press, 2002); Ben Ross Schneider, "Varieties of Semi-Articulated Capitalism in Latin America" (paper presented at the Annual Meeting of the American Political Science Association, Chicago, September 2–5, 2004); Jonathon Perraton and Ben Clift, eds., *Where Are National Capitalisms Now?* (Hampshire, UK: Palgrave, 2004); and David Choates, ed., *Varieties of Capitalism, Varieties of Approaches* (Hampshire, UK, and New York: Palgrave Macmillan, 2005).

2. Jacint Jordana and David Levi-Faur, "The Politics of Regulation in the Age of Governance," in Jacint Jordana and David Levi-Faur, eds., *The Politics of Regulation* (Cheltenham, UK: Edward Elgar, 2004), 6. The accompanying trends of decentralization and privatization are captured in a broad literature. See Daniel Yergin and Joseph Stanislaw, *The Commanding Heights: The Battle between Government and the Marketplace That Is Remaking the Modern World* (New York: Simon and Schuster, 1998).

3. Scott, for example, has argued that modern independent regulators are characterized by fragmentation and inefficiency. Colin Scott, "Analysing Regulatory Spaces: Fragmented Resources and Institutional Design," *Public Law* (2001), 329–353. The famous critique of "independence from business" with the alternative theory of "regulatory capture" is George Stigler, "The Theory of Economic Regulation," *Bell Journal of Economics and Management Science* 6:2 (1971), 3–21.

4. See, for example, the newsletter *The Better Regulator*, from the private consultancy Jacobs and Associates; retrieved on April 26, 2006, from www.regulatoryreform .com/newsletter/Jun-2005-06-09-05-E.pdf

5. David Levi-Faur, "The Global Diffusion of Regulatory Capitalism," *The Annals of the Academy of Political and Social Science* 598 (2005), 6–9.

6. Giandomenico Majone, "The Rise of Statutory Regulation in Europe," in Giandomenico Majone, ed., *Regulating Europe* (London: Routledge, 1996), 47. See also Fabrizio Gilardi, "Spurious and Symbolic Diffusion of Independent Regulatory Agencies in Western Europe" (paper presented at the workshop "The Internationalization of Regulatory Reforms," Center for the Study of Law and Society, University of California, Berkeley, April 25–28, 2003).

7. On direct pressure from the U.S. government after World War II, see Giandomenico Majone, "Cross-National Sources of Regulatory Policy-Making in Europe and the United States," *Journal of Public Policy* 11:1 (1991), 79–106.

8. Carlos Rufin and Evanán Romero, "Sustainability of Regulatory Reform in Latin America: Unraveling of Commitments" (paper presented at the 2004 Annual Research Conference of the Association for Public Policy Analysis and Management, Washington DC, November 6–8, 2004), 20–21.

9. For further discussion of the influence of international development organizations on China's choice of models see: Margaret M. Pearson, "The Business of Governing Business in China," *World Politics* 57:2 (January 2005), 296–322; OECD, *China in the World Economy: The Domestic Policy Challenges* (Geneva: OECD, 2002); and World Bank, *Building Institutions for Markets: World Development Report 2002* (New York: Oxford University Press, 2002).

10. Fabrizio Gilardi, "Institutional Change in Regulatory Policies: Regulation through Independent Agencies and the Three New Institutionalisms," in Jacint Jordana and David Levi-Faur, eds., *The Politics of Regulation* (2004): 75–77.

11. Joel D. Aberbach and Tom Christensen, "Translating Theoretical Ideas into Modern State Reform: Economics-Inspired Reforms and Competing Models of Governance," *Administration & Society* 35:5 (2003), 491–509.

12. The notion of three tiers shares similarities with Studwell's depiction of "parallel economies." However, while Studwell characterizes the state economy (as opposed to the private economy) as a failure to dismantle the old economy, I characterize the top tiers as an effort to reconstitute the former state sector. See Joseph Studwell, *The China Dream* (New York: Atlantic Monthly Press, 2002), 219–244.

13. On the process of corporatization of state enterprises, see: Donald Clarke, "Corporate Governance in China: An Overview," *China Economic Review* 14:4 (2003), 494–507; and Stoyan Tenev and Chunlin Zhang, *Corporate Governance and Enterprise Reform in China: Building the Institutions of Modern Markets* (Washington, DC: The World Bank, 2002), 5–28. Although corporatized state firms are managed by a board of directors, the state, in its capacity as major shareholder, appoints members of the board. The idea is that the state exercises its rights as a shareholder with a primary interest in distributable profits, rather than through direct control of managerial decisions.

14. "The Quest for Global Champions," *China Economic Quarterly* 7:3 (2003), 21.

15. These goals also apply to firms in China's middle tier.

16. For more extensive analysis of regulation in China's strategic industries, see Pearson, "The Business of Governing Business in China."

17. "Governing China's Boards: An Interview with John Thornton," *McKinsey Quarterly* (21 February 2007). Retrieved on February 21, 2007, from www.mckinsey quarterly.com/article_page.aspx?ar=1920&L2=39&L3=3&srid=17&gp=0

18. Ibid. See also Pearson, "The Business of Governing Business in China"; and Barry Naughton, "SASAC Rising," *China Leadership Monitor* 14 (Spring 2005).

19. Barry Naughton, *The Chinese Economy: Transitions and Growth* (Cambridge, MA: MIT Press, 2007), 314.

20. On the same phenomenon in food regulation, see the discussion on the following pages.

21. In the case of the civil aviation sector, a massive breakup of CAAC came with radical deregulation, but it was followed by reorganization into a small number of large airlines. See Jae Ho Chung, "The Political Economy of Industrial Restructuring in China: The Case of Civil Aviation," *The China Journal* 50 (July 2003).

22. It was rumored that China Mobile, which is generally considered "too big," would be the target of this reorganization. The change, expected prior to October 2006 when some crucial WTO commitments in telecom were to be phased in, did not happen, yet rumors continue to abound about yet another major reorganization.

23. On the auto industry, see Eric Thun, *Changing Lanes in China* (Cambridge, UK: Cambridge University Press, 2006).

24. See Yukyung Yeo and Margaret Pearson, "Regulating Decentralized State Industries: China's Auto Industry," *China Review* 8:2 (Fall 2008), 231–259.

25. Adam Segal and Eric Thun, "Thinking Globally, Acting Locally: Local Governments, Industrial Sectors, and Development in China," *Politics and Society* 29:4 (December, 2001), 557–588.

26. FAW (Changchun, belongs to the center). SAIC and BAIC are owned by Shanghai and Beijing municipal governments, respectively. Yeo and Pearson, "Regulating Decentralized State Industries."

27. Many in this category are, of course, township and village enterprises that were begun and often still exist under the purview of local governments via local government or collective ownership. See Barry Naughton, *Growing Out of the Plan: Chinese Economic Reform, 1978–1993* (New York: Cambridge University Press, 1995).

28. Not exempt from the corporatization movement, many of these firms are being leased by local governments to existing management or turned into joint stock companies with a mixture of government and employee ownership. Studwell, *The China Dream*, 236.

29. These "negative" regulations are well summarized in Studwell, *The China Dream*, 228–231. There are also major restrictions on the access of these firms to bank capital and the ability to be listed on stock exchanges. See Yasheng Huang, *Selling China: Foreign Direct Investment During the Reform Era* (New York: Cambridge University Press, 2003); and Kellee Tsai, *Back Alley Banking: Private Entrepreneurs in China* (Ithaca, NY: Cornell University Press, 2002).

30. See Andrew Mertha, "China's Soft Centralization: Shifting Tiao/Kuai Authority Relations," *China Quarterly* 184 (2005), 791–810.

31. Waikeung Tam and Dali Yang, "Food Safety and the Development of Regulatory Institutions in China," *Asian Perspective*, 29:4 (2005), 5–36.

32. See: Fubing Su, "Political Economy of Industrial Regulation in China's Coal Industry, 1992–1999,"in Barry Naughton and Dali L. Yang, eds., *Holding China Together* (New York: Cambridge University Press, 2004); and Shaoguang Wang, "Regulating Death at Coalmines: Changing Mode of Governance in China," *Journal of Contemporary China* 15:46 (February 2006), 1–30. The Bureau of Coal Mining was abolished in 2000.

33. The identification of institutional complementarities is a key focus of the "varieties of capitalism" literature. Hall and Soskice, *Varieties of Capitalism*, 17–19.

34. A key distinction is made between "coordinated market economies" such as Japan's, characterized by substantial nonmarket coordination (such as negotiation) within and between institutional actors (labor, business associations, and the state), and "liberal market economies," such as the United States, characterized by a greater degree of market-based coordination between these actors. Note that two points of comparison in this essay, France and Brazil, are not considered in a core way in the "varieties" literature, as their key features do not fit in either of the main categories. France is considered too statist, more like a "national capital economy." Brazil is not considered because it is not an advanced capitalist economy. Hall and Soskice, *Varieties of Capitalism*, 19–21.

35. Although this chapter focuses on the top tiers of China's economy, future research comparing economic governance in small-scale services and retail will be extremely valuable for completing the picture.

36. In truth, the emphasis in this analysis on the role of state is explicitly *not* sympathetic to the varieties of capitalism literature. Rather, the focus of that

literature is explicitly on the level of the firm as the key actor. In the study of China's top tier industries, it is not yet possible to avoid emphasis on the state.

37. See: Motoshige Itoh, "Regulatory Reform: An Experience of the Japanese Distribution System," in OECD Proceedings: Regulatory Reform and International Market Openness (Paris: OECD, 1996), 99–100; OECD, *China in the World Economy: Domestic Policy Challenges* (Paris: OECD, 2002), 365–366; and T. J. Pempel, "Regime Shift: Japanese Politics in a Changing World Economy," *Journal of Japanese Studies* 23:2 (1997).

38. In the "Varieties of Capitalism" literature, France is considered to be more statist—more in favor of state coordination—than the two most carefully considered categories of countries: liberal market economies (exemplified by the United States and Britain) and coordinated market economies (exemplified by Germany and Japan). Hall and Soskice, *Varieties of Capitalism*, 20.

39. Majone, "The Rise of Statutory Regulation in Europe," 50.

40. Schmidt details the "heroic" role the French government (both on the left under Mitterrand and Chirac) saw for state control of industry. This "heroism" has declined somewhat under pressure from EU integration, and yet the assumption that the state will play a positive role, even if not a direct owner, is deep. See Vivien A. Schmidt, *From State to Market: The Transformation of French Business and Government* (New York: Cambridge University Press, 1996), 163–164; and Schmidt, *The Futures of European Capitalism*, 81–82.

41. Schmidt, *The Futures of European Capitalism*, 220. Schmidt is remarking on the slowness of French discourse to adapt to privatization.

42. Andrea Goldstein, "Brazilian Privatization in International Perspective: The Rocky Path from State Capitalism to Regulatory Capitalism," *Institutional and Corporate Change* 8:4 (1997), 673–711; and Ben Ross Schneider and Blanca Heredia, eds., *Reinventing Leviathan: The Politics of Administrative Reform in Developing Countries* (Miami: North-South Center Press, 2003).

43. Nicholas Lardy, *Integrating China into the World Economy* (Washington, DC: Institute for International Economics, 2002).

44. Majone, "The Rise of Statutory Regulation in Europe," 50.

45. Yergin and Stanislaw, *The Commanding Heights*, 318.

46. Schmidt, *From State to Market*, 369.

47. On the leadership by the U.N. Economic Council for Latin America and emulation of European trends toward deep state intervention of the 1950s, see Luigi Manzetti, *Privatization South American Style* (Oxford, UK: Oxford University Press, 1999), 5–6. On market concentration of Brazilian public enterprises prior to privatization, see Manzetti, *Privatization South American Style*, 165.

48. Manzetti, *Privatization South American Style*, 173, 224, 328–329.

49. Schneider, "Varieties of Semi-Articulated Capitalism in Latin America."

50. See Pearson, "The Business of Regulating Business."

51. Schmidt, *From State to Market*, 166–168.

52. Ben Ross Schneider, *Business Politics and the State in Twentieth-Century Latin America* (New York: Cambridge University Press, 2004), ch. 8.

53. See: Manzetti, *Privatization South American Style*, 184; and Carlos Rufin and Evanán Romero, "Sustainability of Regulatory Reform in Latin America," 21.

54. Hall and Soskice, *Varieties of Capitalism*, 35.

55. Roderic Camp, *Mexico's Mandarins: Crafting a Power Elite for the Twenty-First Century* (Berkeley: University of California Press, 2002).

56. Scott Kennedy, *The Business of Lobbying in China* (Cambridge, MA: Harvard University Press, 2005).

57. On Europe and Latin America, see Schneider, *Business Politics and the State in Twentieth-Century Latin America*, 210. In Japan, the government appears more insulated from business influence and labor.

58. OECD, *China in the World Economy*, 365–366; and Pempel, "Regime Shift."

59. See: T. J. Pempel, "Revisiting the Japanese Economic Model," in Saadia M. Pekkanen and Kellee S. Tsai, eds., *Japan and China in the World Political Economy* (New York: Routledge Press, 2005), 29–44; and Sumner La Croix and James Mak, "Regulatory Reform in Japan: The Road Ahead," in Magnus Blomström, Byron Gangnes, and Sumner La Croix, eds., *Japan's New Economy: Continuity and Change in the Twenty-First Century* (Oxford, UK: Oxford University Press, 2001).

60. Schmidt, *From State to Market*, 271.

61. Ben Clift, "The French Model of Capitalism: *Still* Exceptional?" in Jonathon Perraton and Ben Clift, eds., *Where are National Capitalisms Now?* 91–110.

62. Rufin and Romero, "Sustainability of Regulatory Reform in Latin America," 23.

63. Naughton, *The Chinese Economy*, 106.

64. Clarke, "Corporate Governance in China."

65. Hector Schamis, *Re-Forming the State: The Politics of Privatization in Latin America and Europe* (Ann Arbor: University of Michigan Press, 2002), 4; Manzetti, *Privatization South American Style*.

66. The influence of state ownership in the strategic industries also makes it more difficult to analyze China through the "varieties of capitalism" lens—a lens that is explicitly centered on the firm. Hall and Soskice, *Varieties of Capitalism*, 4.

67. On France, see Schmidt, *The Futures of European Capitalism*, and Schmidt, *From State to Market*. On Latin America, see Manzetti, *Privatization South American Style*.

68. On Latin America, see: Ben Ross Schneider, "Organizing Interests and Coalitions in the Politics of Market Reform in Latin America," *World Politics* 56 (2004), 456–479; and Schneider (2004), ch. 8.

69. Kennedy, *The Business of Lobbying in China*.

NOTES TO CHAPTER THREE

1. The developmental state idea in its general form was described by Alexander Gerschenkron, *Economic Backwardness in Historical Perspective* (Cambridge, MA: Belknap Press, 1962). The classic description of Japan in developmental state terms is Chalmers Johnson, *MITI and the Japanese Miracle* (Stanford, CA: Stanford University Press, 1982). A concise discussion of the broader "East Asian developmental state" and its particularities in the major regional economies is Gordon White and Robert Wade, eds., *Developmental States in East Asia* (Brighton, UK: Institute of Developmental Studies, 1988). My description of the developmental-state model follows White and Wade.

2. In some cases there is evidence of conscious emulation of Japanese or South Korean precedents, but Chinese economic policy makers have imported ideas from many places. Many elements of the Chinese legal and regulatory system refer to models from the United States and Europe; and in the early stages of reform models from other communist countries were used. The 1980 joint-venture law, which created the framework for large-scale foreign participation in the Chinese economy, relied heavily on earlier Yugoslavian joint-venture regulations. Thanks to Mark Cohen (personal communication) for pointing out the genesis of the joint-venture law.

3. These aims are made evident in the large number of sectoral development plans issued by line ministries and/or the State Planning Commission and its successor agencies, as well as by government programs designed specifically to promote the development of an indigenous technological base. The latter include extensive technology-transfer regulations governing Sino–foreign joint venture firms, as well as funding programs such as the "863" program (1986) for funding applied scientific research, and the "973" program (1997) for basic research.

4. "*Women de guojia yiding yao fazhan, bu fazhan jiu hui shou ren qifu, fazhan cai shi ying daoli.*" ("Our country must develop; if we do not develop then we will be bullied. Development is the only hard truth.") Quoted in Xinhua News Service, *Fazhan cai shi ying daoli Xiaoping yiju hua cujin le zhongguo mianmao de gaibian*, August 18, 2004. Available at http://news.xinhuanet.com/newscenter/2004-08/18/content_1816165.htm.

5. The first documented reference to Deng Xiaoping's use of *duiwai kaifang, duinei gaohuo* is at the third plenum of the Twelfth CCP congress, in June 1984. See http://myy.cass.cn/file/200512092780.html. But the emphasis on opening to the outside world clearly dates to the landmark Third Plenum of the Eleventh CCP congress, in December 1978.

6. China's trade figures are distorted by the widespread use of bogus or falsified trade transactions as a means of importing or exporting capital in violation of China's controls on capital flows. Those who wish to send capital abroad routinely over-invoice imports; those who wish to bring capital into the country can

over-invoice exports. For a recent estimate of the value of such bogus transactions, see Stephen Green, "China's Trade: Bermuda Triangle, Accounting Issue or FX Flows?", Standard Chartered Bank research note, April 13, 2006. The relatively depressed trade figures of 1996–1999 are probably too low because of both capital flight and rampant smuggling; the spectacular trade figures of 2003–2005 are probably too high, for the converse reasons. Nonetheless, there is little doubt that WTO entry sparked a sharp increase in China's trade, well above the trend growth pattern of the 1990s.

7. The most systematic analysis of the ownership structure of the Chinese economy is in OECD, *Economic Survey: China* (Paris, 2005), available at www.oecd.org.

8. For Chinese privatization practices, including comparisons to the experiences of the former Soviet bloc, see Stephen Green and Guy Liu, eds., *Exit the Dragon? Privatization and State Control in China* (London: Chatham House/Blackwell Publishing, 2005). For the performance of postrestructuring state enterprises, see Carsten Holz, *China's Industrial State-Owned Enterprises: Between Profitability and Bankruptcy* (Singapore: World Scientific, 2003), and Barry Naughton, "Profiting the SASAC Way," *China Economic Quarterly*, June 2008, 19–26.

9. Central government ownership rights in 196 major state enterprise groups were vested in a new agency, the State-Owned Assets Supervision and Administration Commission (SASAC), in 2003. The number of enterprise groups directly under SASAC has since shrunk to around 140 through mergers (not privatization). SASAC has also asserted regulatory authority over state enterprises at the provincial and lower levels, where it does not exercise direct ownership rights.

10. A noteworthy example of a competitive sector with successful state and private players is the telecoms equipment industry, where private firm Huawei is the clear leader and state-owned ZTE runs a strong second.

11. For details on relations between the Party and private entrepreneurs, see Bruce Dickson, *Red Capitalists in China* (Cambridge, UK: Cambridge University Press, 2003).

12. For Japan, see Chalmers Johnson, *MITI and the Japanese Miracle* (1982). For South Korea, see Richard Luedde-Neurath, "State Intervention and Export-Oriented Development in South Korea," in White and Wade (1988), 68–112.

13. For the importance of liberal–conservative debates in policy formulation, see Barry Naughton, "Deng Xiaoping: The Economist," *China Quarterly*, 135 (September 1993), 491–514. For local state corporatism, see Jean Oi, *Rural China Takes Off* (Berkeley: University of California Press, 1999). For other views of local autonomy in economic development, see Ezra Vogel, *One Step Ahead in China* (Cambridge, MA: Harvard University Press, 1989); and Kellee Tsai, *Back-alley Banking: Private Entrepreneurs in China* (Ithaca, NY: Cornell University Press, 2002). For the role of businesses in influencing the formation of government policy and modifying its effects in practice, see Scott Kennedy, *The Business of Lobbying in*

China (Cambridge, MA: Harvard University Press, 2005), and Andrew Wedeman's contribution to this volume. A useful summary of the tensions in Chinese policy formulation is Shaun Breslin, "China: developmental state or dysfunctional development?" *Third World Quarterly*, 17:4 (1996), 689–706.

14. See Daniel Okimoto, *Between MITI and the Market: Japanese Industrial Policy for High Technology* (Stanford, CA: Stanford University Press, 1989).

15. An interesting example of a Chinese national champion taking it on the chin is Chinalco, the state-owned aluminum producer, which until 2006 also enjoyed an almost total monopoly on domestic production of alumina, the bauxite derivative that is the raw material for aluminum smelting. Five small private companies, supported by local governments, stole Chinalco's technology and in the space of three years cut its share of the domestic alumina market in half. See Richard McGregor, *The Party: The Secret World of China's Communist Rulers* (New York: HarperCollins, 2010), 223–226.

16. To pick only the most obvious examples: Wang Yong-ching's Formosa Plastics Group in Taiwan, Li Ka-shing's Cheung Kong group in Hong Kong, and the business empires of Robert Kwok, Mochtar Riady's Lippo group, and the Chaeranavont family in Malaysia, Indonesia, and Thailand respectively. In most cases, these conglomerates got their start by gaining preferential or monopoly concessions on key commodities and then used the guaranteed cash flows from these monopolies to build up diversified business empires. See Joe Studwell, *Asian Godfathers* (London: Profile Books, 2007). This corporate development path is foreclosed in China because the state has defined resource extraction (including ultimate control over land sales) as a state activity. Arguably, this is a good thing: Asian family conglomerates tend to specialize in asset trading and high-rent monopoly activities, generating high profits for themselves but doing little to promote broad-based economic development. By keeping high-rent sectors in state hands, China at least in theory enables the state to use those rents to finance the creation of industrial infrastructure. And by allowing small-scale private firms to dominate many manufacturing sectors, China has created more dynamic markets for consumer goods and a far faster pace of technological innovation than is characteristic of Southeast Asian economies.

17. My treatment of the Chinese auto industry differs in perspective from, but I believe is complementary to, the analysis presented by Wedeman elsewhere in this volume. He focuses on the factors that enabled China to establish a competitive and dynamic car market, in contrast to the technologically static and gangster-dominated black market in cars that emerged in post-Soviet Russia. My concern is to understand why the Chinese policy of creating national-champion auto assemblers like Toyota and Hyundai has so far failed to bear fruit. Wedeman's discussion of how fragmented local production structures led first to local protectionism and then to robust competition is very helpful in explaining why the Chinese car mar-

ket evolved into a diversified, competitive market rather than into the cozy oligopoly of centrally controlled state-run firms envisaged by policy makers in Beijing.

18. In 1979, the Hyundai Pony cost US$3,745 to produce and was sold in South Korea for US$4,980 and in export markets at US$2,150. I have taken my account of the Korean and Taiwanese car industries, including this data, from Rhys Jenkins, "The Political Economy of Industrial Policy: Automobile Manufacture in the Newly Industrializing Countries," *Cambridge Journal of Economics*, 1995, 625–645.

19. A key difference is that FAW and Dongfeng are controlled by the central government, while SAIC is owned by the Shanghai municipal government. One consequence was that SAIC was far more nimble in restructuring its supplier network in the late 1990s, with the result that its joint ventures wound up more efficient.

20. FAW has joint ventures with VW and Toyota; SAIC with VW and GM; and Dongfeng with Nissan and Honda.

21. By 2005 China was a modest net exporter of vehicles, mainly thanks to the export of trucks and other commercial vehicles to other developing countries. Vehicle imports, liberalized in 2002, remain limited because of the low and falling prices of domestically made cars.

22. Eric Thun, *Changing Lanes in China* (Cambridge, UK: Cambridge University Press, 2005); also Thun, "National Champions-or Chumps?" *China Economic Quarterly*, Q4 (December) 2005, 34–42.

23. A recent examination by the author of the China-based supply chain of a major U.S. personal computer company revealed that there were no domestic Chinese firms among first-tier suppliers, and even at the second tier Chinese participation consisted almost entirely of suppliers of nonelectronic goods such as packaging (Author research, 2006). Recent studies also show that Chinese electronics firms badly lag the China-based operations of Taiwanese and other foreign firms in measures of research and development, such as patent filings. See Douglas B. Fuller, "The New Bamboo Network," *China Economic Quarterly*, Q3 (September) 2006, 29–33.

24. Arthur Kroeber, "China's Push to Innovate in Information Technology," in Linda Jakobson, ed., *Innovation with Chinese Characteristics: High-Tech Research in China* (Basingstoke, UK: Palgrave Macmillan, 2007), 37–70. Huawei is arguably becoming an exception to this rule because an increasing number of its products contain proprietary technology. Other notable exceptions are in certain types of industrial equipment where China has long had a well-established domestic market, for instance in high-efficiency thermal power plant equipment. Chinese firms are now exporting this equipment on a large scale and on occasion licensing technology to foreign users.

25. A good example of the success of these policies is the development of high-quality supercomputers by two domestic firms, Legend (parent of Lenovo) and Dawning, both of which are spinoffs from state scientific research institutes.

26. See for instance Hu Angang and Wang Yahua, eds., *Guoqing yu fazhan* (National Prosperity and Development) (Beijing: Tsinghua University Press, 2005).

NOTES TO CHAPTER FOUR

1. Available at www.imf.org/external/pubs/ft/weo/2005/02/data/index.htm.

2. Pei Minxin, "The Dark Side of China's Rise," *Foreign Policy* (March/April 2006); and Lance L. P. Gore, *Market Communism: The Institutional Foundation of China's Post-Mao Hyper-Growth* (New York: Oxford University Press, 1998).

3. Jean C. Oi, *Rural China Takes Off: Institutional Foundations of Economic Reform* (Berkeley, CA: University of California Press, 1999), 191; Andrew G. Walder, "Local Governments as Industrial Firms: An Organizational Analysis of China's Transitional Economy," *The American Journal of Sociology* 101:2 (September 1995), 267–268; and Jane Duckett, "The Emergence of the Entrepreneurial State in Contemporary China," *The Pacific Review* 9:2 (1996), 182.

4. Kwok-sing Li (compiler) and May Lok (translator), *A Glossary of Political Terms of the People's Republic of China* (Hong Kong: The Chinese University Press, 1995): 281.

5. See Keith Griffin and Azizur Rahman Khan, "The Chinese Transition to a Market Guided Economy," *Contention* 3:2 (Winter 1994), 86; Barry Naughton, *Growing Out of the Plan: Chinese Economic Reform, 1978–1993* (New York: Cambridge University Press, 1996), 7, 309; John McMillan and Barry Naughton, "How to Reform a Planned Economy: Lessons from China," *Oxford Review of Economic Policy* 8:1 (Spring 1992), 130–143.

6. Jin Dengjian and Kingsely E. Haynes, "Economic Transition at the Edge of Order and Chaos: China's Dualist and a Leading Sector Approach," *Journal of Economic Issues* 31:1 (March 1997), 83–84.

7. Charles M.A. Clark, "Spontaneous Order versus Instituted Process: The Market as Cause and Effect," *Journal of Economic Issues* 27:2 (June 1993), 377.

8. Geoffrey M. Hodgson, "Economic Evolution: Intervention Contra Pangloss," *Journal of Economics Issues* 25:2 (June 1991), 528; William J. Baumol and Jess Benhabid, "Chaos: Significance, Mechanism, and Economic Applications," *The Journal of Economic Perspectives* 3:1 (Winter 1989), 77–105; and Michael J. Radzicki, "Institutional Dynamics, Deterministic Chaos, and Self-Organizing Systems," *Journal of Economic Ideas* 24:1 (March 1996), 67–68.

9. Irene van Staveren, "Chaos Theory and Institutional Economics: Metaphor or Model?" *Journal of Economic Ideas* 33:1 (March 1999), 142.

10. Hodgson, "Economic Evolution," 526.

11. Richard Nelson, "Recent Evolutionary Theorizing about Economic Change," *Journal of Economic Literature* 33:1 (March 1995), 48–90.

12. Mainstream economists, however, reject deterministic, single equilibrium models, arguing instead that there are generally multiple rival equilibrium outcomes.

13. David Carrier, "A Methodology for Pattern Modeling Nonlinear Macroeconomic Dynamics," *Journal of Economic Ideas* 26:1 (March 1992), 226.

14. Hodgson, "Economic Evolution:" 528.

15. Carrier, "A Methodology for Pattern Modeling," 227.

16. Scott Kennedy, "Comrade's Dilemma: Corruption and Growth in Transition Economies," *Problems of Post-Communism* (March/April 1997), 28.

17. Fourin, "China Auto Weekly," February 7, 2005; available at www.fourin.com.

18. *Kyodo*, March 30, 2001.

19. *South China Morning Post*, August 7, 2000.

20. *"Industrial Policy for Automotive Industry* Promotes the Development of Automotive Industry," March 2002; available at www.cacauto.com.

21. See Eric Thun, "Industrial Policy, Chinese-Style: FDI, Regulation, and Dreams of National Champions in the Auto Sector," *Journal of East Asian Studies* 4:3 (September–December 2004).

22. Huachen (aka Brilliance), Hunan Jiangnan, Jilin Tongtian, Yuejin, Dongnan, BYD, and Chery.

23. Victor F. S. Sit and Weidong Liu, "Restructuring and Spatial Change of China's Auto Industry under Institutional Reform and Globalization," *Annals of the Association of American Geographers* 90:4 (December 2000), 661.

24. Huang, *Selling China*: 264-270. According to Thun, SAIC remained locally oriented longer than FAW or Dongfeng because, whereas they were linked to the central government and could turn to it, it was faced with local protectionism. SAIC was owned by the Shanghai municipal government, which could provide it little support outside of the city. See Eric Thun, *Changing Lanes in China: Foreign Direct Investment, Local Governments, and Auto Sector Development* (New York: Cambridge University Press, 2006), 189.

25. The SAIC Chery relationship ended badly. *Shenzhen Daily*, October 8, 2004; *China Daily*, December 18, 2005; and *Xinhuanet*, October 1, 2004.

26. FAW's Jilin operations included FAW Jiefang (trucks), FAW Automotive (producer of the Hongqi Red Flag), FAW Volkswagen (JV, producing the Jetta and Bora), FAW Bus, FAW Special Purpose Automotive, FAW Fengyue Co. (JV, producing Toyota Land Cruisers), Jilin FAW Sanyou (trucks); and Changchung FAW (light-duty trucks).

27. Wayne W. J. Xing, "Shifting Gears," *The China Business Review*, November–December 1997.

28. Shanghai Stock Exchange website (sse.com.cn), Shenzhen Stock Exchange website (szse.com.cn), and the Hong Kong Stock Exchange website (hkex.com.hk).

29. *Xinhua News Agency*, February 26, 1992, and November 7, 1994.

30. *Xinhua News Agency*, January 31, 1997, June 18, 1997, June 22, 1997, and December 10, 1997.

31. *China Online*, September 15, 1998, and May 22, 2001.

32. *China Online*, April 7, 2000; July 28, 2000; July 24, 2000; July 21, 2000; July 18, 2000; August 31, 2000; and December 13, 2000.

33. Chun-Li Lee and Takahiro Fujimoto, "The Chinese Automobile Industry," manuscript (May 2003).

34. Based on sales data from the Beijing Yayuncun Auto Sales Center, available at www.cheshi.com.cn.

35. Wayne W. J. Xing, "Automakers in the Fast Lane," *China Business Review*, July–August 2002, p. 12.

36. Virtually all taxicabs in Shanghai, for instance, are locally built Santanas.

37. Thun, *Changing Lanes*: 181–182.

38. See Andrew Wedeman, "Cutting Our Own Throats: Local Protectionism and Price Wars in China." Paper presented at Association for Asian Studies (Chicago), April 2005.

39. The Great Leap Forward led to rapid increase in the number of "automakers," as local governments converted auto repair shops and other enterprise in to "assemblers." Most were, however, assembling few (ten or so a year) vehicles, often based on farm equipment. Most were shut down during the 1961–1963 retrenchment. During the Cultural Revolution, political turmoil and the breakdown of central supply systems led to a doubling in the number of carmakers as local government sought to alleviate chronics shortages. See Sit and Liu, "Restructuring and Spatial Change of China's Auto Industry," 657–658.

40. Gregory W. Noble, John Ravenhill, and Richard F. Doner, "Executioner or Disciplinarian: WTO Accession and the Chinese Auto Industry," *Business and Politics* 7:2 (2005), 6.

41. Thun, *Changing Lanes*, 54–55, 59. Local governments were, however, generally able to pressure local public security bureaus to license locally produced vehicles. In the case of Wuhu-based Chery, which began producing passenger cars without having obtained the approval of the central government in 1999 using a secondhand assembly line illegally purchased from Ford-UK, for example, the municipal government sided stepped Beijing's ban by issuing regulations allowing Chery's cars to be registered as taxicabs Liu and Yeung, "China's Dynamic Industrial Sector," 544.

42. Noble, Ravenhill, and Doner, "Executioner or Disciplinarian," 6–7.

43. Weidong Liu and Henry Wai-chung Leung, "China's Dynamic Industrial Sector: The Automobile Industry," *Eurasian Geography and Economics* 49:5 (September 2008), 525–426.

44. Thun, *Changing Lanes*, 56–7.

45. "The Tenth Five-Year Plan of the Automotive Industry and its Development," retrieved on April 29, 2009, from http://bizchina.chinadaily.com.cn/guide/industry/industry2.htm.

46. Committee on the Future of Personal Transport Vehicles in China, National Research Council, National Academy of Engineering, Chinese Academy of

Engineering, *Personal Cars and China* (Washington, DC: National Academies Press, 2003), 8, retrieved on April 20, 2009, from www.nap.edu/catalog/10491.html.

47. Thun, *Changing Lanes*, 83–99.

48. Tak-Wing Ngo and Yilin Chen, "Rent Production and Industrial Governance in the Auto Industry," in Tak Wing Ngo and Yongping Wu, eds., *Rent Seeking in China* (New York: Routledge, 2009), 178.

49. For a more fully developed model of the role of rent seeking and local protectionism in driving China from the plan to the market see Andrew Wedeman, *From Mao to Market: Rent Seeking, Local Protectionism, and Marketization in China* (New York: Cambridge University Press, 2003), Chapter 2.

50. See James Mulvenon, *Soldiers of Fortune: The Rise and Fall of the Chinese Military-Business Complex, 1978–1998* (Armonk, NY: M. E. Sharpe, 2001).

51. See Noble, Ravenhill, and Doner, "Executioner or Disciplinarian: WTO Accession and the Chinese Auto Industry"; Lily Lin Qiu, Lindsay Turner, and Lindsay Smyrk, "A Study of Changes in the Chinese Automotive Market Resulting from WTO Entry," *The Asia Pacific Journal of Economics & Business* 8:2 (2004), 60–77; and Eric Harwit, "The Impact of WTO Membership on the Automobile Industry in China," *The China Quarterly* 167 (September 2001), 655–670.

52. See Le-Yin Zhang, "Chinese Central-Provincial Fiscal Relationships, Budgetary Decline and the Impact of the 1994 Fiscal Reform: An Evaluation," *China Quarterly* 157 (March 1999), 115–141; and Shougang Wang, "China's 1994 Fiscal Reform: An Initial Assessment," *Asian Survey* 37:9 (September 1997), 801–817.

53. Jerry Flint and Paul Klebnikov, "Would You Want to Drive a Lada?" *Forbes*, August 26, 1996.

54. Savinov, "Where Are We Going, Sir-Comrade?"

55. In 1992–1993, AvtoVAZ reportedly exported 40 percent of its production to markets in the former Soviet Union, South America, the Middle East, and Europe. *Financial Times*, November 25, 1993; and *Moscow News*, August 16, 1992.

56. Based on data from www.globalautoindex.com/; www.autosoviet.altervista .org/; and Ernst & Young, *The Russian Automotive Market: Industry Overview 2006*.

57. AvtoVAZ Vice President Nikolai Lyachenchov, for example, had a stake in Lada Broker, one of the largest automobile distributors in Russia. See Carol Matlack, "Anatomy of a Russian Wreck," *Business Week*, August 7, 1998; and *Current Digest of the Post-Soviet Press*, January 14, 1998. In 1998, 80 percent of AvtoVAZ's output was reportedly controlled by organized crime syndicates.

58. "Russia TV Channel," Moscow, October 23, 1997, in *BBC Summary of World Broadcasts*, October 25, 1997; *Komsomolskaya Pravda*, February 16, 1999, in *BBC Summary of World Broadcasts*, February 18, 1999; and *Moscow News*, July 26, 2000.

59. In January 1996 Kadannikov replaced Atantoly Chubias as first vice premier but was then dismissed by Yelstin in August following his reelection as president.

New York Times, January 26, 1996; and Nodari Simonia, "The Formation of Bureaucratic Capitalism in Russia 1992–1998," *Social Sciences* 32:1 (2001).

60. David E. Hoffman, *The Oligarchs: Wealth and Power in the New Russia* (New York: Public Affairs, 2002): 144–149; Paul Klebnikov, *Godfather of the Kremlin: Boris Berezovski and the Looting of Russia* (New York: Harcourt, 2000); Chrystia Freeland, *Sale of the Century: Russia's Wild Ride From Communism to Capitalism* (New York: Crown Business, 2000): 135–137; "Turin Meets Detroit-On the Volga," *The Economist*, March 7, 1995; "Godfather of the Kremlin?" *Forbes*, December 30, 1996; and Radio Free Europe, "Russia's Financial Empires," January 1998, available at www.rferl.org/.

61. Hoffman, *The Oligarchs*, 209.

62. *Current Digest of the Post-Soviet Press*, January 14, 1998.

63. *Current Digest of the Post-Soviet Press*, August 1, 1999.

64. *Financial Times*, May 8, 1999.

65. Matlack, "Anatomy of a Russian Wreck."

66. Russian Business Forecast Report, "Russia Q4 2005," 24–31; and The Economic Intelligence Unit, "Automotive Forecast," June 2005.

67. "Russians Bought 575,000 New Foreign-Made Cars Past Year," *Kommersant*, January 13, 2006; and "Lada Can Hear Its Rivals Gaining," *Businessweek*, November 14, 2005.

68. "Home Auto Industry 1991–2000," *Kommersant*, March 2, 2004.

69. The state-owned Rosoboronexport arms corporation held a controlling stake in AvtoVAZ, while Rosimushchestvo and other state-controlled banks owned a majority of KamAZ's stock. There was even talk of merging AvtoVAZ, KamAZ, and GAZ into a national automotive consortium. "AvtoVAZ, KAMAZ, GAZ to Consolidate into National Automobile Corporation," *Kommersant*, January 27, 2006; and "Lada Maker Slips Back under State Influence," *Automotive Business*, November 28, 2005.

NOTES TO CHAPTER FIVE

1. Barry Naughton, *The Chinese Economy: Transitions and Growth* (Cambridge, MA: MIT Press, 2007), 212–214. The per capita GDP figures are based on the World Bank's constant-price (year 2000) purchasing power-parity U.S. dollar equivalents. Naughton also provides valuable explanations for why we should treat poverty measures with great care. A World Bank study states that when measured as those consuming less than one U.S. dollar per day in purchasing power parity terms (of 1993 dollars), those in poverty fell from 652 million in 1981 to 135 million in 2004. See World Bank, "From Poor Areas to Poor People: China's Evolving Poverty Reduction Agenda; An Assessment of Poverty and Inequality in China" (Washington, DC: World Bank, 2009), 6.

2. "China to Become a Welfare State by 2049," *Xinhua*, November 2, 2008.

3. Gordon White, "Social Security Reforms in China: Towards an East Asian Model?" in Roger Goodman, Gordon White, and Huck-ju Kwon, eds., *The East Asian Welfare Model: Welfare Orientalism and the State* (London: Routledge, 1998), 175–197; Ian Holliday and Paul Wilding, "Conclusion," in Ian Holliday and Paul Wilding, eds., *Welfare Capitalism in East Asia: Social Policy in the Tiger Economies* (New York: Palgrave Macmillan, 2003), 161–182.

4. Simon Kuznets, "Economic Growth and Income Inequality," *American Economic Review* 45:1 (March 1955): 1–28.

5. Stephan Haggard and Robert R. Kaufman, *Development, Democracy, and Welfare States: Latin America, East Asia, and Eastern Europe* (Princeton, NJ: Princeton University Press, 2008).

6. Ibid., 29–78.

7. Ibid., 64.

8. Gordon White, "Social Security Reforms in China," 178.

9. Jean Oi, *Rural China Takes Off: Institutional Foundations of Economic Reform* (Berkeley: University of California Press, 1999).

10. State Statistics Bureau and Ministry of Labor and Social Security, ed., *China Labor Statistical Yearbook 2004* (Beijing: Zhongguo tongji chubanshe, 2004), 23.

11. Sarah Cook and Margaret Maurer-Fazio, eds., *The Workers' State Meets the Market: Labor in China's Transition* (London: Frank Cass, 1999); Dorothy Solinger, "Labor Market Reform and the Plight of the Laid-Off Proletariat," *The China Quarterly* 170 (June, 2002), 304–326; Jane Duckett, "State, Collectivism and Worker Privilege: A Study of Urban Health Insurance Reform," *The China Quarterly* 177 (March 2004), 155–173; Mark W. Frazier, "After Pension Reform: Navigating the 'Third Rail' in China," *Studies in Comparative International Development* 39:2 (Summer 2004), 43–68.

12. Mary Gallagher, *Contagious Capitalism. Globalization and the Politics of Labor in China* (Princeton, NJ: Princeton University Press, 2005).

13. *China Labor Statistical Yearbook 2004*, 4.

14. Ibid., 7.

15. Dorothy Solinger, "Path Dependency Reexamined: Chinese Welfare Policy in the Transition to Unemployment," *Comparative Politics* 38:1 (October 2005), 88.

16. Linda Wong, *Marginalization and Social Welfare in China* (London: Routledge, 1998).

17. Pension expenditures from social insurance funds for 2004 represented about 2.15 percent of GDP, compared to 0.53 percent for health care payments from social insurance. State Statistics Bureau, ed., *China Statistical Yearbook 2005* (Beijing: Zhongguo tongji chubanshe, 2005).

18. Mark W. Frazier, *Socialist Insecurity: The Politics of Uneven Development in China*, (Ithaca, NY: Cornell University Press, 2010).

19. World Bank, "From Poor Areas to Poor People," 118, 144.

20. Shaoguang Wang, "China's Health System: From Crisis to Opportunity," *Yale-China Health Journal* 3 (2004), 5–49.

21. Catherine Jones, "The Pacific Challenge: Confucian Welfare States," in Catherine Jones, ed., *New Perspectives on the Welfare State in Europe* (London: Routledge, 1993), 198–217; Kwong-Leung Tang, *Social Welfare Development in East Asia* (New York: Palgrave, 2000).

22. Wong, *Marginalization and Social Welfare in China*.

23. The HDI combines data on income, education, and life expectancy into a single measure.

24. Adam Schwarz, *A Nation in Waiting: Indonesia's Search for Stability* (Boulder, CO: Westview Press, 2000), 79–81; Anne Booth, "Development: Achievement and Weakness," in Donald Emmerson, ed., *Indonesia Beyond Suharto: Polity, Economy, Society, Transition* (Armonk, NY: M. E. Sharpe, 1999), 119–123; Joydeep Mukherji, "The Causes of Differential Development: Beyond Regime Dichotomies," in Edward Friedman and Bruce Gilley, eds., *Asia's Giants: Comparing India and China* (New York: Palgrave MacMillan, 2005), 59–60.

25. World Bank, *World Bank Development Indicators* (Washington, DC: World Bank 2005).

26. Jeremy Seekings, "Prospects for Basic Income in Developing Countries: A Comparative Analysis of Welfare Regimes in the South," *Centre for Social Science Research*, Working Paper No. 104 (2005), 23–24.

27. Jeremy Seekings, "Not a Single White Person Should Be Allowed to Go Under: Swartgevaar and the Origins of South Africa's Welfare State, 1924–1929," *Journal of African History* 48 (2007), 375–394.

28. Seekings, "Prospects for Basic Income," 27.

29. Ibid., 28.

30. Nicoli Natrass, "Trading off Income and Health? AIDS and the Disability Grant in South Africa," *Journal of Social Policy* 35 (2005), 3–19.

31. Ibid., 3.

32. Franco Barchiesi, "South African Debates on the Basic Income Grant: Wage Labor and the Post-Apartheid Social Policy," *Journal of Southern African Studies* 33:3 (2007), 562.

33. Armando Barrientos, "Non-Contributory Pensions and Poverty Reduction in Brazil and South Africa," Institute for Development Policy and Management Working Paper, University of Manchester (2005), 4.

34. Peter Lloyd-Sherlock, "Formal Social Protection for Older People in Developing Countries: Three Different Approaches," *Journal of Social Policy* 31:4 (2004), 700–701.

35. Natrass, "Trading off Income and Health," 3.

36. Lloyd-Sherlock, "Formal Social Protection," 688–689.

37. Seekings, "Prospects for Basic Income," 40.

38. James Malloy, *The Politics of Social Security in Brazil* (Pittsburgh: University of Pittsburgh Press, 1979), 129.

39. Ibid., 107–113.

40. Barrientos, "Non-Contributory Pensions and Poverty Reduction," 4.

41. Kurt Weyland, "Obstacles to Social Reform in Brazil," *Comparative Politics* 29 (1996), 1–22.

42. Sara Miller Llana, "Brazil Becomes Antipoverty Showcase," *Christian Science Monitor*, November 13, 2008.

43. "Unions v. Jobs," *The Economist*, May 26, 2005.

44. "Fixing the Finances," *The Economist*, February 20, 2003.

45. United Nations Development Program (UNDP), *Human Development Report 2007*, available at http://hdr.undp.org/en/statistics/data/.

46. Ashutosh Varshney, "India's Democratic Challenge," *Foreign Affairs* 86:2 (2007), 93–106.

47. Pranab Bardhan, "India and China: Governance Issues and Development," *Journal of Asian Studies* 68:2 (2009), 349–350.

48. S. Bhattacharjya, "Organized Mess," *India Today*, May 22, 2006.

49. Ibid.

50. Ramgopal Agarwala and Zafar Dad Khan, "Labor Market and Social Insurance Policy in India: A Case of Losing on Both Competitiveness and Caring" (Washington, DC: World Bank, 2002), 2.

51. Ibid., 15.

52. UNDP, *Human Development Report 2007.*

53. Robert Holzmann, Ian W. MacArthur, and Yvonne Sin, "Pension Systems in East Asia and the Pacific: Challenges and Opportunities," The World Bank, Social Protection Discussion Paper, No. 14 (June 2000), 77.

54. Alex Arifianto, "The New Indonesian Social Security Law: A Blessing or a Curse for Indonesians?" *ASEAN Economic Bulletin* 23:1 (2006), 57–75.

55. Ibid.

56. Ridwan Max Sijabat, "Employers, Trade Unions Oppose Social Security Bill," *The Jakarta Post*, February 13, 2004.

57. Arifianto, "New Indonesian Social Security Law."

58. "Enemies of Promise," *The Economist*, December 9, 2004.

59. John McBeth, "Jakarta's Labour Reforms a Tough Sell," *The Straits Times*, April 28, 2006.

60. Isabela Mares, "The Sources of Business Interest in Social Insurance: Sectoral versus National Differences," *World Politics* 55:2 (2003), 254–255.

61. James W. McGuire, "Labor Union Strength and Human Development in East Asia and Latin America," *Studies in Comparative International Development* 33:4 (1999), 3–34.

NOTES TO CHAPTER SIX

1. Zhilong Tian and Gao Haitao, *Goutong chuangzao jiazhi: qiye zhengfu gong-guande celue yu anli* (Communication creates value: tactics and cases of government public relations by enterprises) (Beijing: Qinghua University Press, 2007), 1–16.

2. Dorothy Solinger, "Urban Entrepreneurs and the State: The Merger of State and Society," in Arthur Lewis Rosenbaum, ed., *State and Society in China: The Consequences of Reform* (Boulder, CO: Westview Press, 1992), 121–141; Ying Lun So and Anthony Walker, *Explaining Guanxi: The Chinese Business Network* (New York: Routledge, 2006).

3. Scott Kennedy, *The Business of Lobbying in China* (Cambridge, MA: Harvard University Press, 2005).

4. For example, see Aseema Sinha, "Understanding the Rise and Transformation of Collective Action in India," *Business and Politics* 7:2 (2005). For important exceptions, see Harmon Zeigler, *Pluralism, Corporatism, and Confucianism: Political Association and Conflict Regulation in the United States, Europe, and Taiwan* (Philadelphia: Temple University Press, 1998); and Gregory W. Noble, *Collective Action in East Asia: How Ruling Parties Shape Industrial Policy* (Ithaca, NY: Cornell University Press, 1998).

5. Peter A. Hall and David W. Soskice, eds., *Varieties of Capitalism: The Institutional Foundations of Comparative Advantage* (Oxford, UK: Oxford University Press 2001), 8–9.

6. Mancur Olson, *The Logic of Collective Action: Public Goods and the Theory of Groups* (Cambridge, MA: Harvard University Press, 1965).

7. An excellent overview of Olson and others who have tested his propositions is found in Thomas. See Clive S. Thomas, *Research Guide to U.S. and International Interest Groups* (Westport, CT: Praeger, 2004), 97–104. Also see Wyn Grant, Alberto Martinelli, and William Paterson, "Large Firms as Political Actors: A Comparative Analysis of the Chemical Industry in Britain, Italy and West Germany," *West European Politics* 12:2 (April 1989), 72–90; Neil J. Mitchell, "The Decentralization of Business in Britain," *Journal of Politics* 52:2 (1990), 622–637; Franz Traxler and Brigette Unger "The Dairy Sector," in J. Rogers Hollingsworth, Phillipe Schmitter, and Wolfgang Streeck, eds., *Governing Capitalist Economies: Performance and Control of Economic Sector* (New York: Oxford University Press, 1994), 183–214; Jesse Biddle and Vedat Milor, "Economic Governance in Turkey: Bureaucratic Capacity, Policy Networks, and Business Associations," in Sylvia Maxfield and Ben Ross Schneider, eds., *Business and the State in Developing Countries* (Ithaca, NY: Cornell University Press, 1997), 277–309.

8. Andrew Shonfield, *Modern Capitalism: The Changing Balance of Public and Private Power* (London: Oxford University Press, 1965); Mauro F. Guillen, *The Limits of Convergence: Globalization and Organizational Change in Argentina, South Korea,*

and Spain (Princeton, NJ: Princeton University Press, 2001); and Noble, *Collective Action in East Asia*.

9. Ben Ross Schneider, *Business Politics and the State in Twentieth-Century Latin America* (Cambridge, UK: Cambridge University Press, 2004).

10. Interviews were carried out between 1998 and 2009 with representatives from Chinese and foreign industry, industry associations, and government agencies. To protect the interview sources, they must remain anonymous.

11. Philippe C. Schmitter, "Still the Century of Corporatism?" *The Review of Politics* 36:1 (1974), 85–131.

12. The key current regulation governing associations is the 1998 "Regulations on the Registration and Regulation of Social Organizations" (*shehui tuanti dengji guanli tiaoli*), which replaced a 1989 law of the same name. The 1998 version, issued October 25, 1998, is carried in *Fazhi Ribao* (Legal Daily), November 4, 1998, 3.

13. SELA is a government-controlled organization to which all small proprietors belong on registration. SELA officially represents their interests, but it acts more as a watchdog for government regulators. The CEC-CEDA officially represents large state-owned enterprises (and some large private ones as well), but it is essentially moribund.

14. Guosheng Deng and Scott Kennedy, "Big Business and Industry Association Lobbying in China: The Paradox of Contrasting Styles," *The China Journal*, 63 (2010), 101–125.

15. Cai Dingjian, *The National People's Congress Institution System, Fourth Edition* (Beijing: Legal Affairs Press, 2004).

16. The only part of the steel industry where associations make a real difference in the sector's ability to organize and coordinate is in the stainless steel subsector, which is dominated by small and medium-sized private companies.

17. Scott Kennedy, "Transnational Political Alliances: An Exploration with Evidence from China," *Business & Society*, 2 (2007), 174–200.

18. Scott Kennedy, "China's Porous Protectionism: The Changing Political Economy of Trade Policy," *Political Science Quarterly* 120:3 (2005), 407–432.

19. Ted C. Fishman, *China, Inc.: How the Rise of the Next Superpower Challenges America and the World* (New York: Scribner, 2005); Jonathan Unger and Anita Chan, "Corporatism in China: A Developmental State in an East Asian Context," in Barrett L. McCormick and Jonathan Unger, eds., *China after Socialism: In the Footsteps of Eastern Europe or East Asia?* (Armonk, NY: M. E. Sharpe, 1996), 95–129.

20. For a recent study that examines the logic of lobbying Diet members and bureaucrats, see Megumi Naoi and Ellis Krauss, "Who Lobbies Whom? Special Interests Politics under Alternative Electoral Systems," *American Journal of Political Science* 53:4 (2009), 874–892.

21. Ulrike Schaede, "The 'Old Boys' Network and Government-Business Relationships in Japan," *Journal of Japanese Studies* 21:2 (1995), 293–317.

22. James Babb, *Business and Politics in Japan* (Manchester, UK: Manchester University Press, 2001), 114–115. For a view that sees a contentious relationship between Japanese business and government already common during the high-growth era, see Gregory W. Noble, "The Japanese Industrial Policy Debate," in Stephan Haggard and Chun-In Moon, eds., *Pacific Dynamics: The International Politics of Industrial Change* (Boulder, CO: Westview Press, 1989), 53–95; and Scott Callon, *Divided Sun: MITI and the Breakdown of Japanese High-Tech Industrial Policy, 1975–1993* (Stanford, CA: Stanford University Press, 1993).

23. Ibid., 116.

24. Calder and Schaede find that *amakudari* was more common in sectors with prominent intraindustry policy problems, such as when regulators must decide between how to divvy up export quotas among an industry's firms. The nature of the issue raises the stakes for individual firms to seek advantage against their competitors. See Kent E. Calder, "Elites in an Equalizing Role: Ex-Bureaucrats as Coordinators and Intermediaries in the Japanese Government-Business Relationship," *Journal of Comparative Politics* 21:4 (1989), 379–403; and Schaede, "The Old Boys' Network."

25. In mid-2007, senior officials from the central bank and other agencies were appointed to head three of China's state-owned banks. Jamil Anderlini, "Chinese Walls Have Not Yet Been Built in Beijing," *Financial Times*, June 22, 2007, 14.

26. Takeshi Ishida, "Interest Groups under a Semipermanent Government Party: The Case of Japan," *Annals of the American Academy of Political and Social Science* 413 (1974), 1–10.

27. Babb, *Business and Politics in Japan*, 37.

28. Jeff Kingston, *Japan's Quiet Transformation: Social Change and Civil Society in the Twenty-First Century* (London: Routledge, 2004), 70–78.

29. Edward J. Lincoln, *Arthritic Japan: The Slow Pace of Economic Reform* (Washington, DC: Brookings, 2001).

30. Mark Tilton, *Restrained Trade: Cartels in Japan's Basic Materials Industries* (Ithaca, NY: Cornell University Press, 1996).

31. Scott Kennedy, "The Price of Competition: Pricing Policies and the Struggle to Define China's Economic System," *The China Journal*, 49 (January 2003), 1–30.

32. Joydeep Mukherji, "India's Long March to Capitalism," *India Review*, 1:2 (April 2002), 29–60.

33. Stanley A. Kochanek, "The Transformation of Interest Politics in India," *Pacific Affairs* 68:4 (Winter 1995–1996), 543; Stanley A. Kochanek, "Liberalisation and Business Lobbying in India," *Journal of Commonwealth and Comparative Politics* 34:3 (November 1996), 155–173.

34. Kochanek, "Liberalisation and Business Lobbying in India," 159–160.

35. Ibid., 157–158.

36. Ibid., 159–160.

37. Kochanek, "The Transformation of Interest Politics in India," 530.

38. Aseema Sinha, "Understanding the Rise and Transformation of Collective Action in India," 13.

39. More information about CII is available from its website, www.ciionline.org.

40. Kochanek, "The Transformation of Interest Politics in India," 546.

41. Sinha, "Understanding the Rise and Transformation of Collective Action in India," 8.

42. "Lobbying: India's Newest Industry," *India Business Intelligence*, October 1998, 5–6; and Anand Giridharadas, "India's New Lobbyists use American Methods," *International Herald Tribune*, May 18, 2006.

43. Sinha, "Understanding the Rise and Transformation of Collective Action in India"; Kochanek, "Liberalisation and Business Lobbying in India"; Jorgen Dige Pedersen, "Explaining Economic Liberalization in India: State and Society Perspectives," *World Development* 28:2 (February 2000), 265–282.

44. Devish Kapur, "The Causes and Consequences of India's IT Boom," *India Review* 1:2 (April 2002), 91–100.

45. Suma Athreye and Sachin Chaturvedi, "Industry Associations and Technology-Based Growth in India," *European Journal of Development Research* 19:1 (March 2007), 156–173.

46. Nyay Bhushan, "India Steps Up C'right Protection," *Billboard* 110:40 (October 3, 1998), 59–60.

47. Dine Butler, "India's New Millenium Salvo to Wal-Mart and Resistance to Re-Colonialization," *Social Policy*, 36:1 (Fall 2005), 28–31.

48. Peter A. Rutland, "Introduction: Business and the State in Russia," in Peter Rutland, ed., *Business and the State in Contemporary Russia* (Boulder, CO: Westview, 2001), 1–32.

49. Sergei Peregudov and Irina Semenenko, "Lobbying Business Interests in Russia," *Democratization*, 3:2 (Summer 1996), 115–139.

50. Rutland, "Introduction: Business and the State in Russia," 15.

51. David Lane, "What Kind of Capitalism for Russia? A Comparative Analysis," *Communist and Post-Communist Studies* 33 (2000), 485–504; Paul Hutchcroft, "Booty Capitalism: Business–Government Relations in the Philippines," in Andrew MacIntyre, ed., *Business and Government in Industrialising Asia* (Ithaca, NY: Cornell University Press, 1994), 216–243.

52. Rutland, "Introduction: Business and the State in Russia," 25–26; Peter A. Rutland, "Business and Civil Society in Russia," in Alfred B. Evans et al., eds., *Russian Civil Society: A Critical Assessment* (Armonk, NY: M. E. Sharpe, 2006), 87–88.

53. Peregudov and Semenenko, "Lobbying Business Interests in Russia," 133.

54. Timothy Frye, "Capture or Exchange? Business Lobbying in Russia," *Europe-Asia Studies* 54:7 (2002), 1017–1036.

55. Peregudov and Semenenko, "Lobbying Business Interests in Russia," 127–128.

56. Steven Fish, "The Emergence of Independent Associations and the Transformation of Russian Political Society," *Journal of Communist Studies* 7:3 (September 1991), 299–334.

57. Peter Rutland, *Business Elites and Russian Economic Policy* (London: Royal Institute for International Affairs, 1992), 20–21.

58. William Pyle, "Collective Action and Post-Communist Enterprise: The Economic Logic of Russia's Business Associations," *Europe-Asia Studies* 58:4 (June 2006), 491–521.

59. Barbara Lehmbruch, "Managing Uncertainty: Hierarchies, Markets and 'Networks' in the Russian Timber Industry, 1991–1998," *BOFIT Discussion Papers*, 4 (1999); and Paul Kubicek, "Variations on a Corporatist Theme: Interest Associations in Post-Soviet Ukraine and Russia," *Europe-Asia Studies* 48:1 (January 1996), 27–46.

60. Dinissa Duvanova, "Bureaucratic Corruption and Collective Action: Business Associations in the Post-Communist Transition," *Comparative Politics* 37:4 (July 2007).

61. Philip Hanson and Elizabeth Teague, "Big Business and the State in Russia," *Europe-Asia Studies* 57:5 (July 2005), 657–680.

62. Hanson and Teague, "Big Business and the State in Russia," 673–674.

63. Rutland, "Business and Civil Society in Russia," 87–88.

64. Pyle, "Collective Action and Post-Communist Enterprise," 491–521; Hanson and Teague, "Big Business and the State in Russia," 662.

65. Rutland, "Business and Civil Society in Russia," 86.

66. Pyle, "Collective Action and Post-Communist Enterprise," 491–521.

67. Duvanova, "Bureaucratic Corruption and Collective Action."

68. Pyle, "Collective Action and Post-Communist Enterprise."

69. Richard F. Doner and Ben Ross Schneider, "Business Associations and Economic Development: Why Some Associations Contribute More Than Others," *Business and Politics* 2:3 (2000), 261–288.

70. I was unable to locate research materials that shed light on policy coalitions in Russia and so prefer to refrain from speculating about this issue with regard to that country.

NOTES TO CHAPTER SEVEN

A National Science Foundation grant (INT-0107326) provided funding for the research in this paper. While many people have commented on the larger project, I would like to thank Stephan Haggard, Scott Kennedy, Kevin O'Brien, Margaret Pearson, Aseema Sinha, and three anonymous readers for more recent and detailed input. They are, of course, absolved from its inadequacies.

1. *China Daily*, December 18, 2007, and January 29, 2008.

2. Xiaoqin Guo, *State and Society in China's Democratic Transition: Confucianism, Leninism, and Economic Development* (New York: Routledge, 2003), 220.

3. Yongnian Zheng, *Will China Become Democratic? Elite, Class and Regime Transition* (Singapore: Eastern Universities Press, 2004), 311. Those who expect democratization in China usually mean a liberal democracy, including competitive and fair elections, and protection of civil and political liberties by rule of law. See Suisheng Zhao, ed., *China and Democracy: Reconsidering the Prospects for a Democratic China* (New York: Routledge, 2000) and the special issue, "Will China Democratize?" *Journal of Democracy* 9:1 (January 1998).

4. Carles Boix and Susan C. Stokes, "Endogenous Democratization," *World Politics* 55:4 (2003): 517–549; and Adam Przeworski and Fernando Limongi, "Modernization: Theories and Facts," *World Politics* 49 (1997), 155–183.

5. For example, Larry Diamond and Marc F. Plattner, eds., *The Global Resurgence of Democracy* (Baltimore: Johns Hopkins University Press, 1996).

6. Bruce J. Dickson, *Wealth into Power: The Communist Party's Embrace of China's Private Sector* (New York: Cambridge University Press, 2008); Bruce J. Dickson, *Red Capitalists in China: The Party, Private Entrepreneurs, and the Prospects for Political Change* (New York: Cambridge University Press, 2003); Scott Kennedy, *The Business of Lobbying in China* (Cambridge, MA: Harvard University Press, 2005); and Margaret M. Pearson, "Entrepreneurs and Democratization in China's Foreign Sector," in Victoria E. Bonnell and Thomas B. Gold, eds., *New Entrepreneurs of Europe and Asia: Patterns of Business Development in Russia, Eastern Europe, and China* (Armonk, NY: M. E. Sharpe, 2002).

7. Note, however, that this chapter does not address the broader issue of whether China's apparently emerging middle classes are likely to support democracy. My research focused on private entrepreneurs, which spans both the higher and lower ends of the socioeconomic spectrum.

8. The full version of the argument is presented in Kellee S. Tsai, *Capitalism without Democracy: The Private Sector in Contemporary China* (Ithaca, NY: Cornell University Press, 2007).

9. Barrington Moore Jr., *Social Origins of Dictatorship and Democracy: Lord and Peasant in the Making of the Modern World* (Boston: Beacon Press, 1966), 418. Political scientists writing about the "third wave" of democratization in the late 1970s and early 1980s identified multiple paths for authoritarian breakdown and democratic consolidation. See Ruth Berins Collier, *Paths Toward Democracy: The Working Class and Elites in Western Europe and South America* (New York: Cambridge University Press, 1999); Samuel P. Huntington, *The Third Wave: Democratization in the Late Twentieth Century* (Norman: University of Oklahoma Press, 1991); Guillermo O'Donnell, Philippe Schmitter, and Laurence Whitehead, eds., *Transitions from Authoritarian Rule: Tentative Conclusions about Uncertain Democracies* (Baltimore: Johns Hopkins University Press, 1986); and Dietrich Rueschemeyer, Evelyn

Huber Stephens, and John D. Stephens, *Capitalist Development and Democracy* (Chicago: University of Chicago Press, 1992).

10. Many accounts of democratization draw on both structural and individual-level variables. For example, Michael Bratton and Nicolas van de Walle, *Democratic Experiments in Africa: Regime Transitions in Comparative Perspective* (New York: Cambridge University Press, 1997); Collier, *Paths Toward Democracy*; Stephen Haggard and Robert Kaufman, *The Political Economy of Democratic Transitions* (Princeton, NJ: Princeton University Press, 1995); and Huntington, *The Third Wave*. The applicability of these "third wave" explanations to postcommunist societies is questionable; see Michael McFaul, "The Fourth Wave of Democracy *and* Dictatorship: Noncooperative Transitions in the Postcommunist World," *World Politics* 54:2 (2002), 212–244.

11. The logic of structural approaches resonates with modernization theory, which has experienced a revival in light of post–Cold War notions of convergence towards global norms of capitalism and democracy. Although structural explanations of democratic development also emphasize the new middle classes as a force for democratization, this chapter focuses on the specific hypothesis that private business owners comprise a prodemocratic capitalist class in China.

12. Eva Bellin, "Contingent Democrats: Industrialists, Labor, and Democratization in Late-Developing Countries," *World Politics* 52:2 (2000), 175–205.

13. Andrew MacIntyre, *Business and Politics in Indonesia* (Sydney: Allen and Unwin, 1991).

14. Carter J. Eckert, "The South Korean Bourgeoisie: A Class in Search of Hegemony," in Hagen Koo, ed., *State and Society in Contemporary Korea* (Ithaca, NY: Cornell University Press, 1993), 95–130; Hagen Koo, *Korean Workers: The Culture and Politics of Class Formation* (Ithaca, NY: Cornell University Press, 2001); and cf. Leigh A. Payne, *Brazilian Industrialists and Democratic Change* (Baltimore: Johns Hopkins University Press, 1994).

15. Josep Colomer, *Strategic Transitions: Game Theory and Democratization* (Baltimore: Johns Hopkins University Press, 2000); O'Donnell, Schmitter, and Whitehead, *Transitions from Authoritarian Rule*; Adam Przeworski, *Democracy and the Market: Political and Economic Reforms in Eastern Europe and Latin America* (New York: Cambridge University Press, 1991); and Dankwart A. Rustow, "Transitions to Democracy: Toward a Dynamic Model," *Comparative Politics* 2:2 (1970), 337–363.

16. Guillermo O'Donnell, "Substantive or Procedural Consensus? Notes on the Latin American Bourgeoisie," in Douglas Chambers, Mariado Carmo Campello de Souza and Atilio A. Boron, eds., *The Right and Democracy in Latin America* (New York: Praeger, 1992).

17. Payne, *Brazilian Industrialists and Democratic Change*; and William C. Smith, *Authoritarianism and the Crisis of Argentine Political Economy* (Stanford, CA: Stanford University Press, 1989).

18. Lisa Anderson, ed., *Transitions to Democracy* (New York: Columbia University Press, 1999); Diamond and Plattner, eds., *The Global Resurgence of Democracy*; Huntington, *The Third Wave*; O'Donnell et al., *Transitions from Authoritarian Rule*; and Przeworski, *Democracy and the Market*.

19. Most theories of institutional change rely either on the presence of external shocks or highly motivated political leaders to explain institutional transformations. For example, Stephen D. Krasner, "Approaches to the State: Alternative Conceptions and Historical Dynamics," *Comparative Politics* 16:2 (1984), 223–246; Margaret Levi, "A Logic of Institutional Change," in Karen S. Cook and Margaret Levi, eds., *The Limits of Rationality* (Chicago: University of Chicago Press, 1990); and George Tsebelis, *Nested Games: Rational Choice in Comparative Politics* (Berkeley: University of California Press, 1990).

20. Paul Pierson, *Politics in Time: History, Institutions, and Social Analysis* (Princeton, NJ: Princeton University Press, 2004).

21. Ibid., 73.

22. James Mahoney, "Path Dependent Explanations of Regime Change: Central America in Comparative Perspective," *Studies in Comparative International Development* 36:1 (2001), 111–141.

23. Cf. examples of the difference between self-reinforcing and self-destructing institutions in Avner Greif and David Laitin, "A Theory of Endogenous Institutional Change," *American Political Science Review* 98:4 (2004), 633–652.

24. Eric Schickler, *Disjointed Pluralism: Institutional Innovation and the Development of the U.S. Congress* (Princeton, NJ: Princeton University Press, 2001).

25. Robert C. Lieberman, "Ideas, Institutions, and Political Order: Explaining Political Change," *American Political Science Review* 96:4 (2002), 703.

26. Ibid., 704.

27. Kathleen Thelen, *How Institutions Evolve: The Political Economy of Skills in Germany, Britain, the United States, and Japan* (New York: Cambridge University Press, 2004).

28. Ibid., 292.

29. In the Chinese context, X. L. Ding refers to a similar phenomenon as "institutional amphibiousness." See X. L. Ding, "Institutional Amphibiousness and the Transition from Communism: The Case of China," *British Journal of Political Science* 24:3 (1994), 293–318. This notion of organizational appropriation may be traced back to Philip Selznick's classic study of the Tennessee Valley Authority See Philip Selznick, *TVA and the Grassroots: A Study in the Sociology of Formal Organization* (Berkeley: University of California Press, 1949.)

30. Douglass C. North, *Institutions, Institutional Change, and Economic Performance* (Cambridge, UK: Cambridge University Press, 1990), 91. This definition draws from Helmke and Levitsky but also includes public policies because they typically have institutional consequences. See Gretchen Helmke and Steven

Levitsky, "Informal Institutions and Comparative Politics: A Research Agenda," *Perspectives on Politics* 2:4 (2004), 727. Pierson suggests that "it makes good sense to think of public policies as important institutions. For the individuals and social organizations that make up civil society, public policies are clearly very central rules governing their interactions." Pierson, *Politics in Time*, 165.

31. The survey was conducted in collaboration with the Private Economy Research Center of the Chinese Academy of Social Sciences. The sampling frame was a stratified multistage area probability sample. In the first stage, the PSUs were ten provinces stratified by region according to the relative development of the private sector. Within each province, two cities/counties were randomly selected, and within each county two townships were randomly selected. At the township level, registration lists from the Industrial and Commercial Management Bureau were used to select private businesses (both *getihu* and *siying qiye*) according to PPS measures. A total of 1,600 surveys were administered in 2002–2003, and the response rate was 84.7 percent, yielding a total of 1,525 completed questionnaires. In addition to the national survey, I conducted 317 interviews with private entrepreneurs (including unregistered business owners), rank-and-file bureaucrats, government officials, bankers, and researchers in eight provinces/municipalities over the course of 2001–2005.

32. Class formation may be defined as the process through which individuals engage in collective action to defend interests generated by class structure. On the distinction among class structure, class consciousness, class formation, and class practices, see Erik Olin Wright, *Class Counts* (New York: Cambridge University Press, 2000), 185–215.

33. Harley Balzer, "Routinization of the New Russians?" *The Russian Review* 62:1 (2003), 17.

34. Simeon Djankov, Edward Miguel, Yingyi Qian, Gerard Roland, and Ekaterina Zhuravskaya, "Who Are Russia's Entrepreneurs?" *Journal of the European Economic Association* 3:2–3 (2005), 587–597.

35. Ibid.

36. David Smallbone and Friederike Welter, "The Distinctiveness of Entrepreneurship in Transition Economies," *Small Business Economics* 16 (2001), 249–262.

37. Kellee S. Tsai, *Back-Alley Banking: Private Entrepreneurs in China* (Ithaca, NY: Cornell University Press, 2002).

38. For other ways of identifying local variation, see William Hurst, "Understanding Contentious Collective Action by Chinese Laid-Off Workers," *Studies in Comparative International Development* 39, 2 (Summer 2004), 94–120; Jean C. Oi and Andrew G. Walder, eds., *Property Rights and Economic Reform in China* (Stanford, CA: Stanford University Press, 1999); and Susan H. Whiting, *Power and Wealth in Rural China* (New York: Cambridge University Press, 2001).

39. Also see Jianjun Zhang, "Business Associations in China: Two Regional Experiences," *Journal of Contemporary Asia* 37:2 (2007), 209–231.

40. Indeed, in the sociologist Lu Xueyi's delineation of the ten social strata in contemporary China, different types of business owners are classified into four different socioeconomic ranks: the upper social strata (owners of large private enterprises), upper middle strata (owners of private enterprises), middle middle strata (owners of small enterprises), and lower middle strata (self-employed *getihu*) Xueyi Lu, ed., *Dangdai zhongguo shehui jieceng yanjiu baogao* (Report on social strata in contemporary China) (Beijing: shehui kexue wenxian chubanshe, 2001).

41. Dickson, *Wealth into Power*, and Dickson, *Red Capitalists in China*.

42. To analyze how members and leaders in formal political institutions differ from nonmembers, I created two variables from the data set, "political member" and "political elite," respectively, to distinguish among respondents who were members of the NPC, CPPCC, CCP, and/or village committee, respondents who held leadership positions in those organizations, and respondents who were not members in any formal political institution.

43. But they are more likely than regular entrepreneurs to report that they encounter disputes with local government agencies and residents. This is probably because they actually interact with local officials more frequently and feel more empowered/confident about voicing their complaints.

44. Note that that members of business associations are also more likely to be Party members ($r = 0.38$, $p < 0.01$). Although I have not presented my data on association members in this chapter, they complement Kennedy's findings. Kennedy, *The Business of Lobbying in China*.

45. The other categories of political coping strategies in my typology are grudgingly acceptant, avoidant, and assertive. Tsai, *Capitalism without Democracy*, Chapter 5.

46. Martin Gainsborough, "Political Change in Vietnam: In Search of the Middle-Class Challenge to the State," *Asian Survey* 42:5 (2002), 700.

47. *China Daily*, July 17, 2007, and *People's Daily*, October 31, 2006, respectively. On the growing political influence of China's private sector, also see Dickson, *Wealth into Power*, Chapter 5.

48. Zhongguo gongshang guanli ju (China State Administration for Industry and Commerce), *Zhongguo siying jingji nianjian* (China private economy yearbook) (Beijing: Beijing zhigong chubanshe, various years).

49. In my 2002–2003 survey, 23.5 percent of the respondents indicated that they were Party members; and of this group, 85.7 were already Party members when they registered their private enterprises. In other words, only 14.3 percent of the entrepreneurs who are Party members joined after they registered their businesses. My 2002–2003 finding falls within the range of the percentage of private entrepreneurs with Party membership in Dickson's 1999 and 2005 surveys, at 13.1 percent and 15.7 percent, respectively. Dickson, *Wealth into Power*, and *Red Capitalists in China*.

50. Dickson, *Wealth into Power* and *Red Capitalists in China*; and Joseph Few-smith, "Rethinking the Role of the CCP: Explicating Jiang Zemin's Party Anni-versary Speech," *China Leadership Monitor* 1, Part 2 (2002), 1–11.

51. Donald Clarke, Peter Murrell, and Susan Whiting, "Law Institutions, and Property Rights in China," *Asia Program Special Report* (Washington DC: Wood-row Wilson Center for International Scholars, July 2005), 42–47.

52. Avner Greif, "Reputation and Coalitions in Medieval Trade: Evidence from the Maghribi Traders," *Journal of Economic History* 49:4 (1999), 857–882; John McMillan and Christopher Woodruff, "Dispute Prevention without Courts in Vietnam," *Journal of Law, Economics, and Organization* 15:3 (1999), 637–658; and Tsai, *Back-Alley Banking*.

53. One prominent example of adaptive institutional "failure" is the ongoing popularity of informal finance among private entrepreneurs despite official efforts to ban their "illicit financial activities." The reason for continued resistance to genuine commercialization of the banking system is political: the formal financial sector remains beholden to public sector firms and entities that employ millions of employees and require subsidization.

54. Rose Brady, *Kapitalizm: Russia's Struggle to Free its Economy* (New Haven, CT: Yale University Press, 1999); and Edmund Malesky, "Leveled Mountains and Broken Fences: Measuring and Analysing de facto Decentralisation in Vietnam," *European Journal of East Asian Studies* 3:2 (2004), 307–336.

55. James C. Scott, *Weapons of the Weak: Everyday Forms of Resistance* (New Ha-ven, CT: Yale University Press, 1985).

56. Benedict J. Tria Kerkvliet, *The Power of Everyday Politics: How Vietnamese Peasants Transformed National Policy* (Ithaca, NY: Cornell University Press, 2005); R. K. Murphy Frydman and Andrzej Rapaczynski, *Capitalism with a Comrade's Face* (Budapest: Central European University Press, 1998); and Vadim Volkov, *Violent Entrepreneurs: The Use of Force in the Making of Russian Capitalism* (Ithaca, NY: Cor-nell University Press, 2002).

NOTES TO CHAPTER EIGHT

1. "Lao Bushe Lijian Huaqi Yinhang Guangfahang Jinggou Zhizheng Yuelai-yue Weimiao" (Senior Bush's Lobbying on Behalf of Citibank in the Bid for Guangdong Development Bank Brought about Interesting Development), China Financial Net, March 20, 2006; available online at www.zgjrw.com.

2. Feng Xia, "Guangfahang Jinggouzhan: Yinjianhui Wuyi 'Puoxian' Huaqi Huo Gaifang'an," *Shanghai Securities News*, April 20, 2006.

3. Before Citibank's acquisition of Banamex in 2001, Menezes went to Mexico City and discussed the acquisition with Vincente Fox, the president of Mexico. See John Barham, "Citigroup's Latin Platform," *LatinFinance* 2001, 39 (2001).

4. Bruce Bueno de Mesquita et al., *The Logic of Political Survival* (Cambridge, MA: MIT Press, 2003).

5. Peter B. Evans, *Embedded Autonomy: States and Industrial Transformation* (Princeton, NJ: Princeton University Press, 1995).

6. Scott Kennedy, *The Business of Lobbying in China* (Cambridge, MA: Harvard University Press, 2005); and Scott Kennedy, "China's Porous Protectionism: The Changing Political Economy of Trade Policy," *Political Science Quarterly* 120:3 (Fall 2005), 407–432.

7. Mancur Olson Jr., *The Logic of Collective Action* (Cambridge, MA: Harvard University Press, 1965).

8. J. Alexander Caldwell, "Financial System in Taiwan: Structure, Function, and Issues for the Future," *Asian Survey* 16:8 (1976); Negar Roshanzamir, "Iran to Privatise but Cling to Big Oil Companies," *Financial Times*, July 3, 2006; Tun-jen Cheng, "Guarding the Commanding Heights: The State as Banker in Taiwan," in Stephan Haggard, Chung H. Lee, and Sylvia Maxfield, eds., *The Politics of Finance in Developing Countries* (Ithaca, NY: Cornell University Press, 1993).

9. Allen N. Berger et al., "Bank Concentration and Competition: An Evolution in the Making," *Journal of Money, Credit and Banking* 36:3 (2004).

10. See Evans, *Embedded Autonomy: States and Industrial Transformation*; Stephan Haggard and Chung H. Lee, "The Political Dimension of Finance in Economic Development," in Stephan Haggard, Chung H. Lee, and Sylvia Maxfield, *The Politics of Finances in Developing Countries*; and Chalmers Johnson, *MITI and the Japanese Miracle: The Growth of Industrial Policy, 1925–1975* (Stanford, CA: Stanford University Press, 1982).

11. Victor Shih, "Partial Reform Equilibrium, Chinese Style: Political Incentives and Reform Stagnation in Chinese Financial Policies," *Comparative Political Studies*, 10 (2007); David C. Kang, *Crony Capitalism: Corruption and Development in South Korea and the Philippines* (New York: Cambridge University Press, 2002); Timothy P. Kessler, *Global Capital and National Politics: Reforming Mexico's Financial System* (Westport, CT: Praeger, 1999); Sylvia Maxfield, *Governing Capital: International Finance and Mexican Politics* (Ithaca, NY: Cornell University Press, 1990).

12. Maxfield implies that the need to attract foreign capital drove financial policies in many Latin American countries. Sylvia Maxfield, *Gatekeepers of Growth: The International Political Economy of Central Banking in Developing Countries* (Princeton, NJ: Princeton University Press, 1997).

13. Lee J. Alston and Andres A. Gallo, "Banking System under Convertibility: The Roles of Crises and Path Dependence," in *NBER Working Paper*, ed. NBER (Cambridge, MA: NBER, 2000).

14. "Understanding China's Bank Bailout," *China Economic Bulletin* 1 (2004).

15. Peter Fritsch, "Going South: How Citibank's Deal to Buy Mexican Bank Turned into a Standoff," *Wall Street Journal*, September 20, 2000.

16. Kessler, *Global Capital and National Politics: Reforming Mexico's Financial System*.

17. Although the conventional explanation of increasing power of capital is increasing ease of capital flow, capital account convertibility is itself endogenous to the success of capital lobbying. Maxfield, *Governing Capital: International Finance and Mexican Politics*.

18. Kessler, *Global Capital and National Politics: Reforming Mexico's Financial System*, 55.

19. Timothy Kessler, "Political Capital: Mexican Financial Policy under Salinas," *World Politics* 51:1 (1998).

20. Haluk Unal and Miguel Navarro, "The Technical Process of Bank Privatization in Mexico," in Wharton Financial Institutions Center, ed., *FIC Working Papers* (Philadelphia: Wharton School of Business, 1999).

21. Ibid.

22. Ibid.

23. Kessler, "Political Capital: Mexican Financial Policy under Salinas."

24. Kessler, *Global Capital and National Politics: Reforming Mexico's Financial System*, 122.

25. Ibid.

26. Bank of Mexico, "Financial Support Programs for the Banking System and Its Debtors," available at www.banxico.org.mx/gpublicaciones/mexicaneconomy/mexecon96/m96iv2.html.

27. Brian Caplen, "A House Built on Sand," *Euromoney* 351 (1998).

28. Fritsch, "Going South: How Citibank's Deal to Buy Mexican Bank Turned into a Standoff"; and Kessler, *Global Capital and National Politics: Reforming Mexico's Financial System*, 126.

29. Unal and Navarro, "The Technical Process of Bank Privatization in Mexico."

30. Caplen, "A House Built on Sand"; Kessler, *Global Capital and National Politics: Reforming Mexico's Financial System*.

31. Kessler, *Global Capital and National Politics: Reforming Mexico's Financial System*, 134.

32. Tim Weiner, "After a Bailout, a Wedding," *New York Times*, May 27, 2001.

33. "Hernandez, Harp and Aguilera Laughing All the Way between Banks," *El Economista*, 2001.

34. Richard Jacobsen, "Citibank, Banacci Roots Tangled in Mexican History," *Reuters*, May 17, 2001.

35. Kessler, *Global Capital and National Politics: Reforming Mexico's Financial System*, 52.

36. Ben Ross Schneider, "The Career Connection: A Coparative Analysis of Bureaucratic Preferences and Insulation," *Comparative Politics* 25:3 (1993); Ben Ross

Schneider, "Big Business and the Politics of Economic Reform: Confidence and Concertation in Brazil and Mexico," in Sylvia Maxfield and Ben Ross Schneider, eds., *Business and the State in Developing Countries* (Ithaca, NY: Cornell University Press, 1997).

37. Fritsch, "Going South: How Citibank's Deal to Buy Mexican Bank Turned into a Standoff."

38. "Some See Fruits of Globalization, Some US Domination in Citibank's Mexican Buyout," *Associated Press Newswires*, August 3,2001.

39. Byung-sun Choi, "Financial Policy and Big Business in Korea: The Perils of Financial Regulation," in Stephan Haggard, Chung H. Lee, and Sylvia Maxfield, eds., *The Politics of Finance in Developing Countries*, (Ithaca, NY: Cornell University Press, 1993). *Chaebols* are large industrial conglomerate headed by a flagship company, which acts as a holding company. For further details, see Stephan Haggard, Wonhyuk Lim, and Euysung Kim, *Economic Crisis and Corporate Restructuring in Korea: Reforming the Chaebol* (Cambridge, UK, and New York: Cambridge University Press, 2003).

40. Chung H. Lee and Stephan Haggard, "Introduction: Issues and Findings," in Chung H. Lee and Stephan Haggard, eds., *Financial Systems and Economic Policy in Developing Countries* (Ithaca, NY: Cornell University Press, 1995).

41. Choi, "Financial Policy and Big Business in Korea: The Perils of Financial Regulation"; Kang, *Crony Capitalism: Corruption and Development in South Korea and the Philippines.*

42. Choi, "Financial Policy and Big Business in Korea: The Perils of Financial Regulation"; Wonhyuk Lim, "The Emergence of the Chaebol and the Origins of the Chaebol Problem," in Stephan Haggard, Wonhyuk Lim, and Euysung Kim, eds., *Economic Crisis and Corporate Restructuring in Korea: Reforming the Chaebol* (New York: Cambridge University Press, 2003).

43. Choi, "Financial Policy and Big Business in Korea: The Perils of Financial Regulation."

44. Ibid.

45. Lim, "The Emergence of the Chaebol and the Origins of the Chaebol Problem."

46. More research is needed to discern why *chaebols* did not succeed in gaining greater control over banks given their powerful clout (Joon-ho Hahm, "The Government, the Chaebol and Financial Institutions before the Economic Crisis," in Stephan Haggard, Wonhyuk Lim, and Euysung Kim, eds., *Economic Crisis and Corporate Restructuring in Korea*).

47. Ibid.

48. Stephan Haggard, *The Political Economy of the Asian Financial Crisis* (Washington, DC: Institute for International Economics, 2000), 35–36.

49. Ibid., 1.

50. This figure is for the top thirty chaebols. See Joseph Bisignano, "Precarious Credit Equilibria: Reflections on the Asian Financial Crisis," *BIS Working Paper* 64 (Basel, Switzerland: Bank for International Settlements, 1999).

51. This assumes a won–dollar exchange rate of 1,000, although the won was much weaker at the beginning of 1998.

52. Kyung-Gon Ro, "Banking Industry Consolidation in Korea," in *BIS Working Paper* (Basel: Bank for International Settlements, 2001).

53. Ibid.

54. Kyung Suh Park, "Bank-Led Corporate Restructuring," in Stephan Haggard, Wonhyuk Lim, and Euysung Kim, eds., *Economic Crisis and Corporate Restructuring in Korea.*

55. Ibid.

56. Chungwon Kang, "From the Front Lines at Seoul Bank: Restructuring and Reprivatization," in *IMF Working Paper* (Washington, DC: International Monetary Fund, 2003).

57. Ibid.

58. Ibid.

59. Ibid.

60. Ibid.

61. Kang, "From the Front Lines at Seoul Bank: Restructuring and Reprivatization."

62. Kookmin Bank, "Major Shareholders of New Kookmin before and after Merger," available at http://inf.kbstar.com/quics?page=A001193&cc=a005049: a005049.

63. On why corruption never got out of hand in Korea, there are at least two versions, mutual hostage and embedded autonomy. See Alice H. Amsden, *Asia's Next Giant: South Korea and Late Industrialization* (New York: Oxford University Press, 1989); Kang, *Crony Capitalism: Corruption and Development in South Korea and the Philippines*; and Evans, *Embedded Autonomy: States and Industrial Transformation.*

64. Kang, *Crony Capitalism*; James Schopf, "An Explanation for the End of Political Bank Robbery in the Republic of Korea: The T & T Model," *Asian Survey* 41:5 (2001).

65. Kang, *Crony Capitalism*, 100.

66. Ibid.

67. Ibid., 162.

68. Ibid., 72; Evans, *Embedded Autonomy.*

69. Byung-kook Kim, "The Politics of Chaebol Reform: 1980–1997," in Stephan Haggard, Wonhyuk Lim, and Euysung Kim, eds., *Economic Crisis and Corporate Restructuring in Korea*; and Wonhyuk Lim, Stephan Haggard, and Euysung Kim, "Introduction: The Political Economy of Corporate Restructuring," in Stephan Haggard, Wonhyuk Lim, and Euysung Kim, eds., *Economic Crisis and*

Corporate Restructuring in Korea: Reforming the Chaebol (New York: Cambridge University Press, 2003).

70. Shirk makes the argument that Central Committee members are in the selectorate, while others disagree. See Susan Shirk, *The Political Logic of Economic Reform in China* (Berkeley, CA: The University of California Press, 1993).

71. Nicholas Lardy, *China's Unfinished Economic Reform* (Washington, DC: Brookings Institution Press, 1998).

72. Laurence W. Berger, George R. Nast, and Christian Raubach, "Fixing Asia's Bad-Debt Mess: A Banking Crisis Crippled Asia's Economies in 1997. A Bad Debt Crisis Threatens to Do So Again Unless Governments and Banks Crack Down on Nonperforming Loans," *McKinsey Quarterly* 2002:139 (2002).

73. Victor Shih, "Dealing with Non-Performing Loans: Political Constraints and Financial Policies in China," *The China Quarterly*, 180 (2004).

74. PBOC Monetary Policy Committee, "Zhongguo Renminyinhang Huobi Zhengce Weiyuanhui Diwuci Huiyi Jiyao" (Summary of the Fifth Meeting of the PBOC Monetary Policy Committee), in PBOC Monetary Policy Committee, ed., *Zhongguo Renmin Yinhang Huobi Zhengce Weiyuanhui Huiyi Jiyao (A Summary of Meetings of the PBOC Monetary Policy Committee)* (Beijing: China Finance Publisher, 2000).

75. Haiyan Hu, "Zhongyang Huijin Gongsi Jinrong Bantu Qiemi" (Unveiling the Secret Design of the Central Huijing Company) *Zhongguo Qiyejia (Chinese Entrepreneur)*, July 7, 2005.

76. China Economic Quarterly, "Understanding China's Bank Bailout."

77. Victor Shih, "Beijing's Bailout of Joint-Stock and State-Owned Banks," *China Brief* 5:18 (2005).

78. "Senior Bush's Lobbying on Behalf of Citibank in the Bid for Guangdong Development Bank Brought about Interesting Development."

79. Yuan Li, "Huaqi Yinhang De Zhongguo Jinrong Zhanlue" (Citibank's China Strategy), *Jingji Cankaobao*, February 6, 2006; Yanzheng Lu, "Guangfa Feichang Congzu, Dianfu Zhongguo Shangye Yinhang Yinzi Chongzu Moshi" (The Unusual Restructuring of Gdb Scrambles the Usual Mode of Recapitalization and Restructuring in the Chinese Commercial Banking Sector), *Caijing*, October 5, 2005.

80. Kathy Chen, "Foreigners Face Backlash in China—In an Echo of Beijing's Problems in the West, Criticism Grows of Overseas Investors' Influence on Its Home Turf," *Asian Wall Street Journal*, April 3, 2006.

81. Ibid.

82. Xia, "Guangfahang Jinggouzhan: Yinjianhui Wuyi 'Puoxian' Huaqi Huo Gaifang'an."

83. "Huaqi Yingqu Zhongguo Yinhangye Zuihou Dadangao" (Citibank Wins the Large Big Cake in the Banking Sector), *Nanfang Zhoumo (Southern Weekend)*, November 24, 2006.

84. Victor Shih, "Partial Reform Equilibrium, Chinese Style: Political Incentives and Reform Stagnation in Chinese Financial Policies," *Comparative Political Studies* 40:10 (2007).

85. Edward S. Steinfeld, *Forging Reform in China: The Fate of State-Owned Industry* (Cambridge, UK: Cambridge University Press, 1998).

NOTES TO CHAPTER NINE

1. Samuel P. Huntington, *Political Order in Changing Societies* (New Haven, CT: Yale University Press, 1968).

2. Two contributions are Yanqi Tong, *Transitions from State Socialism: Economic and Political Change in Hungary and China* (Lanham, MD: Rowman & Littlefield, 1997); and Regina Abrami, Edmund Malesky, and Yu Zheng, "Accountability and Inequality in Single-Party Regimes: A Comparative Analysis of Vietnam and China," HBS Working Paper 08-099 (May 2008), available online at http://hbswk .hbs.edu/item/5948.html.

3. Two rare exceptions are Kellee S. Tsai, "Debating Decentralized Development: A Reconsideration of the Kerala and Wenzhou Models," *Indian Journal of Economics and Business* (Special Issue: India and China, 2006), 47–67; and Lynn T. White, *Political Booms: Local Money and Power in Taiwan, East China, Thailand, and the Philippines* (Singapore: World Scientific, 2009).

4. For an example, see Andrew C. Mertha and William R. Lowry, "Unbuilt Dams: Seminal Events and Policy Change in China, Australia, and the United States," *Journal of Comparative Politics*, 39:1 (October 2006), 1–20.

5. Gregory J. Kasza, *The Conscription Society: Administered Mass Organizations* (New Haven, CT: Yale University Press, 1995).

6. For example, see Suzanne Ogden, *China: Global Studies*, eighth edition (Guilford, CT: Dushkin/McGraw-Hill, 1999), 30.

7. *Facts and Figures of Japan 2002* (Tokyo: Foreign Press Center, 2002), 167.

8. From the U.S. Department of Justice, Bureau of Justice Statistics, "Criminal Case Processing Statistics," available online at www.ojp.usdoj.gov/bjs/cases.htm. Also see J. Mark Ramseyer and Eric B. Rasmusen, "Why Is the Japanese Conviction Rate so High?" *Journal of Legal Studies*, 30:1 (January 2001), 53–88.

List of Contributors

Mark W. Frazier (PhD, Political Science, University of California, Berkeley) is the ConocoPhillips Professor of Chinese Politics and Associate Professor of International and Area Studies at the University of Oklahoma. His research examines the politics of labor and social policy in China. He is the author of *Socialist Insecurity: Pensions and the Politics of Unevern Development in China* (Cornell University Press, 2010) and *The Making of the Chinese Industrial Workplace: State, Revolution, and Labor Management* (Cambridge University Press, 2002).

Gregory J. Kasza (PhD, Political Science, Yale University) is Professor in the Departments of East Asian Languages & Cultures and Political Science at Indiana University. His scholarship analyzes Japanese politics from a broad comparative perspective, and his interests include state–society relations, war and politics, fascism, and welfare policy. He is the author of *The State and the Mass Media in Japan, 1918–1945* (University of California Press, 1988), *The Conscription Society* (Yale University Press, 1995), and *One World of Welfare: Japan in Comparative Perspective* (Cornell University Press, 2006).

Scott Kennedy (PhD, Political Science, George Washington University) is Associate Professor, Departments of East Asian Languages & Cultures and Political Science; and Director, Research Center for Chinese Politics and Business, Indiana University. He is author of *The Business of Lobbying in China* (Harvard University Press, 2005) and editor of *China Cross Talk: The American Debate over China Policy since Normalization, A Reader* (Rowman & Littlefield, 2003). His current research projects are on the growing role of Chinese industry and government in global governance and on the evolution of corporate political activity in China.

Arthur R. Kroeber (AB, Harvard University) is editor of the *China Economic Quarterly* and managing director of GKDragonomics, an economic research firm specializing in China and its impact on the world economy.

Margaret M. Pearson (PhD, Political Science, Yale University) is Professor of Government and Politics at the University of Maryland, College Park. She has focused her research on China's domestic and international political economy. Her publications include the books *Joint Ventures in the People's Republic of China* (Princeton University Press, 1991) and *China's New Business Elite: The Political Results of Economic Reform* (University of California Press, 1997). Her numerous other publications include articles in *World Politics*, *Public Administration Review*, *The China Journal*, *Modern China*, and *China Business Review*. Her most recent work is on China's role in the WTO and on the politics of economic regulation in China.

Victor Shih (PhD, Government, Harvard University) is an Associate Professor of Political Science at Northwestern University specializing in China. An immigrant to the United States from Hong Kong, Dr. Shih researched banking sector reform in China with the support of the Jacob K. Javits Fellowship and the Fulbright Fellowship while a doctoral student at Harvard. He is the author of *Factions and Finance in China: Elite Conflict and Inflation* (Cambridge University Press, 2008). It is the first book to inquire into the linkages between elite politics and banking policies in China. He is also the author of numerous articles appearing in academic and business journals, including *The China Quarterly*, *Comparative Political Studies*, and *The Far Eastern Economic Review*, and is a frequent adviser to the private sector on the banking industry in China. His current research concerns elite political dynamics in China and Chinese policies toward ethnic minorities.

Kellee S. Tsai (PhD, Political Science, Columbia University) is Professor of Political Science and Vice Dean for Humanities, Social Sciences, and Graduate Programs at Johns Hopkins University. Her most recent book is *Capitalism without Democracy: The Private Sector in Contemporary China* (Cornell University Press, 2007). She is also the author of *Back-Alley Banking: Private Entrepreneurs in China* (Cornell University Press, 2002), coauthor of *Rural Industrialization and Non-Governmental Finance: Insights from Wenzhou* (Shanxi Economics Press, 2004), coeditor of *Japan and China in the World*

Political Economy (2005), and author of various journal articles. Tsai's professional experience includes working at Morgan Stanley and Women's World Banking and consulting for the World Bank's Consultative Group to Assist the Poorest and various other organizations.

Andrew Wedeman (PhD, Political Science, UCLA) is Professor, Department of Political Science, University of Nebraska. He has served as a visiting professor at the Johns Hopkins–Nanjing University Center for Chinese and American Studies, a visiting Fulbright Researcher at National Taiwan University, and a visiting scholar at Peking University. His research focuses on the political economy of reform in China and specifically on the relationship between corruption and development, both in China and elsewhere in the developing world. His publications include *The Double Paradox of Corruption and Rapid Development in China* (Cornell University Press, forthcoming), *From Mao to Market: Rent Seeking, Local Protectionism, and Marketization in China* (Cambridge University Press, 2003) and articles in *China Quarterly*, the *Journal of Contemporary China*, and the *China Review*.

Index

Japan: economic regulation in (*continued*) 203n57, 218n24; electoral politics in, 123, 125; foreign investment in, 20, 125–26; imports, 49, 50, 125; Keidanren/Japanese Federation of Economic Organizations, 123, 124–25, 127; Liberal Democratic Party (LDP), 11, 123; lobbying in, 114, 122–26; Ministry of International Trade and Industry/MITI, 40, 53, 114, 124; myths regarding, 11; *Nikkei* newspapers, 124–25; population of, 114; practice of *amakudari* in, 124, 218n24; privatization in, 42; protectionism in, 125; relations with United States, 20; social welfare policies in, 11; trade ratio of, 48; uniqueness of, 10–11; vs. United States, 195n28, 201n34, 202n38
Jenkins, Rhys, 207n18
Jiangsu, 73
Jiangxi, 74
Jiang Zemin: on "Three Represents," 154
Jilin Light Duty Vehicles, 73
Jilin Tongtian, 209n22
Jin, Dengjian, 67, 208n6
Jinan, 78
Johnson, Chalmers: *Change in Communist Systems*, 193n14; *MITI and the Japanese Miracle*, 196n38, 204n1, 205n12
Johnston, Michael, 194n17
joint stock companies, 29, 75, 81, 88, 201n28
joint ventures, Sino-foreign, 32, 33, 48, 57, 58, 204nn2,3; in automotive industry, 55–56, 73, 75, 77, 79, 207nn19,20
Jones, Catherine, 214n21
Jordana, Jacint, 198n2

Kadannikov, Vladimir, 83, 85, 211n59
KamAZ, 83, 85, 86, 212n69
Kang, Chungwon, 230nn56–61
Kang, David C.: *Crony Capitalism*, 227n11, 229n41, 230nn63–68
Kapur, Devish, 219n44
Kasza, Gregory J.: *The Conscription Society*, 198n51, 232n5; on Japan's

welfare policies, 11; *One World of Welfare*, 195n28, 198n51
Kaufman, Robert R., 92; *Development, Democracy, and Welfare States*, 213nn5–7; *The Political Economy of Democratic Transitions*, 222n10
Kennedy, Scott, 43, 161, 209n16, 217nn14,17,18, 218n31; *The Business of Lobbying in China*, 43, 192n10, 198n50, 203nn56,69, 205n13, 216n3, 221n6, 225n44, 227n6
Kerala, 103
Kerkvliet, Benedict J. Tria: *The Power of Everyday Politics*, 226n56
Kessler, Timothy P., 228nn19,23; *Global Capital and National Politics*, 227n11, 228nn16,18,24,25,31,35
Khan, Azizur Rahman, 208n5
Khan, Zafar Dad, 215nn50,51
Khodorkovsky, Mikhail, 132
Kia, 55, 83, 86
Kim, Byung-kook, 230n69
Kim Dae-jung, 170
Kim, Euysung: *Economic Crisis and Corporate Restructuring in Korea*, 229n39, 230n69
Kim Young-sam, 171
Kingston, Jeff: *Japan's Quiet Transformation*, 218n28
Klebnikov, Paul, 211n53; *Godfather of the Kremlin*, 212n60
Kochanek, Stanley A., 128, 218nn33–36, 219nn37,40
Kolodko, Grzegorz: *From Shock to Therapy*, 195n30
Koo, Hagen: *Korean Workers*, 222n14
Krasner, Stephen D., 223n19
Krauss, Ellis, 217n20
Kroeber, Arthur, 207n24
Kubicek, Paul, 195n29, 220n59
Kuznets, Simon, 90, 213n4
Kwok, Robert, 206n16

labor market, 35, 102, 104, 105–6
labor unions, 105, 108
La Croix, Sumner, 203n59
Laitin, David, 223n23
Lane, David, 130, 197n46, 219n51

East-West Center Series on

CONTEMPORARY ISSUES IN ASIA AND THE PACIFIC

Japan's Dual Civil Society: Members Without Advocates
By Robert Pekkanen
2006

Protest and Possibilities: Civil Society and Coalitions for Political Change in Malaysia
By Meredith Leigh Weiss
2005

Opposing Suharto: Compromise, Resistance, and Regime Change in Indonesia
By Edward Aspinall
2005

Blowback: Linguistic Nationalism, Institutional Decay, and Ethnic Conflict in Sri Lanka
By Neil DeVotta
2004

Beyond Bilateralism: U.S.-Japan Relations in the New Asia Pacific
Edited by Ellis S. Krauss and T.J. Pempel
2004

Population Change and Economic Development in East Asia: Challenges Met, Opportunities Seized
Edited by Andrew Mason
2001

Capital, Coercion, and Crime: Bossism in the Philippines
By John T. Sidel
1999

Making Majorities: Constituting the Nation in Japan, Korea, China, Malaysia, Fiji, Turkey, and the United States
Edited by Dru C. Gladney
1998

Chiefs Today: Traditional Pacific Leadership and the Postcolonial State
Edited by Geoffrey M. White and Lamont Lindstrom
1997

Political Legitimacy in Southeast Asia: The Quest for Moral Authority
Edited by Muthiah Alagappa
1995